Praise for *Woman Up*

"In the media studies scholarship analyzing the torrent of recent female-centered television, Julia Havas's book stands out for its rigorous examination of series whose formal experimentation is matched by self-conscious engagement with popular feminism. Her sterling contribution to this literature reminds us how exciting it is to see new feminist research frontiers being mapped and charted."

—Diane Negra, professor of film studies and screen culture,
University College Dublin

"Julia Havas opens provocative questions about television series like *30 Rock* that have been progressive favorites in the postfeminist era. Her savvy insights about marketable feminism and the meanings of 'quality' TV will have you re-watching and re-thinking your favorite episodes. Exploring the politics and aesthetics of both television and representations of feminism, *Woman Up* is an original and refreshing read for fans and scholars alike."

—Linda Mizejewski,
Ohio State University

"In this essential reading for anyone interested in television studies, Julia Havas spotlights the field's two most vital approaches: feminism and formalism. *Woman Up*'s deep dive into recent feminist quality TV theorizes and exemplifies how these critical lenses function optimally in tandem, rather than (all too often) in opposition."

—Julia Leyda, professor of film studies,
Norwegian University of Science and Technology

"Showing how profoundly and insistently quality television calls on feminist tropes, *Woman Up* challenges a predominate masculinist emphasis in scholarly accounts. An evocative reading of feminist quality television, and a powerful engagement with landmark shows, Havas's book is a vital source for both television and feminist media studies."

—Yvonne Tasker, professor of media and communication,
University of Leeds

GW00499924

WOMAN UP

Contemporary Approaches to Film and Media Series

A complete listing of the books in this series can
be found online at wsupress.wayne.edu.

GENERAL EDITOR

Barry Keith Grant
Brock University

WOMAN UP

INVOKING
FEMINISM
IN QUALITY
TELEVISION

JULIA HAVAS

Wayne State University Press
Detroit

Copyright © 2022 by Wayne State University Press, Detroit, Michigan, 48201.
All rights reserved. No part of this book may be reproduced without formal
permission.

ISBN (paperback): 978-0-8143-4656-3
ISBN (hardcover): 978-0-8143-4655-6
ISBN (e-book): 978-0-8143-4657-0

Library of Congress Control Number: 2021943070

Cover illustration by Miriam Kent. Cover design by Genna Blackburn.

Wayne State University Press rests on Waawiyaataanong, also referred to as Detroit,
the ancestral and contemporary homeland of the Three Fires Confederacy. These
sovereign lands were granted by the Ojibwe, Odawa, Potawatomi, and Wyandot
nations, in 1807, through the Treaty of Detroit. Wayne State University Press af-
firms Indigenous sovereignty and honors all tribes with a connection to Detroit.
With our Native neighbors, the press works to advance educational equity and
promote a better future for the earth and all people.

Wayne State University Press
Leonard N. Simons Building
4809 Woodward Avenue
Detroit, Michigan 48201-1309

Visit us online at wsupress.wayne.edu.

CONTENTS

ACKNOWLEDGMENTS

This book grew out of a doctoral research project carried out at the University of East Anglia between 2013 and 2016. I wish to express my gratitude to Diane Negra and Yvonne Tasker, whose mentorship over the years has been invaluable for transitioning the project from doctoral thesis to book. Thanks are also due to colleagues at De Montfort University for forging a supportive research atmosphere, especially Simon Mills, Heather Savigny, Justin Smith, and Paul Smith.

I also want to thank my wonderful editor, Marie Sweetman, for her continuous support and her patience with me, and to all at Wayne State University Press. My thanks also to series editor Barry Keith Grant and the two anonymous reviewers for their constructive criticism and helpful comments on the manuscript.

For their instrumental help, inspiration, support, and academic friendship, I am grateful to Julia Leyda, Linda Mizejewski, and Maria Sulimma. Special thanks to Miriam Kent for her support and solidarity through the years and especially for designing the book's unique cover art.

I want to express my heartfelt gratitude to Vicky Ball, my friend and colleague at De Montfort University: Lacey to my Cagney (Thelma to my Louise?) without whose personal-professional support and friendship through thick and thin I could not have completed this book and who helped me get through a great deal of professional, mental, emotional, and even medical struggles in the last couple of years.

Special thanks to my friends Mártonfi Anna and Gergely Gábor for always being there for me. I am especially thankful to Gábor for patiently answering my incessant flow of questions about all manner of issues from the banal to the complex and for his selfless support, guidance, mentorship, and crystal-clear advice. Anna, I am forever grateful for our productive and chatty brainstorming sessions and online hangouts, especially in times of acute emotional need and hardship. Thank you for always having my back.

Finally, I want to thank my family at home in Szeged. I would not have been able to finish (let alone start) this work without the loving support of my parents Ilona and Miklós, and my brother Péter and his family: Henni, Hanga, Kincső, and the youngest member of the gang, Villő.

This book is dedicated to the memory of my late father, Havas Miklós, who passed away during the development of this project. I am forever grateful for his encouragement and his dogged confidence in me. Köszönöm, Apa.

Passages from chapters 2, 3, and 4 were first published in substantially revised form in the anthology *Hysterical! Women in American Comedy*, ed. Linda Mizejewski and Victoria Sturtevant (University of Texas Press, 2017). Sections of chapters 5 and 6 first appeared in a piece co-written with Maria Sulimma: "Through the Gaps of My Fingers: Genre, Femininity, and Cringe Aesthetics in Dramedy Television," *Television and New Media* 21, no. 1 (January 2020): 75–94.

INTRODUCTION

Woman, writer, New York: those are all on my list of "TV no-no words."

Kenneth Parcell, *30 Rock* ("Hogcock!")

Kenneth Parcell (Jack McBrayer), the NBC page turned network president, speaks these words in the NBC series *30 Rock* (2006–2013), the American metasitcom set backstage on a fictional sketch comedy show whose main protagonist is the show's head writer, Liz Lemon (Tina Fey). Kenneth's remark comes in response to Liz's pitch for a series based on her life as a female TV writer working in New York. To elaborate on his dismissal of Liz's pitch, Kenneth presents her with a piece of paper containing a list of words, titled "Kenneth's TV No-No Words," and explains American network television's imperative to provide easy entertainment for audiences. The list, which the viewer can examine by pausing the image, includes the following expressions: urban, woman, shows about shows, writer, dramedy, politics, high concept, complex, niche, quality, edgy. To Liz's objection that "TV can be successful without sacrificing quality," Kenneth disapprovingly points at the word. Liz retorts, "Maybe I shouldn't bring my ideas to NBC. I'll go to cable where you can swear and *really* take time to let moments la——." We never hear her finish the word *land* because the scene abruptly ends to cut to the next one.

This sequence's satire assumes and plays into the audience's awareness of American "quality" television culture and the dualism between the features and cultural values assigned to network and cable television. It also assumes the underlying genderedness of these distinctions: Progressive female representations in this setup belong in the "edgy" world of cable television. Yet as an NBC series about a woman writer and as urban showbiz comedy,

30 Rock's satire reassures viewers that it *is* all of these things: edgy (frequently thematizing contentious political and cultural issues), self-reflexive (offering itself to be interpreted as an autobiographical rendering of Tina Fey's career), and complex quality comedy. Further, it treats its audiences as savvy, smart observers who practice what Jason Mittell (2015a) calls forensic fandom (fans will freeze-frame the image for extra jokes on Kenneth's list and get the hall-of-mirrors metacommentary) while centralizing the politics of urban white womanhood, sending up popular debates about feminism. That such layered material appears on *network* television is crucial for the series' institutional positioning: *30 Rock*'s satire of both NBC and other networks allows the company to appear different from its competitors with their supposedly mediocre and sexist programming, an effort involving the centering of a female comedian to reposition comedy's status on legacy television. After all, upon Fey's success with *30 Rock*, NBC continued this strategy by commissioning the comedy *Parks and Recreation* (2009–2015), starring Amy Poehler. The *30 Rock* scene, then, and the whole series take television's negotiations of cultural value, aesthetics, and gender politics as their central theme and treat them as fundamentally intertwined.

In this book I examine the issues that *30 Rock* thematizes and is a prominent example of. I investigate the emergence after the millennium of a group of programs in American television whose categorization as quality television is predicated on their status as feminist television. Although the strategic association between cultural value and gender politics is nothing new in American television—it might even be called a staple of its heritage—the postmillennial makeup of this connection deems it unique enough to call for an in-depth examination. The tendency became widespread enough in the 2010s to form patterns, and television scholarship has started to examine these from a feminist perspective (Nygaard and Lagerwey 2016; Lagerwey et al. 2016). This phenomenon is described in TV journalism as a new era of "feminist quality television" (Blay 2015), and, in keeping with the critical tradition of evaluating cultural products in a negotiation of their socially realistic representation and artistic expression, it is credited with subverting two dominant phenomena simultaneously, one linked to identity politics and the other to aesthetics. The social-political subversion targets the previous (millennial) era's comparatively limited representations of female subjectivity associated with postfeminist ideology, whereas the aesthetic subversion upsets the value hierarchies of a masculinist and "nontelevisual" quality television.

My primary goal in this book is to understand the relationship between these two discourses of subversion in an era in which feminism has once again become a popular and contested concept (Banet-Weiser 2018) and in which the most recent golden age of television is both celebrated for its aesthetic innovations and criticized for its reliance on patriarchal ideals of cultural value. I examine this relationship from two distinct but related vantage points to critically analyze the emergence and characteristics of the feminist quality television phenomenon. The first area of investigation is this programming's touted subversion and negotiation of postfeminist politics and this subversion's links to aesthetic and genre conventions. The second aspect reverses the focus and concentrates on the "quality" descriptor, asking in what particular ways feminist quality television mobilizes patterns of aesthetic-formal innovation to engage with the discursive struggle between postfeminism and feminism. My analysis of these aspects is governed by the key conviction that the meanings of the phrase *feminist quality television* and the individual words within it singly and in their interrelations are discursively produced in a nexus of institutional, textual, journalistic, audience, and scholarly discourses, accounting for their constantly shifting cultural understandings.

I use four American programs as case studies to examine these issues. To highlight the role that the established modalities of television genres and their cultural work play in the attribution of value, I consider two comedies and two dramas. The comedies are *30 Rock* and *Parks and Recreation*, and the dramas are *The Good Wife* (2009–2016) and *Orange Is the New Black* (2013–2019). *Orange* is an outlier on this list for two reasons. First, it is one of the first flagship series of streaming giant Netflix, and, second, its genre features have created much confusion in industry and press discourses, vacillating between comedy, drama, and dramedy without consensus. The interdependence between these two aspects of *Orange*—its institutional position in the changing television landscape and its blurring of genre descriptors—is examined in depth and undergirds my argument about discursive negotiation processes around cultural value, genre, and gender. Overall, journalistic discourse positions these four programs as both negotiating the masculinism of millennial quality television and foregrounding themes of gender politics and feminism as a historic political movement.

In my examination of the discursive interlink between political and aesthetic value in these programs, I draw on similarly two-pronged scholarly traditions of television studies: a feminist approach on the one hand, and the emerging but popular field of television aesthetics on the other. Television studies, as a still young and somewhat amorphous field of scholarly interest—itself bound up in anxieties over academic legitimation—has in its short history been a territory fraught with power struggles over the legitimacy of analytical approaches, a problem exacerbated by popular and often academic declarations about the new age of aesthetically valuable television or the "aesthetic turn" (Lury 2016, 120). I outline these theoretical debates later in this introduction, but here I want to signal a wariness around the either-or understandings that typically organize the debate. I argue throughout this book that the emergence of feminist quality television provides an opportunity to demonstrate the necessity of combining these approaches: A program's cultural work cannot be understood without acknowledging and unpacking the profound genderedness of television's cultivation of aesthetic value in this latest "golden age of television"; and similarly, the political implications of this programming cannot be unearthed without considering the aesthetic-generic and institutional context. My argument recognizes that each of these approaches has had a definitional struggle over a popularly coined term at its core—*postfeminism* and *quality television*, respectively—that has structured their postmillennial development and academic utility. In the next section I briefly detail these definitional struggles. Moreover, given the rich theoretical and historic background of American quality television and gender, I devote a longer discussion to it in chapter 1.

POSTFEMINISM AND QUALITY TELEVISION IN SCHOLARSHIP

As noted, the term *feminist quality television* signals feminist television analysis on the one hand and academic discourses about aesthetic evaluative practices (i.e., the quality television debate) on the other. Although the two fields occasionally overlap, recent academic interest in the aesthetics of television has resulted in a renewed tension between them concerning the limits of validity and the usefulness of their respective analytical methods. As stated, I call for their combination, or even for abolishing the discursive opposition that limits scholarly analysis. Nonetheless, I discuss each approach and the dominant term operating in it in turn here.

Anglo-American feminist scholarship has, at least since the 1990s, been governed by debates about the cultural dominance of postfeminism, a concentration inevitably central to feminist *television* scholarship as well, given the phenomenon's strong ties to and roots in popular media representation. The term *postfeminism* and its cultural influence have been described by critics as, historically, a cultural and political backlash against Western second-wave feminism (Faludi 1991) and as a popularized—and therefore distorted and simplified—understanding of and response to its political, economic, and cultural struggles against the patriarchal makeup of modern Western societies. Because the most visible and public strand of second-wave feminism concentrated on the liberation of one social group—white heterosexual middle-class women—the movement has become associated with this privileged cohort and has been criticized for ignoring other, less visible identity formations. Scholars also argue that the way that feminism's struggles have become incorporated into Western culture in the postfeminist era follows logically from the political and economic necessities of late modern neoliberal capitalism (Tasker and Negra 2007; Gill 2007; McRobbie 2009; Negra 2009), which continues to have a strong hold on feminism's public utilization by constantly shape-shifting to adapt to rapidly transforming contexts (Negra and Tasker 2014b; Gill 2016). The entering of a narrow subset of American women into the education system and labor market since the 1960s created a new consumer group whose emergence in turn required new marketing strategies, ones that make use of the seemingly commonsense aspects of feminist ideas—those most marketable and realizable as well as unthreatening to the status quo—while producing a type of consumer-spectator who is constantly in search of self-betterment through consumption.

In Angela McRobbie's (2009) influential formulation, this is the post-feminist process of "feminism taken into account" (2) in most areas of Western culture and policymaking. Popular media's perpetuation of the image of the economically and emotionally independent, sexually liberated, and empowered woman ensures the maintenance and reproduction of this structure, so long as the idea of empowerment is understood in individualized, intimate ways and does not entail political solidarity across social groups. This postfeminist culture (re)produces an ideological struggle between women's sexual and professional empowerment on the one hand and the social primacy of coupledom, heterosexual romance, and the nuclear family on the other, promoting the importance of individual "choice," self-surveillance, and status anxiety for female agency and happiness to deflect attention from larger social-political forces at work (Negra 2009, 153).

These theorizations of postfeminism have become widely accepted in feminist cultural criticism but are also being debated for their broader consequences for Western societies' gender politics, particularly with respect to postfeminism's links to popular media's cultural work and logics. Scholars contesting this criticism have argued that, historically, feminism's sociocultural power has always been entangled in its popular media presence and that feminist academics' widespread critique of postfeminism neglects the legacy of this entanglement, or indeed the ever-present negotiations of gender scripts in cultural products and issues of audience engagement (Lotz 2001, 2007; Hollows and Moseley 2006; Johnson 2007b).

The 2010s have seen a renewed popular cultural interest in feminism both as a marketable term and a political tool, aided by the increased significance of social media platforms as sites of politicized public communication. These phenomena signal a growing cultural unhappiness with the utility of postfeminism, especially its premise on narrow definitions of ideal womanhood, consumer citizenship, and prosperity. This rebooted feminism, its intense contestations, and its instrumentalizations in popular media have been seen partly as responses to transformative economic, political, and cultural events, such as the 2008 financial crisis (Negra and Tasker 2014b), Donald Trump's ascendance to the U.S. presidency in 2016, and the Me Too movement (Banet-Weiser 2018). Thus the scholarly debates around the usefulness of postfeminism as a concept have in recent years intensified at the same time as its critique became prominent in simultaneously emerging popular feminist media products. This is tightly linked to television culture and to the analysis of quality television, not only because the medium is commonly regarded as a prime indicator of a society's structures of feeling but also because a key commonality between postfeminist media and quality television culture is their production of and appeal to upmarket consumer-viewers. Therefore the status of the gendered public sphere, signaling an unease with the postfeminist premise of narrowly defined female subjectivities, is linked with the increased promotional value of diversity politics and dramatizations of a problematic postfeminism in prestige television culture.

The scholarly debates about postfeminism and its usefulness as an analytical term are thus mirrored in the contradictions that characterize popular culture's relationship with feminism. Popular discourses about the role of gender in neoliberal capitalism have started to reemerge and to echo the debates that have preoccupied feminist academia since the establishment of the postfeminist paradigm in the 1980s, a development that to some extent follows from the economic and political upheavals of the Global West. Heated discussions about the problematic nature of privileged womanhood and its representations and of systemic oppression and marginalization on the basis of gender, race, body image, sexual orientation, and other nonnormative identities permeate the Anglo-American public sphere and cultural imagination, also sparking new interests in discussions about feminism's role in addressing these issues. This renewed popular interest reflects decades-long academic debates and has crystallized around well-identifiable issues to the extent that they have become available for fictional dramatizations. Again, television is a prominent site of negotiating these conflicts—unsurprisingly, considering the medium's claims to immediacy and realism, amicability to liberal feminist politics and female talent, and its suitability for portraying cultural conflicts in an endlessly reproducible fashion.[1]

Anglophone feminist media scholarship's interrogation of the renewed popular cultural fascination with feminism has paid attention to its impact on various phenomena in the cultural industries, media production, social media, celebrity culture, corporate branding practices, and so on. Representatively, the figure of the "feminist celebrity" (Hamad and Taylor 2015) and the sporadically appearing Hollywood blockbuster films marketed for gender swapping or a feminist sensibility (e.g., *Bridesmaids* [2011]) have been examined in feminist academia (Savigny and Warner 2015b). The idea of a rebooted popular feminism continues to be investigated in relation to the overarching theoretical framework of postfeminism and its embeddedness in the neoliberal market economy, highlighting how the culture industries constantly reconfigure and circulate ideals of citizenship, be it in the form of consumer, entrepreneur, or activist. Savigny and Warner (2015a) express skepticism about this popular feminism, emphasizing the interdependence of mediatized feminism and consumer culture that by and large operates to depoliticize the movement and repackage it as a branded product.

Yet the intensified polarization of American political culture and the simultaneous centralization of identity politics, especially in relation to gender, class, and race, have unavoidably produced popular media phenomena that keenly emphasize a politicized approach at odds with millennial (post) feminism. The popularization of the term *intersectionality* (initially coined by legal scholar Kimberlé Crenshaw [1989]) in media punditry is a symptom of this, as are numerous efforts in entertainment media discourses to speak to the increased sociocultural requirement of thematizing identity *as* politics, seen, for instance, in the promotional value of diversity in

---

1   See more on these notions in chapter 1.

media production and advertising (Khamis 2020). Feminist media scholarship interrogates these aspects of popular culture within the interlocking fulcrum of creative labor and market demands (involving postfeminism as governing backdrop), seen, for example, in Linda Mizejewski's (2014) examination of the rising popularity of women's comedy on American television. Similarly, the dubious prominence of the feminist female celebrity has been analyzed through the case of Beyoncé, for instance, whose 2013 coming-out as a *Black* feminist threw into relief the contrast with her preexisting star image as a postrace, postfeminist diva (Durham 2012; Weidhase 2015; Hamad and Negra 2020). Yet another contentious issue is the increased presence of feminist activism on social media platforms, often in conjunction with media branding practices and with celebrity activism (Keller 2015). Previously marginalized strands of emancipatory efforts, such as transgender political activism, have also become more visible and tied to the imperatives of popular media's political economy, as seen in the celebrity activism of Laverne Cox and Janet Mock and in the discourses about reality TV personality Caitlyn Jenner—each highlighting negotiation processes among transgender feminism's efforts to challenge gender binaries, transgender mainstreaming, and homonormativity (Stryker 2008; Irving 2008; Lovelock 2016).

These examples demonstrate the increased focus of American popular discourses on questions that academic reflections on postfeminism have been asking about the relationship between postfeminism and feminist politics, specifically postfeminism's selective incorporation of feminist rhetoric into popular cultural production. The tensions that have long been present in feminist media theory about the relationship between feminism and popular culture have thus shifted onto popular platforms. In a postrecessionary cultural environment the circulation of high-profile debates questioning the use of the feminist label has intensified in popular entertainment, at the same time invoking historically less visible (Black and postcolonial, transgender) feminisms. These debates demonstrate how inquiries that had historically been marginalized for their critique of the working mechanisms of structural oppression and postfeminism have been seeping into popular representations and discourses. However, because these representations continue to be subject to the logic and forces of commercial culture in their interpretations of feminist critique, pessimistic scholarly warnings about popular cultural treatments also continue to be valid. Precisely this circular nature keeps feeding further marketable tensions into these discourses, because the selective and performative tendencies of such thematizations expose which of these marginalized voices and criticisms are deemed fit or unfit for popularization, providing further ground for criticism and productive tensions unsettling the narratives of public discourse.

As discussed, television, with its reputation for being the ideal venue for representing so-called women's issues and other social tensions in long-form narratives, has been at the center of popular discourses about representations of this renewed feminism. Dramatizations of the tension between postfeminism and feminism started to appear in the mid-2000s in the controversial subcategory of quality television, foregrounding feminist politics as a marketable novelty that strives to dialogue with and emphatically distance itself from earlier postfeminist gender representations seen in the likes of *Sex and the City* (1998–2004) and *Ally McBeal* (1997–2002), two series considered blueprints of postfeminist media (Dow 2002; Negra 2004). I analyze this process in detail in this book's individual chapters, but to cite a typical example, consider *Orange*'s promotional strategies and narrative technique. The series and its paratexts insist that its portrayal of women opposes traditional postfeminist representations of womanhood, and *this* is its primary claim for quality status. As discussed in chapters 5 and 6, series creator Jenji Kohan stresses in interviews that the trope of the privileged attractive white woman in a central role was used as a "Trojan horse" to pitch the series to Netflix executives, in order to sell the idea of exploring stories of marginalized women. Similarly, the program's dialogue and narratives frequently reinforce the notion of exposing and ridiculing postfeminist womanhood.

The observation that the examined series use their status as quality TV to explore issues of gender merits further investigation, considering television's historic associations with both feminine *and* low culture—thus, in chapter 1 I look at how the contemporary formation of quality TV, which presumably distances the medium from its connotations with mediocrity and unculturedness, affects its gendered working mechanisms. This inquiry is all the more crucial considering two contradictory aspects of American TV's historical relationship with gendered cultural value. First, in the historic emergence of the term, *quality* as a buzzword was initially used in the 1970s to promote a female-centered and discursively feminist sitcom cycle, starting with *The Mary Tyler Moore Show* (1970–1977). Second and in contrast, the early-twenty-first century establishment of quality television mobilizes ideals of cultural value governed by an underlying masculine-coded understanding of genre and aesthetic judgment. I tease out the details of this apparent contrast by providing a diachronic analysis of the term's gendered development in American culture since the 1970s and then by turning to how the premium cable channel HBO mobilized ideas of transgression to establish its own masculinized quality brand. In so doing, I lay the groundwork for individual analyses of the four selected series and assessments of how they formulate and navigate their gender politics both in the current quality TV landscape and in the historic context.

The term *quality television* has produced a tension in television scholarship similar to that of feminist scholarship's grappling with postfeminism, here in the antagonism between aesthetic and political approaches, or as James Zborowski (2016) describes these, the "TV aesthetics" and "media and cultural studies" groups (see also Lury 2016). This contestation is partly due to the term's coinage in industry and journalistic discourses, which makes it unstable and subject to constant strategic reappropriations (akin to postfeminism's constant adaptation to new cultural-economic contexts). Given feminist scholarship's historic contributions to the establishment of television studies' concepts, behind the tension between political and aesthetic approaches looms large the antagonism between the tools of *feminist* and aesthetic analysis. And as Newman and Levine (2012) show, the advancement since the early 2000s of primarily aesthetic analyses of television texts is intertwined with the American television industry's redefinition of quality television as "cinematic," a moniker carrying implicit notions of masculinism.[2] Thus a gendered binary of aesthetic value becomes reproduced where the masculine-coded cinematic appropriates the spaces of the feminine-coded televisual.

Because television's significance for academic research is historically rooted in the medium's political, economic, and institutional practices, suspicions about the recent rise of aesthetic analysis follow from such analyses' perceived close ties to industry and journalistic discourses. More bluntly, television's aesthetic analysis is seen to be a servile follower to the masculinist elitism underlying the emergence of convergence-era quality television (Newman and Levine 2012, 153–71). But as I will show, debates about the gendered and classed elitism of academic discussions of cultural distinctions and hierarchies have been a staple of television scholarship at

---

2 See also Helen Wheatley's *Spectacular Television* (2016), which meticulously demolishes the notion that visually interesting television is inherently "cinematic."

least since the 1980s and grew in significance in concordance with cultural critics' theorizations of postmodern culture. Academics heralding the millennial emergence of an aesthetically and narratively different television culture and feminist scholars' suspicion of this enthusiasm fall into this earlier pattern of debates, which includes the self-perceived underdog status of each group. A power struggle is evident in this academic conflict, one that similarly structured the field in the 1980s and 1990s—with the difference that feminist television studies was then struggling for academic emancipation and for the legitimation of studying a whole medium and its derided forms, whereas it is now often seen as the dominant approach that forecloses others by being bogged down in questions of political representation and ideological processes of canonization. Scholars such as Jason Mittell (2015) and Sudeep Dasgupta (2012) warn against television studies "limit[ing] itself to defending popular culture against 'Quality TV'" (Dasgupta 2012) on the basis of the field's deeply embedded political agenda; in contrast, feminist critics Taylor Nygaard and Jorie Lagerwey (2016) call for a "challenge [to] the hierarchies of value placed on all modes of TV in order to reclaim TV studies' feminist roots and re-center feminine subjects."

My analysis intervenes in these debates, which seem to correspond to American television culture's categorizations of cultural value divided along the lines of aesthetics and politics. Precisely these demarcations collide in the emergence of postmillennial feminist quality television: Each program that I examine takes the masculinism of contemporaneous quality television culture for granted and establishes its discursively feminist aesthetics in response to this, a practice that is featured with specific significance in traditional and streaming television companies' institutional self-branding and promotion. But the feminism that is thus mobilized also involves the rhetorical contestation of preceding postfeminist representational strategies linked with genre traditions. This trait of the programs deems them central to feminist television scholarship, which has a historically rich literature examining the ramifications of postfeminist television culture for the creation of the new female subject both as consumer-spectator and protagonist. Because the four series I examine incorporate so prominently in their generic and narrative features the signifiers of the quality brand and the politics of female-targeted television, their analysis needs to combine these apparently conflicted approaches to begin to unearth their cultural work. Although this argument echoes Zborowski's (2016) in its conciliatory tenor, unlike his, it highlights the necessity of considering the specific findings of feminist scholarship.[3]

CONTEXTUALIZING FEMINIST QUALITY TELEVISION

In this book I demonstrate how gender politics and the foregrounding of popular feminism are used in the four series' branding as quality TV and tease out their (often contradictory) negotiations of gendered cultural value and aesthetic signifiers, an undertaking that ultimately signals larger theoretical debates and the necessity of rethinking analytical methods in television studies. To this end, I approach the four programs by means of a combined analysis of the TV texts, promotional and institutional discourses, and critical reception, the last of which includes both journalistic and academic writings. Focusing on only four shows allows for a detailed analysis of their forms and political features and the characteristics of their circulation in public discourses.

The four programs exemplify feminist quality television in several ways. The first aspect is production context: All are American series commissioned between 2005 and 2013, when feminist quality television was emerging and becoming increasingly and discursively visible. Three of the four case studies are network programs and provide an example of being a symbolic first for a specific phenomenon: *30 Rock* originated American postmillennial quality comedy that centralized feminism as a political force and key theme; *The Good Wife* was the first prominent quality drama to operate in a similar capacity; *Orange Is the New Black* was the first series to continue this trend on nonterrestrial, nonlegacy TV, serving as a template for Netflix to configure its position in the quality industry through the invocation of feminism for branding purposes in the streaming era. Although *Parks and Recreation* is hardly a first in these terms, its inclusion is justified by the intense media discourse about the series as feminist quality comedy par excellence and, crucially, by this discourse's frequent evaluative contrasting of *Parks* with *30 Rock* because of the two series' different engagements with feminism, complicated by the media promotion of the discursively feminist friendship between Amy Poehler and Tina Fey, the two shows' central stars. Juxtaposing *Parks* with *30 Rock* in an examination of quality comedy

---

3   I return to Zborowski's argument in the Conclusion.

provides an opportunity to unpack the shifts in popular evaluative practices around what counts as ideal feminist comedy.

Although I am aware of the increasing transnationalization of (prestige) television in the globalized streaming age, my aim to map the emergent period of the feminist quality TV trend calls for concentrating on American television. This is partly because the by now ubiquitous globalized quality TV culture that developed in the late 1900s and early 2000s originates in the American TV industry; as such, its institutional, aesthetic, and political traits are embedded in this national context. Further, and following from this, the first and most prominent examples of postmillennial feminist quality TV (those analyzed here) perform their cultural work in this context: The distinct Americanness of the series' institutional settings (the American TV show business, local government, the legal-political system, and the prison industrial complex) is a key aspect of their aesthetic and political efforts to dispute, reflect on, but also appropriate those notions of cultural value for which the foregoing period's quality television is renowned.

Second, the central themes of these series involve a specific appeal to (American) feminist politics. All four series are widely regarded as mobilizing feminist rhetoric at odds or dialoguing with postfeminist discourses by highlighting a political narrative context that centralizes female protagonists in public and political environments and dramatizes and reflects on feminism as a historic and mediated political movement. This shift in focus and rhetoric around representations of womanhood can be linked partly to the recessionary cultural environment (Negra and Tasker 2014a; Lagerwey et al. 2016), in which the postfeminism of earlier texts predicated on prosperity and classed consumerism was no longer viable and required a reconfiguration of the meanings of women's empowerment. The political and social impact of the recession is considered a contributor to these programs' emergence, but it is not fundamental to my analysis, because I see the recession as one of a group of interacting factors. *30 Rock*'s 2006 start predates the recession by two years—in addition, the series was in preproduction for at least another year—and its political satire consistently treats feminism, postfeminism, capitalism, race politics, and so on as central to its narration. Rather than an exceptional precursor to recessionary women-centered media, it signals the growing anti-authoritarian politicization of comedy in American culture after the millennium (Imre 2016, 242–50), which gave more space to women comedians' focus on gender politics (Mizejewski 2014), a process that only intensified during the recession. Again, I see the cultural shift that the recession brought about as an important factor in this development but not a defining one.

Third, all four programs are regarded in media and industry discourses as quality television, a descriptor in which aesthetic exceptionality and novel gender politics converge. Although the terms of this criterion are admittedly vague and would allow for the inclusion of a number of other programs, I identify a specific feature in these programs that justifies their unique usefulness for my purposes: They each upset gendered conventions of genre, narrative, and aesthetics in ways that effect a cultural unease around either their generic-aesthetic positioning or the purported progressiveness of their gender politics, or both, which is consequential for the discursive allocations of their cultural value. The issue of genre hybridity affected by gender politics is evident in other, more recent programming as well, but in keeping with my interest in the phenomenon as it is *emerging*, I concentrate on those that provide the earliest examples.

A number of programs created after those analyzed here can be (and have been) understood as prominent instances of female-centered quality programming foregrounding genre hybridity and feminist discourses. These include *Girls* (2012–2017), *The Fall* (2013–2016), *Top of the Lake* (2013–2017), *Transparent* (2014–2019), *Jessica Jones* (2015–2019), *Crazy Ex-Girlfriend* (2015–2019), *Unbreakable Kimmy Schmidt* (2015–2020), *Veep* (2012–2019), *Broad City* (2014–2019), *Masters of Sex* (2013), *Homeland* (2011–2020), *Fleabag* (2016–2019), *Good Girls Revolt* (2015), *The Good Fight* (2017–), *The Handmaid's Tale* (2017–), and *Mrs. America* (2020). Indeed, the rapid spread of the feminist quality TV phenomenon after the recession and in the mid- to late 2010s demonstrates the increasing viability of the strategic marriage between foregrounded gender (and other identity) politics and aesthetic exceptionalism for the industry. Although I do not provide an analysis of this blooming state of feminist quality TV, my strategy of retracing the features of its emergent period provides a methodological framework for other media scholars engaging with the aforementioned and other programs. In this perspective my analysis of *Orange Is the New Black*, the last series in the examined emergent period and in a different programming context from the others, provides a model for theorizing my key series' proliferating successors: *Orange*'s inclusion allows me to show the cultural traction of feminist rhetoric by means of the streaming platform Netflix's reliance on it as an early brand identifier. Contrasted with the other three programs, which were produced for broadcast television, it also demonstrates the significance of technological shifts and changing viewer habits in the streaming era, which has also influenced the ways in which feminist rhetoric is mobilized.

This book consists of two parts, preceded by a chapter (chapter 1) discussing my theoretical perspective on the gendered history, politics, and aesthetics of quality television. In chapter 1 I examine in detail the quality brand's specificities as a category of television, focusing on both the term's academic and popular history and the debate that revolves around gendered and classed processes of canonization. I highlight the relevance of gender politics for these processes through a historical examination of the term's shifting meanings and its gendered implications in the United States. I also pay attention to the question of culturally sanctioned transgressions ("edginess"), an aspect of quality television that carries heightened significance for its branding power. By examining the masculinism of the post-1990s quality paradigm, developed by the premium cable channel HBO, from the perspective of its cultivated subversion of traditional television's content regulations, I contrast this kind of subversion with the issue of *political* transgression, specifically, American television's legacy of feminist-coded transgressions of expectations of femininity. As I argue, such feminist transgressions have their own historical connection with assignations of cultural value. This chapter's findings underpin the individual discussions of the programs' appeals to transgressions of gendered political and aesthetic traditions.

Chapters 2, 3, and 4 and chapters 5 and 6 discuss the two comedies and two dramas, respectively. This structure around genre (comedy versus drama) corresponds to my focus on the connection between questions of aesthetics and gender politics and also aligns with the programs' categorization in industry and media discourses according to their genre signifiers. Genre categorization is central to my discussion because the series' feminist credentials are produced in the specific contexts of their genre positioning. Both comedy and drama are explored thematically through a cross-cutting discussion of cultural value, genre, and aesthetics on the one hand and the negotiation of feminist rhetoric and postfeminism on the other. Each theme is a focus of a chapter. My concentration on these aspects of feminist quality television stems from the twofold theoretical approach of the book, aiming to show the interconnection of aesthetics and politics in the series' appeals to cultural value. In each chapter I provide close analyses of each series and their comparative elements as appropriate.

My discussion of comedy includes an extra chapter (chapter 4), which explores body politics, acknowledging the discursive centrality of the body in the genre. In the academic literature on comedy, physical humor and embodied comic performance are a key concern to theorizing the genre's expressive power and cultural value and, crucially, the ways in which women's comedy uses the body as a site of politics. As such, the significance of this discussion is the treatment of the comic female body in quality comedy's modes of expression. As discussed in chapter 1, a key feature of the quality brand is its subversion of American television's regulations of visual depictions of the corporeal, and the setup of these institutional regulations and subversions (the network versus cable/streaming dichotomy) is profoundly gendered. Therefore the two network comedies' treatment of the comic female body, already a site of cultural anxieties, is essential to their appeal to cultural value. My discussion of the two dramas also pays attention to the question of embodied performance and sexual politics as signifiers of feminist quality, but these discussions are integrated into chapters 5 and 6.

I do not evaluate the four series' feminism or postfeminism; nor do I champion their inclusion into the quality television canon, whether on aesthetic or political grounds. My interest lies in examining how the series and their promotional and institutional contexts mobilize these terms to produce novelty programming in an age of television frequently described in TV journalism with the slightly ominous phrase "Peak TV" (Garber et al. 2015). Doubtlessly, American television has undergone profound aesthetic shifts in need of interrogation; but I agree with critics of the "TV aesthetics" camp that canonization processes continue to be problematically gendered and with feminist criticism's contention that this gendering is informed by postfeminism's and feminism's popular cultural presence and promotional power. In this book I explore the nexus of those complex phenomena, which has allowed for Kenneth's "TV no-no list" to become the industry's "yes-yes list."

1

QUALITY TV, GENDER, AND THE POLITICS OF CULTURAL TRANSGRESSION

THE QUALITY TELEVISION DEBATE

Television scholars have been intensely debating the definition and usefulness of the term *quality television* at least since the turn of the millennium. To some extent this debate derives from the fact that the phrase—similar to postfeminism—originates in popular discourse and thus eludes rigorous definitions. The term itself is not new—it has been circulating in American popular discourses and in scholarship since the 1970s—but its understanding has changed significantly in the postnetwork era, in concord with shifts in the industry and in the medium's public image.

Even though quality TV is considered a distinct category of television, scholars also acknowledge that traditional televisual genres continue to operate within it, and they frequently distinguish between quality comedy and quality drama. Nonetheless, when describing characteristics of "quality" in terms of what sets it apart from other TV forms, academics tend to emphasize commonalities among quality programs to highlight definitive features. For instance, Jason Mittell (2006) analyzes in detail both quality drama and quality comedy programming to demonstrate how "narrative complexity" works in each form. Similarly, when Janet McCabe and Kim Akass (2007b) examine HBO programs' strategies of using explicit content, their examples include both *The Sopranos* (1999–2007) and *Curb Your Enthusiasm* (2000–). However, despite considerations of different form and genre traditions in these examples, theories about quality TV tend to concentrate on quality *drama* as the default genre on which its working mechanisms are most effectively illustrated. This follows from drama and comedy's historically different cultural estimations: Comedy, being a genre of lower cultural status, may gain the "quality" descriptor, but because drama and tragedy are positioned in Western culture on a "higher dramatic plane" (Rowe Karlyn 1995b, 97), in the longitudinal evolution of quality television, the quality drama's emergence is considered television's artistic peak.

Jonathan Bignell (2013) identifies three main characteristics of quality television. First, quality programs have an aesthetic ambition "with the literary values of creative imagination, authenticity and relevance" that differentiates them from other, "generic" and "conventional" programming. Second, such programs exhibit high production values that "prioritize strong writing and innovative *mise-en-scène*." Third, they are targeted to "valuable" or quality (middle-class, educated, affluent) audiences, ensuring these programs' economic value (179). Bignell's definition is aligned with earlier television scholars' discussions of the term, including the argument that quality television is best understood as a genre (R. J. Thompson 1997; Mittell 2006; Cardwell 2007). Its theorization as a genre, then, contradictorily involves the notion that it resists the "generic," or formulaic, dimensions of television narration. Sarah Cardwell (2007) in particular goes to great lengths to conceptualize quality TV in these terms, arguing for stripping the word of its evaluative implications and highlighting specific genre features instead, which presumably creates a more democratic and objective atmosphere for critical judgments about any type of television (23, 32–33). Such an argument thus sidesteps the term's origins in evaluative critical judgments and cultural hierarchies, which are predicated on privileging certain types of evaluative subjectivities. This becomes clear in the term's historical development, to which I now turn.

Before the 1990s, American quality TV primarily meant programming aimed at the "quality" demographic (Feuer et al. 1984). This definition also cultivated an aesthetic that was "clean," "least objectionable," and profoundly televisual (Lentz 2000). Mittell (2006), in explaining the emergence of "narrative complexity" (his influential term for a new feature of American TV programs), provides an exhaustive account of the factors that changed institutional practices in the 1990s to facilitate a different kind of programming. In his book *Complex TV* (2015a), Mittell expresses his disapproval of the term *quality* for its hierarchical connotations, instead proposing *complex TV*, an expression signifying a TV text's aesthetic efforts while, purportedly, avoiding an elitist hierarchy between "complex" and "simple" TV, similar to Cardwell's (2007) concept.[1] Narrative complexity is partly facilitated by creative personnel's new understanding of television as a territory of artistic freedom, explaining why so many of them arrive from careers in cinema. Mittell's (2006) explanation for the trend of cinema personnel's discovery of television is the medium's presumed amicability toward innovative *storytelling*, as opposed to Hollywood cinema's preference for *visual* spectacle (31–32). The move of film directors and screenwriters toward television is thus mutually beneficial: Film creatives gain more room for artistic experimentation, and the television industry capitalizes not only on new and innovative products but also on the higher regard in which these producers and creators are held, given their association with cinema. Quality in television is therefore formulated in relation to cinema, rooted in the latter medium's cultural estimation as superior to television. As such, the transition toward television by cinema directors and writers is a form of cultural colonization, a process in which representatives of the putatively aesthetically superior medium appropriate the spaces, discourses, and working mechanisms of the conquered medium, which is deemed inferior for its practitioners' assumed incapability to realize its full potential. Inherent in quality television discourses about saving television from mediocrity by excavating its aesthetic capacities is, then, a continued contempt for existing television culture.

Jane Feuer's (2007) critical analysis of quality television further specifies the importance of television and cinema's different cultural status. She postulates that when creative personnel are lured away from cinema and toward television, they arrive with an aspiration to associate quality television with art cinema (as opposed to formulaic genre cinema). Thus what is regarded as certain television programs' higher artistic value and originality than the assumed norm implies a cultural hierarchy between the two media that is extended to a parallel hierarchy among television genres and programs. Feuer's criticism of this cultural hierarchy is echoed by a number of television theorists (e.g., Newman and Levine 2012; Mills 2013).

A further aspect of the role that cultural hierarchies play in the emergence of millennial quality TV is the medium's relationship to so-called explicit content. McCabe and Akass (2007b) highlight that the process in which HBO created its "not TV" brand in the 1990s involved capitalizing on its exempt status from broadcasting regulation practices as a subscription-based

---

1   I examine Mittell's arguments in more detail in chapter 6.

premium cable channel. That is, the graphic sexuality and violence that is a frequent feature of HBO's (and, later, other cable channels') original programming contributes to its brand identity as a trailblazer of quality television. In HBO's practice of "courting controversy," the discourses about the quality of such series as *The Sopranos* and *Deadwood* (2004–2006) justify the explicitness through "creative risk-taking and artistic integrity" (McCabe and Akass 2007, 69). HBO and its auteur producers legitimate "illicit" content by linking it to exceptional aesthetics, authenticity, and "dramatic verisimilitude" (70–75). Although McCabe and Akass (2007) do not emphasize it, their case studies also illustrate how the idea of cinema as the bearer of higher cultural value surfaces for *The Sopranos* and *Deadwood* in genre terms. Both series draw on American cinema's legacies of so-called tough genres (the gangster film and the western) and as such are deeply embedded in discourses about nation and masculinity.[2] However, HBO's self-promotion, which constantly seeks to reconfirm its headliner programming's high cultural status through associations of the illicit with cinematic and literary values and authenticity, betrays an anxiety about the cultural positioning of illicit content (73). A clear sign of this in the 1990s and 2000s was the channel's much more muted promotion of its consequently lesser known but just as explicit programming, such as its sex documentaries; HBO's "internal regulation is cautious in handling the salacious and gratuitous, and absorbs the illicit into the serious business of making original groundbreaking programs" (73).

HBO's frequent rationalization of the incorporation of explicit content into its flagship programs exemplifies the anxiety with which industry and media discourses about quality TV (not just on cable) strain to reposition and redefine the term's meanings. The appeal to the cinematic or "above TV" status creates a paradoxical situation, because scholars and TV critics praise quality TV as profoundly televisual in maximizing medium-specific characteristics, as seen in Mittell's analysis of narrative complexity. Mittell (2006) describes this as "a redefinition of episodic forms under the influence

---

2 To jump ahead in my argument, the justification of portrayals of explicit sex and violence as a claim to realism recalls the discursive positioning of legendary TV producer Norman Lear's "relevance" sitcoms in the 1970s, invoking the "authenticity" of profanity as a masculine trait. I detail this historic discourse later in this chapter, drawing on Lentz (2000). A crucial difference is that the relevance sitcom's significance is limited to its claim to televisual realism (as opposed to cinematic aesthetic), and thus it becomes positioned as nonquality through its attachment to racial politics and working-class profanity.

of serial narration" that uses the seriality of soap operas, while "rejecting . . . the melodramatic style" (32).[3] Although highlighting the legacy of the culturally derided soap opera in the formation of narrative complexity, and as such contending that it uses narrative forms specific to television, Mittell's rhetoric also asserts the relative cultural position of these two types of TV: "While certainly soap opera narration can be quite complex and requires a high degree of audience activity . . . , narratively complex programming typically foregrounds plot developments far more centrally than soaps, allowing relationship and character drama to emerge from plot development in an emphasis reversed from soap operas" (32). Because Mittel's purpose is to demonstrate how this new type of TV is "innovative" as opposed to "conventional" programming (29), he makes clear which kind of storytelling practice (foregrounding plot versus foregrounding relationship drama) is deemed more valuable. At the same time, Mittell rhetorically distances complex TV from soap traditions by drawing comparisons with cinema. By defining complex TV's "operational aesthetic" as a set of narrative devices that bring viewer attention to the mechanics of plotting, he juxtaposes this with the cinema of attractions: television's "narrative special effects" appeal to viewer appreciation akin to cinema's narrative-stopping visual spectacle (35).

Mittell's account of narrative complexity is representative of the discursive struggles around positioning quality TV in the cultural hierarchy of the two media. These discourses regularly invoke the cinematic to provide aesthetic validation and downplay the television heritage to insist that quality TV may have grown out of this heritage but has definitely outgrown it. Quality television's decades-long aesthetic validation, championed prominently by Mittell, has effected an intense debate, evidenced in rebuttals from Feuer (2007), Kackman (2008), Imre (2009), Newman and Levine (2012), Mills (2013), and Nygaard and Lagerwey (2016), among others. These scholars problematize the notion of quality or complex television by bringing attention to the inherent elitism of its discursive development on the grounds of classed and gendered ideals of cultural value. The influence of melodramas and soap operas on television's generic

---

3   Mittell changes his stance on melodrama's influence in *Complex TV* (2015a), but gendered evaluative judgments continue to govern it. See chapter 6. For an incisive examination of the relationship between gender and television seriality, see Sulimma (2021).

and political traditions features significantly in these arguments, evoking Lynne Joyrich's (1988) interrogation of similar phenomena two decades earlier.[4] Patrice Petro (1986) and Charlotte Brunsdon (1990) also brought attention to these questions through examinations of cultural valuations of Anglo-American media just when our current understanding of quality TV was about to emerge. Joyrich's, Petro's, and Brunsdon's arguments are echoed in contemporary critics' *political* interrogations of television's aesthetics, stressing that quality TV emerges from a rhetorical distancing from feminized and classed television culture. Their interventions stress how gendered and classed power structures operate in the canonization of a category whose common defining point derives from critical and institutional gatekeeping and whose concentration on aesthetics glosses over this practice's profoundly political nature.

GENDERED QUALITY TV CULTURE IN THE 2000S

As discussed, one strand of television scholarship contends that the evolution of contemporary quality TV is embedded in gendered and classed understandings of cultural value. There is some consensus about quality TV's rootedness in the narrational and characterization heritage of soap operas and melodrama, even in the discursive distancing from these lesser valued forms on narrative-generic grounds. Kackman (2008) also reminds us that discursive formulations of quality TV, by "re-embracing the gendered hierarchies that made the medium an object of critical and popular scorn," sidestep in the process feminist scholars' historic contribution to the emergence of television studies (see also Nygaard and Lagerwey 2016). But even though gendered hierarchies previously manifested through contrasting evaluations of different *media* (TV versus cinema), now that TV has become eligible for aesthetic judgments, this differentiation continues *within* television, in the gendered cultural hierarchy between quality and "other" programming.

The emergence of contemporary quality TV is therefore founded on classed and gendered differentiations from so-called average TV, igniting a debate in television studies between scholars celebrating television's

---

4 Joyrich's concepts about the relationship between television, cultural value, and gender are discussed later in this chapter.

aesthetic revolution and those criticizing its gendered and classed hierarchies using cultural studies approaches (Zborowski 2016). In the following discussion, I combine the aesthetic and political approaches to map how the gendered hierarchy works not only in the quality versus conventional opposition but also *within* the millennial quality TV paradigm. This gendered differentiation follows from the economic incentives, governed by fragmented audience targeting, of multichannel-era television: Quality TV's appeal to urban, high-income, educated viewers involves a gendered division (among others) of viewership. The history of quality TV since the 1970s is founded on differentiations between the feminine and the masculine in terms of target audiences, production practices, genre and textual features, and journalistic discourse. In the postnetwork era the industry's gendering of audiences produces a dualistic formation of quality TV texts: masculine-coded quality drama on one hand and feminine-coded quality television (mostly dramedy) on the other.

The quality television of the 1990s and 2000s links high aesthetic and production values with the exploration of white masculinities (Lagerwey et al. 2016; Nygaard and Lagerwey 2016). Series that helped to shape this canon, such as *The Sopranos*, *The Wire* (2002–2008), *24* (2001–2010), *Breaking Bad* (2008–2013), *Lost* (2004–2010), *Mad Men* (2007–2015), *Game of Thrones* (2011–2019), *Boardwalk Empire* (2010–2014), *Deadwood*, and *True Detective* (2014–2019), share not only obvious generic-aesthetic features (markers of their quality) but also a preference for concentrating on and dissecting variously troubled masculinities. These programs introduced the figure of the complex hero or antihero whose stories reflect changing ideas of American masculinity, society, family, and identity (Lotz 2014; Albrecht 2015; Mittell 2015b). Although these texts offer themselves for analyzing the complexity of their portrayals of troubled masculinities in relation to broader crisis narratives about social, political, and cultural changes (Albrecht 2015), omitted from their examinations are critical inquiries into how and why these cultural anxieties appear to be embedded in quality television's genre-hybridizing and cinematic apparatus as profoundly male experiences. Lacking this scrutiny, masculinity remains an inherently assumed (whether celebrated or lamented) feature of quality drama's novelty aesthetics.

But postnetwork TV also produced feminine-coded quality television, characterized by the use of female leads and an ideological connection to postfeminist cultural discourses. The emergence of postfeminist TV programming has its own extensive literature in feminist television theory, with

scholars investigating its relationship to neoliberal consumer culture, (post)
feminist gender politics, and American television history's relationship with
feminism, among other concerns. Representatively, two urtexts of postfeminist television, *Sex and the City* and *Desperate Housewives* (2004–2012), have
been the objects of study in McCabe and Akass's anthology series *Reading
Contemporary Television* (2004, 2006), which features TV programs based
on their prominence in shaping television culture. Yet studies of millennial
postfeminist television from the perspective of its relationship with quality TV discourses have been scarce. One exception is Diane Negra's (2004)
work on *Sex and the City*, which examines the program's articulation of
quality through its address to upscale female audiences and its connections
to postfeminist consumer culture. Negra's argument that quality here has to
be understood in the series' relationship to postfeminism means that quality becomes defined by the text's treatment of gender politics, that is, by its
representation of contemporaneous concerns about the millennial female
subject and by its ambiguous relationship to (post)feminist politics. In other
words, quality here is defined not so much as an aesthetic category but as a
political one: Questions of aesthetics and narrative are articulated through
questions of gender politics.

This observation can be extended to other female-led quality series
that emerged after *Sex and the City*'s trendsetting success, even its short-
lived copycats *The Lipstick Jungle* (2008–2009) and *Cashmere Mafia* (2008)
or the more lasting *Desperate Housewives* and *Grey's Anatomy* (2005–). In
these programs the notion of quality is tied to their negotiation of issues
of womanhood, tailored to the target demographic's assumed interests;
and their cultural value hinges on whether and how their representational
politics transgress boundaries of the gendered status quo. This becomes
clear in the programs' relationships to genre. Their concentration on the
political rather than on the aesthetic articulation of quality implies that
female-led quality television locates its expressive modes in the frameworks
of melodrama and dramedy, because it is not so interested in transgressions of genre and form, and as such remains in the domain of what are
typically called women's genres. Thus the soap opera's televisual heritage is
more visible (less concealed aesthetically) because the notion of quality
is not primarily expressed through intended narrative and artistic invention.
Consequently, this programming becomes discursively inferior in relation
to the quality associated with masculine-coded television. In this setup the
idea of subversion is split along gendered lines between the aesthetic form

and the political, with the aesthetic subversion carrying more cultural currency than the political intent.

The concentration of postfeminist quality television on the new female subject spawned a number of female-targeted series on premium cable that present various kinds of troubled white womanhood, such as *Nurse Jackie* (2009–2015), *United States of Tara* (2009–2011), *Weeds* (2005–2012), *The L Word* (2004–2009), *Enlightened* (2011–2013), or *The Big C* (2010–2013). These programs use their cable TV environment to express subversions of traditional images of women, exemplified in cable channel Showtime's "ladies with problems" programming formula (Nygaard 2013). These subversions are tied to the half-hour dramedy form and revolve around the complexity of middle-class white womanhood, tapping into discourses about the messy and complex lives of middle-class white women whose narratives explore this identity in a generically and aesthetically fixed form. Postfeminist quality TV's roots in the explicitly political explains why its representation practices—namely, its focus on women fitting into particular social categories (housewife, career woman, mother)—become crucial questions in their critical evaluations. Contrastingly, the protagonist of male-focused quality drama is mostly identified by profession (mafia leader, small-town sheriff, chemistry-teacher-turned-meth-cook), which in turn is associated with plot and transgressive aesthetics. His identity, unlike the postfeminist woman's, becomes articulated through these aesthetic practices. The postfeminist protagonist signals concerns about women's shifting domestic identities, and this focus determines generic and aesthetic practices; consequently, issues of progressiveness and representational politics override aesthetic concerns, both for the programs and for the discourses about them.

Because high production values and the targeting of select demographics are given features for both masculine-coded and postfeminist quality TV, the distinguishing factor between these categories becomes the specific methods in articulating cultural value. As seen, for masculine-coded programming this means foregrounding aesthetics, genre, and plot, whereas postfeminist quality TV defines cultural value through the politics of characterization of a culturally recognizable female protagonist, rendering issues of genre, plotting, and aesthetics subordinate to characterization practices. A gendered difference is also recognizable in these categories' textual-discursive modes of audience address. Male-centered quality drama, despite its focus on troubled masculinities, is still interested in attracting other-than-white-male audiences, as indicated by the trope of so-called strong female and minority supporting characters, which the narratives of ensemble series tend to exhibit. The appeal to universal aesthetic values invites a degendered appreciation of these forms, at the same time veiling the gender dynamics inherent in their construction. This universal quality is also linked to high-concept serialization's emergence on television, which promises a contrast to traditional TV's ephemeral and episodic patchwork structure; the appeal to a superior grand narrative assumes a lack of gendered cultural hierarchies. This programming is putatively universally appealing to any discerning viewer on account of its aesthetic values. In contrast, postfeminist programming openly targets a female or feminine-coded audience segment, and the quality that it claims to carry emerges in its political address to this group.

The gendered split in millennial definitions of quality TV can be further illuminated through the term's historical examination. In the following section I trace how the idea of quality television was constructed in the 1970s (a period when the promotional vernacular started to mobilize the term) and how both programs and contemporaneous discourses invoked gender politics. By tracing the historic genealogy of the relationship between American quality TV and gender, I highlight the changing contexts in which this relationship evolved over time.

QUALITY DISCOURSES IN THE NETWORK ERA

The diachronic trajectory of quality from the 1970s to the postnetwork era is a gradual shift from a political understanding of the term toward an aesthetic one. In their engagement with television's relationship with gender and cultural value between the 1970s and 1990s, television historians Jane Feuer et al. (1984), Lynne Joyrich (1988, 1996), Bonnie J. Dow (1996), and Julie D'Acci (1994) emphasize television's early associations with political immediacy and suitability for social-political realism.

In the history of television's relationship with quality, the year 1970 has symbolic importance because it marks the debut of the workplace sitcom *The Mary Tyler Moore Show* on the CBS network. Produced by the production company MTM, the program proved a game changer both in the American television industry's relationship with its popular reputation as low culture and in second-wave feminism's relationship with its popular cultural representations (Feuer et al. 1984). The fact that this happened in the situation comedy genre shows that the idea of quality television in its meaning of social-political innovation was considered better suited for comedic forms, specifically, for a new type of comedy that did not simply provide light entertainment—it also exhibited social consciousness. The TV industry's new directive of creating quality through catching up with the era's social-political upheavals (such as the women's liberation movement) was predicated on a calculated association between feminist politics and the sitcom form (Rabinovitz 1999). Bonnie Dow (1996) notes that in American television history, female-led dramas have long been scarce because of that format's higher cultural regard; consequently, the sitcom "is the type of programming in which women are most often and most centrally represented and from which television's most resonant feminist representations have emerged" (xviii) (see also D'Acci 1994, 14, 71; Rowe Karlyn 1995b, 97–99). The quality discourse emerged in a genre that, because of its low-culture status[5] presented in a low-culture medium, had more freedom to be politically and socially subversive than others—further demonstrating that television quality in this era was primarily associated with political rather than aesthetic meanings.

In *The Mary Tyler Moore Show* and in other female-led sitcoms that followed throughout the 1970s (*Rhoda* [1974–1978], *Phyllis* [1975–1977], *The Betty White Show* [1977–1978]), the television industry began to develop models of capitalizing on its popular associations with topical political issues to remedy its dubious reputation. The feminist sitcom formula that dominated the era was an answer to the social relevance trend characterizing 1970s television, which all three major networks (CBS, NBC, ABC) used in efforts to reach the newly discovered quality demographic (Feuer 1984a, 4; D'Acci 1994, 13–14; Dow 1996, 32). Competing with MTM in reforming television, Norman Lear's Tandem Enterprises launched its race-relations-themed sitcom *All in the Family* (1971–1979) on CBS. Through their competition the two production companies transformed the sitcom form and also "represented a kind of brand differentiation within the same product line" (Feuer 1984a, 8). As Kerr (1984) notes, "Much of *The Mary Tyler Moore Show*'s success has been attributed to its coincidence with the crisis of the nuclear family and the impact of the women's movement, in much the same way that *All in the Family* has been associated with changing liberal attitudes toward race and racial equality" (80).

---

5   For a detailed exploration of the relationship between cultural value and genre, see Rowe Karlyn (1995b, 95–115).

Through the 1970s female-centered sitcom, MTM and CBS produced quality comedy by openly associating it with the women's liberation movement. Mary Richards (Mary Tyler Moore) represented the new female subject who is financially independent, educated, unmarried, and childless. This female characterization was considered revolutionary for its time (Kerr 1984, 80–81) and was aimed to appeal to white professional female audiences, an emerging target demographic for the culture industries. The female character's innovation drove the idea of quality and provided the MTM sitcom's backbone. That is, all other novelty features—the workplace as the main location, the ensemble cast of colleagues, the emphasis on character rather than situation, the untypically fluid camera movements (87–92)—originate in the radicalism of the female lead's gendered characterization. In other words, television's assumed ability to portray social issues and engage with questions of identity provided the foundation of its 1970s configuration of quality. Crucially, this quality was predicated on television's perceived femininity, the idea that television, a signifier of female consumerism, might best draw on this femininity as political capacity to redefine itself as innovative.[6] An element of this is television's perceived closeness with the (female or feminized) viewer: Its domestic presence, as opposed to cinema's putatively masculine distance and voyeurism, is used here as an asset (Joyrich 1988, 146; 1996, 36–39).

However, even this configuration of feminine quality television by means of the MTM sitcom emerged in a dualistic opposition with other, masculinist television, manifested in Norman Lear's *All in the Family*. Lentz (2000) traces how contemporaneous popular discourse set up the dualism between quality and relevance by highlighting the differences between MTM and Tandem's comedy styles. In this relationship *The Mary Tyler Moore Show* became associated with middle-class whiteness, intellectualism, and "sexual modesty" (68), whereas *All in the Family* earned its reputation for political relevance; its centralization of racial issues situated it in "a discourse about the 'real,' not the moral or polite. And reality is allowed to be shocking" (68). Thus the opposition between quality and relevance also became an opposition between feminist politics and racial politics: sexual modesty and white, middle-class femininity against sexual licentiousness, gritty realism, and working-class, lower-culture masculinity. The traditional dualism of

---

6   For more on the television industry's construction of the female audience, see D'Acci (1994, 63–73).

feminine television and masculine cinema was projected onto the 1970s sitcom through these signifiers, and their gendered and racial features reversed their cultural value and also rendered their aesthetics subservient to these politics. Unlike in the TV versus cinema dualism, the MTM sitcom's liberal feminism assumed higher quality than the Tandem sitcom's masculine-coded realism and raced physicality (in addition, this dualism also kept antiracist and gender politics safely separate in the popular consciousness [80]).

Aesthetic-generic differences between the MTM and Tandem sitcoms follow from their political distance, as Feuer et al. (1984) show. In reinventing the sitcom form, MTM developed the character comedy. By abandoning the classic problem/solution narrative format, *The Mary Tyler Moore Show* and its successors foreground the protagonist's psychological journey; the situation is a pretext for character study, effecting a more nuanced televisual style. Further, because of the emphasis on character dynamics, discussions of political issues primarily focus on the intimate, personal dimensions of these problems. In contrast, *All in the Family* foregrounds situation. To present "social issues," it "retains the simplistic, insult-ridden, joke machine apparatus to a far greater extent than did *The Mary Tyler Moore Show*" (Feuer 1984b, 35). Characters are less complex and virtually "stick figures in a political allegory" (46), each standing for an ideological social type, including female stereotypes. The Tandem comedy's overtly political-allegorical nature disallows psychological depth and offers fewer opportunities for identification or sentimentality; it is also less interested in formal innovation, treating style secondary to politics.

In further scrutinizing the MTM workplace comedy's novelty, Bathrick (1984) highlights that in showcasing a new, liberated, and complex female character, *The Mary Tyler Moore Show* simultaneously drives straightforward political discussions into the background: "The presence in the workplace of the humane and accessible woman" might be a political novelty, but it still subdues direct political address. Therefore "whether the TV newsroom as workplace marks a new environment for a new kind of women's work remains to be considered" (105). Bathrick's oblique criticism can provide a springboard for thinking through the different ideological work that the two types of comedies perform in transforming the sitcom formula. By creating the workplace character comedy, or "warmedy" (Feuer 1984b, 43), *The Mary Tyler Moore Show* domesticates the workplace and to some extent depoliticizes it by means of feminization, whereas the domestically set *All in the Family*'s so-called issue comedy brings (racial) politics into the living room and thus masculinizes it by turning it into an arena of public debate. As such, the masculine-coded political-public and the feminine-coded personal-private cross-contaminate in these two contrasting rearrangements of a traditional TV genre—but in the process they still carry their gendered dimensions with them into the ideologically new form and space.

American television's reflection on the ideological, cultural, and economic changes of the 1960s and 1970s thus yielded a new understanding of quality TV whose definition was politically rooted: It mobilized quality TV's femininity as a political trait. This notion is further nuanced in 1970s quality TV's configuration of the political; in contrast to the Norman Lear sitcom, the feminine or feminist sitcom preferred intimate character development and refined aesthetics to the Lear sitcom's direct political satire, masculinism, and disinterest in formal innovation. This period thus established an implicit polarization between a feminine and a masculine television, but the difference emerged as feminine TV's superior aesthetic value, which in turn was rooted in emphasizing the personal within the political. This is in contrast to postnetwork quality television's configuration, which uses the idea of aesthetic-formal innovation and embeds it in a masculinist cultural tradition, concealing its gendered ideological work. However, feminine-coded postfeminist quality dramedy continues to be defined through a politically subversive but individualized characterization practice (fostered by postfeminist discourse) and is realized in the tried and true aesthetics of the half-hour comedy or dramedy. It was in the 1970s when American television first tested out notions of quality in terms of aesthetics, demographics, and the political—and given television's assumed femininity, it is only logical that this happened through forms, styles, and characterization methods associated with the feminine. These experiments and their formulas for success later became used and transformed in television's gradual establishment of the more aestheticized, masculine-coded, and decidedly more prestigious quality drama.

The last few years of the 1970s and early 1980s saw the decline of the feminine character comedy and the rise of the hour-long quality drama. Political and cultural shifts, such as the three networks' new "Family Hour" programming initiative and the Reagan-Bush era's neoconservative atmosphere, effected institutional reluctance to experiment with women's portrayals (Kerr 1984, 85–87). Wary of presenting content that could be considered controversial, television brought back female representations deemed traditional, thus creating the deeply ironic situation in which "ratings were dominated by examples of what were known inside the industry as 'T&A programming,' 'candy-for-the-eyes' and 'jiggle television'" (87). It was in this cultural atmosphere that MTM developed the hour-long dramas *Lou Grant* (1977–1982) and *Hill Street Blues* (1981–1987), both foundational to postnetwork-era quality drama. They concentrated on male characters in professional environments and used masculine-associated genres and associations with cinema. *Hill Street Blues* mixes the cop genre with documentarism. *Lou Grant*'s inception is owed to the cultural impact of the film *All the President's Men* (1976); the series is set at a daily newspaper and follows an ensemble of investigative reporters chasing news stories of great political and social impact (Wicking 1984, 167) using unusual storytelling methods. Yet these series' several formal features originate in the 1970s MTM sitcom, such as the ensemble cast, the workplace as familial space, and the emphasis on characters' psychological development.[7] A crucial difference, however, is that the innovations of the feminine-coded sitcom were politically motivated: The emphasis on character was a consequence of the strive to create identification points for a new, potentially controversial type of protagonist (the female professional, the divorced woman, the single woman) and thereby to avoid alienating audiences. No such motivation facilitates the subsequent hour-long quality drama's characterization methods; rather, the drama uses this style by simultaneously emptying it of its gendered political impetus and incorporating it into other distinguishing markers of quality.

Although *The Mary Tyler Moore Show* is known for spawning a number of spin-offs and launching the careers of its ensemble cast, in a striking sign of the genderedness of quality TV's genre transformation, it is only the male character Lou Grant (Ed Asner) whose eponymous spin-off series is an hour-long drama. In fact, *Lou Grant* is the series through which MTM configured how topicality and issue-oriented storytelling work in a more serious format. In other words, when MTM, in its quest for the next novelty programming, experimented with genres of higher cultural prestige than the sitcom, it turned to masculine-coded cultural traditions, culminating in *Hill Street Blues* as "the new paradigm for television" in terms of innovative

---

7 They are also influenced by the narrative and characterization methods of melodramas and soap operas, evidenced, for instance, in the increased hybridization of the serial and episodic structure.

style and social criticism (Feuer 1984a, 26). Unsurprisingly, *Hill Street Blues* is frequently discussed as *the* progenitor of postnetwork quality drama.[8] This strive for aesthetic value does not necessitate political innovation in gender representations, and this aspect diminishes in the term's shifting meanings.[9] Decentering the idea of radical female portrayals, the increasing masculinization of quality TV also heralded a "feminism taken into account" (McRobbie 2009, 2) type of treatment of women's allocated spaces in ensemble casts. Dow (1996) mentions that in the "professional serial drama" form of the 1980s, "the influence of feminism in American culture is obvious" but limited, naturalizing the postfeminist paradigm via women professionals' obligatory inclusion as supporting characters into masculine-coded forms of quality television (98).

The historic shift in the discursive formation of quality, moving from the feminine or liberal feminist sitcom toward the masculinist, aesthetically driven quality drama in this period, can be best understood through Lynn Joyrich's argument about discursive connections between television, postmodernism, consumerist culture, and femininity (Joyrich 1988, 1996). Joyrich shows how academic cultural criticism historically configures television culture as the primary manifestation of late capitalist mass culture and postmodern chaos, threatening the classic humanist ethos with the collapse of its traditional dualistic values and epistemologies, where this dualism is profoundly gendered: "Rather than the masculine spectator stimulated by the negativity inherent in modernist art, television creates an effeminate viewer, passive and gullible, in need of comfort and support. Within this discourse, TV's mystification becomes almost a castration" (Joyrich 1996, 26). The contradiction in the popular and academic image of a "feminization lurking over all American culture" is that within the constant fear of mass culture's destruction of such traditional values as "the distance between subject and object, active and passive, that upholds the masculine gaze and the primacy of the male subject" resides these values' continued high evaluation (Joyrich

---

8   Producers of such quality dramas as *The Wire, Deadwood,* and *House of Cards* (2013–2018) cite the influence of *Hill Street Blues* on their work (Ryan 2014).

9   The best-known exception that proves this rule with special force is *Cagney and Lacey* (1981–1988), a drama that attempted to mix the tough cop genre with feminist politics and that strove for quality status through this. The concomitant intense anxieties around the female protagonists' political meaning demonstrate the unease with which foregrounded feminist politics were accepted into genres associated with higher cultural value (D'Acci 1994).

1988, 146). Thus postmodern culture is "desperately trying to retrieve and maintain its traditional distinctions," paradoxically using television's low-culture melodramatic storytelling as a privileged formula that "promis[es] the certainty of clearly marked conflict and legible meaning even as it plays on the closeness associated with a feminine spectator-consumer" (147). In this way, postmodern culture "decenters oppositions even as it attempts to resuscitate them" (147).

Joyrich's theorization of the discursive tension between a feminizing, infantilizing, fragmented, consumerist television culture and a masculinist cultural tradition, canonized as carrying great universal value, provides an explanation for the emergence of television's gendered idea of quality drama, a quality that carries associations of the seemingly nontelevisual (because cinematic) and the masculine voyeuristic (consider HBO's use of sexualized explicit content). In this perspective the longitudinal gravitation toward the cultural dominance of the masculine-coded quality drama seems almost inevitable. Joyrich prognosticated in the 1990s how TV culture would increasingly attempt to ease the tension of postmodernity by introducing such features into its meanings. In the poignantly titled essay "Threats from Within the Gates: Critical and Textual Hypermasculinity" (Joyrich 1996), she shows how 1990s "action and crime dramas . . . attempt to deny television's 'feminine' connotations in order to construct a masculine spectator and achieve the status of 'quality' television" (11). The quality drama canon emerging in the 2000s not only fulfills but also brings to its logical next phase this possibility by adapting ideas of exceptionalism, authenticity, authorship, metanarrative, universalism, and other descriptors of modernist artistry to (cable) television's ecosystem, as signifiers of masculinity.

HBO AND THE CULTURAL VALUE OF TRANSGRESSION

In this section I focus on the connection between transgression and cultural value, specifically the discursively gendered divide between ideals of aesthetic and political transgression on TV. Quality television discourses cultivate the idea of edginess, meaning aesthetic uniqueness, narrativizations of divisive themes, and depictions of violent, sexually explicit content. One of my key arguments in this book is that the feminist quality TV trend strategically mixes different modes of transgression by linking discursively novel treatments of form and narrative with novel thematizations of content associated with popular feminism; from this follows a need to examine how American television configures the relationship between ideas of boundary breaking and cultural value.

The institutional and aesthetic paradigm shift that facilitated the emergence of postnetwork quality TV culture is rooted in premium cable company HBO's aggressive brand building in the 1990s (McCabe and Akass 2007b; Leverette et al. 2008b; Edgerton and Jones 2009). HBO's then-novel method of promoting its brand identity by embedding its original programming in discourses about exclusivity, artistry, and explicit content played a crucial role in establishing the association of some television with high(er) cultural value. The idea of subversion cultivated by the company quickly gained currency in the industry and became a key feature of the quality TV paradigm. Considering that the artistic merits of the HBO model are associated with a taboo-breaking use of explicit content, my focus here is primarily on how this is mobilized to evoke the aura of high cultural value, specifically in its relationship with taboos around the gendered body, social mores, and language. I then move on to unpack the legacy of discursively feminist transgressions on TV, both in a historical trajectory and also in the postnetwork paradigm of quality TV. Considering HBO's profound cultural influence, this examination also builds its timeline around the company's treatment of televisual quality and thus outlines a before-and-after relationship of feminist transgressions with it.

As argued, HBO's promotion of a motivated use of explicit content served to emphasize its uniqueness in the 1990s television landscape. McCabe and Akass (2007b) show that the eagerness with which producers of HBO's flagship series validated the sexually explicit or violent content by linking it to authenticity exposes an underlying unease with this content. This nervousness speaks to the cultural status of the explicit, especially if connected to the body and its boundaries, which in itself is inherently suspicious in taste hierarchies. Linda Williams's (1991) key work on cinema's "body" genres is instructive here; she demonstrates that genres defined by their centralization of the physical and by their appeal to viewers' physical and emotional reactions, especially pornography and horror, have historically been categorized as low culture. HBO's promotional treatment of the explicit emphasizes this content's artistic and/or narrative motivation, thus removing the notion of "only physical" entertainment from its function to secure its programs' cultural prestige.

It is not only the explicit content that gains cultural validation by its association with the artistic but also the medium itself. Despite the assertion of its much-quoted slogan ("It's not TV. It's HBO"), HBO remains closely attached to and dependent on television culture; in Avi Santo's (2008, 24–30) term, the cable network is "para-television." In this bartering around cultural prestige, two phenomena—television and representations of explicit content, both of which have been seen as pandering to the masses and thus being denied judgments based on artistic merit—use each other to create culturally validated modes of representation. The crucial difference between these realms, however, is their gendered cultural coding: American television has long been associated with feminizing, emasculating, consumerist, and middle- to lower-class culture, whereas the profane and its associations with bodily or linguistic transgressions are predicated on lower-class masculinity and the exclusion of the feminine or female *subject*, from mainstream pornography to Freudian theorizations of the smut joke. Television's understanding as feminine is linked to its assumed avoidance of excess, to its appeal to a middlebrow, bourgeois regime of taste that hypocritically regulates representations of the corporeal. The sexually excessive or violent, however, is in a reverse yet symbiotic relationship with the feminine. In Williams's (1991) words, "What may especially mark these body genres [pornography, gross-out horror, and melodrama] as low is the perception that the body of the spectator is caught up in an almost involuntary mimicry of the emotion or sensation of the body on the screen along with the fact *that the body displayed is female*" (4; italics mine). In classic pornography and horror the centralization of the female body and the display of physical pleasure or pain causes these genres to be associated with masculine viewing pleasures and to be banned from middle-class tastes, especially from the feminine world of television. Williams's third body genre, the melodrama, is of course not only exempt from this ban but also permeates television as a female-targeted and feminine-coded form (Joyrich 1988), which speaks to the differences in the cultural acceptability, function, and position of the bodily excesses that these genres represent along gendered lines. HBO's quality TV discursively replaces TV melodrama's feminine-coded excess with the similarly low-culture but masculine-coded excess of sex and violence, meanwhile lending cultural prestige to the sexual and violent modes of bodily transgressions.

From its beginnings in the 1970s and well into the mid-1990s, HBO's programming and branding strategies as a cable channel relied primarily on an exclusivity emerging from the combination of television and profanity, two seemingly irreconcilable phenomena. Content that could be broadcast only on subscription cable channels, such as feature films without advertisements and censorship, live sports events (mainly professional boxing), sex documentaries, and stand-up comedy with explicit language, dominated HBO's programming before it started to produce original series (Edgerton 2009). In this era the exclusivity promised to subscribers did not yet include the idea of higher aesthetic value, just the novelty of showing content on television understood to be anathema to its ecosystem. The notion of taboo breaking, then, has been part of the premium cable network's branding policy throughout its history; in its first twenty-odd years this simply meant the cultural clash of a masculinized idea of the daringly explicit and of the feminine televisual. It was in the 1990s that HBO's cultural politics relating to its originally produced programming started to build the notion of an edgy *aesthetic* into the brand by heavily promoting it as a cross-pollination of art and profanity.[10]

Importantly, the 1990s was also the era when Western culture's already brewing ideological and political transformations started to surface in popular culture. In the process of spectacular "post"-ings of cultural and political struggles and ideologies, traditionally low cultural forms gained new meanings in rearrangements of dominant taste regimes. As feminist cultural critics contend, postfeminism and the postmodern inaugurated a new valorization of the pornographic through discourses of feminist empowerment and self-actualization (Levy 2006; Gill 2007; McRobbie 2009; Douglas 2010). Pornography and horror gradually acquired higher positions in the hierarchies of taste in the 1990s and were accepted into the mainstream as ironic and/or artistic. In this regard, HBO's strategy of combining the explicit and the aesthetic can be understood as a recognition of and a tapping into this cultural atmosphere and as contributing to its proliferation in its own institutional context. The obvious yet paradoxical parallel between postfeminism and HBO's policy is that both infuse an initially feminine-coded, suspicious phenomenon (second-wave feminism and the derided medium of television, respectively) with the sexualized and pornographic, transforming them into more digestible or respectable phenomena. In this perspective it is little wonder that postfeminism's Holy Grail text, *Sex and the City*, was an HBO production.

---

10 HBO's establishment of quality TV culture was purely a business decision by its management in the mid-1990s, attributed to then-chairman Chris Albrecht, to best its industry competitors. The marketing tagline "It's Not TV. It's HBO" was introduced in 1996 (McCabe and Akass 2007b, 84; Edgerton 2009, 8).

In HBO's treatment both television and the profane undergo a cultural reevaluation as realms of entertainment whose cultural function becomes distanced from *mere* entertainment. Because I argue that these reevaluations of both TV and the profane hinge on cultural recombination more than actual content, a question arises about the exact nature of content that is associated with breaking established taboos. Setting aside the issue of cultural recombination (the shock factor of pairing the artistically explicit with the televisual), we can ask, What kinds of cultural boundaries is this television understood to break thematically? My interest here is not in interpreting texts or separating theme and aesthetic treatment but in unpacking connections between cultivations of the gendered profane and the politics of cultural (academic and popular) validation. Considering the HBO-style quality text, I suggest that content that is discursively linked with transgression as a result of its illicit connotations is in fact aligned with already familiar themes of the shocking. Consequently, HBO's treatment of the explicit as boundary pushing is less interested in a political subversion of this particular tradition and is in fact conventional in its localizations of the subversive. A scrutiny of critical discourses about such programs confirms this suggestion. To illuminate this argument, I analyze two academic works—Leverette (2008) and Lotz (2014)—that typify the rhetorical repression of the gendered conservativism in putatively edgy TV texts in their efforts to enshrine these texts' extraordinariness.

Marc Leverette's (2008) study of HBO's exceptionality in television for its foregrounding of profanity asserts that the transgressive act lies in questioning the boundaries that separate cultural categories. Leverette discusses how HBO negotiates this boundary crossing of othered or subcultural territories using the example of George Carlin's stand-up comedy, among other programming. First broadcast on HBO in the 1970s and 1980s, Carlin's comedy helped popularize the world of stand-up "as well as having a normalizing effect regarding profanity" (127). Leverette analyzes Carlin's classic monologue about the "seven dirty words that you cannot use on television,"[11] positing that Carlin's method of sociolinguistically dissecting swear words that are taboos for television *on television* is an absolute subversive gesture. But Leverette's argument, amplified with a demonstrative writing style that mixes academic language with expletives, leaves untouched the question

----

11   See https://www.youtube.com/watch?v=kyBH5oNQOS0 (accessed July 23, 2020).

of where exactly the political subversion lies beyond the gesture of using profane language where it traditionally does not belong. His argument overlooks the point that Carlin's monologue, although it breaks certain taboos (the contextually classed nature of profane and proper language), does not upset more deep-lying ones linked with sexualized power relations. Symptomatically, in discussing a sequence about the word *cocksucker*, Leverette writes, "For Carlin, the real danger of puritanical linguistic relativism can be seen here as he asks how did cocksucker come to mean 'a bad man,' when it's really 'a good woman.' How did they do that?" (130). Although Leverette deems this bit of the monologue characteristic enough to merit specific mention for its ridiculing of classist puritanism, the misogyny and homophobia in the word's shifting derogatory function and in Carlin's rhetoric go unmentioned. This is revealing, considering that both Carlin's humor and Leverette's analysis highlight the *sociolinguistic* aspect. The monologue is of course a product of its time, meaning that this act of boundary crossing had its own contemporaneous political contradictions, but a historic analysis is incomplete without exposing these. A case in point: It is striking that Carlin's wording consistently imagines the ridiculed middlebrow, sanctimonious tastes as female. In his jokes the bourgeois society that deems foul language unacceptable is populated with bishop's wives, mothers, and prim ladies, in accordance with the gendered associations of 1980s television. When Carlin brings his seven dirty words into television, then, the overtly classed taste boundaries he oversteps are implicitly gendered. Leverette's statement that HBO "sells a subculture" (125) sidesteps the question of where exactly the political subversion of bringing the subcultural out of the margins lies. After all, the subcultural art to which Leverette compares Carlin is Jean Genet's "style as revolt, style as refusal, crime as art" (125), which is motivated by concrete social marginalization, mostly that of gay masculinities. Leverette's omission is all the more conspicuous here because his essay's next section examines HBO's broadcasting practices of boxing matches as raced and sexualized mediations of masculine-coded spectator sports.

A similarly conspicuous absence of inquiry into the politics of transgression characterizes Amanda Lotz's (2014) analysis of male-centered quality programs in her book *Cable Guys*. This work endeavors to account for the increased interest in portraying troubled masculinities in prestige TV texts. Lotz finds that programs such as *Sons of Anarchy* (2008–2014), *Breaking Bad*, *Entourage* (2004–2011), or *The Shield* (2002–2008) complicate the patriarchal gender scripts of earlier television by depicting male characters as struggling with contradictions between social expectations of hegemonic masculinity and individual experience. Lotz sees this phenomenon as owing to contemporary "negotiations among aspects of patriarchal and feminist masculinities" (38) in Western culture, influenced by post-second-wave feminism. Lotz locates these texts' transgressive moment in their gender politics: their characterizations of complicated men. She does not bring the boundaries crossed into connection with the popularization of profanity and the explicit, as Leverette does; nor does the analysis interrogate the interplay between depictions of these masculinities and aesthetic-narrative conventions of quality TV. The notion of boundary crossing is focused on institutional differences between cable and network television for Lotz: Cable TV encourages "edgier" characterization practices, whereas network TV emits more reactionary politics, "erect[ing] a big tent that welcomes heterogeneous audiences with content unlikely to easily offend" (61). Because Lotz takes at face value the association of premium cable television with edginess, the analysis unavoidably runs aground in accounting for the cultural anxieties around masculinity that these programs signal.

> Interesting, and still unexplainable in my mind, is the impetus that stimulates stories about men's struggles. Some sort of catalysing event remains elusive, so that these preponderant themes and stories of struggle seem instead to be an organic bubbling to the surface of largely unconsidered and unspoken challenges for men. (Lotz 2014, 81)

Eluding an inquiry into the relationship between cultural hierarchies, gender, and aesthetics, Lotz's analysis cannot explain the existence of these putatively progressively complicated masculinities.[12] Her textual analysis of *Sons of Anarchy* is representative, aiming to demonstrate how the program's gender politics problematize protagonist Jax's (Charlie Hunnam) position in an archetypically patriarchal setting, an outlaw motorcycle club. The series' narrative tensions revolve around Jax's ongoing struggles with expected performances of tough leadership, a position that clashes with his post-second-wave feminist characterization as a sensitive family man

---

12 Albrecht (2015) accounts for some of these questions while still leaving uninterrogated the "artistic risks" (6) taken by masculine-coded quality TV, and the ideological and aesthetic implications of the term *edginess*.

(107–10). Crucially, Lotz notes that the series uses a "Shakespearean" plot in its premise of a power struggle between Jax, the only son of the club's deceased founder John, and Clay (Ron Perlman), who was responsible for John's demise, took over the club's presidency, and married Jax's mother (Katie Segal), a Lady Macbeth–like figure. Hamlet and Macbeth narratives are blueprints of Western storytelling, and Hamlet especially is a shorthand reference in modern cultural history for modernizing the Oedipal narrative. Feminist cultural theory has shown the patriarchal roots of this storytelling tradition, often within psychoanalytic frameworks (Rowe Karlyn 1995a; Bronfen 1996). Considering that *Sons of Anarchy* self-referentially invokes the Hamlet story and that Lotz registers her awareness of this, the analysis of the series' gender dynamics—supposedly a signifier of a daring edginess—would invite an investigation of how it negotiates the openly Oedipal plotting with its main protagonist's characterization, understood as struggling with different—retrograde and progressive—models of masculinities.

Leverette's inquiry ties the profane's transgressive use to the interaction between two culturally incongruous realms of entertainment without considering the underlying gendered aspect. Lotz foregrounds gender (masculinities) in locating the progressive elements of so-called edgy programs while neglecting to interrogate this characterization's relationship with the gendered coding of narrative-aesthetic conventions. Thus questions such as how and why these transgressions develop in this particular era in this particular cluster of texts remain "unexplainable." Both scholars take the industry-driven valorization of these texts at face value by unquestioningly ascribing politically progressive boundary breaking to their supposed aesthetic edginess.

In sum, although the issue of cultural subversion features as an essential concern in discussions of quality television's value hierarchies, this occurs in concert with strategies of industry and media discourses that configure the transgressive moment as that which combines explicit content (content that would be censored by network TV) with so-called edgy storytelling and characterization techniques (also incompatible with network TV). Because this transgression's articulation hinges on competitive comparisons with network TV (Nygaard and Lagerwey 2016), it eclipses questions about the political nature of such breaches of cultural boundaries, a neglect that influences academic investigations of the quality text. This shift in emphasis is made possible because, in its history, so-called mass TV has been figured as more adept at political rather than aesthetic subversion (Feuer et al. 1984; Ott 2008) and because the idea of political subversion akin to network TV's is muted in the cable context.

The cross-cultural success of discursively transgressive television backfired somewhat for HBO in the late 2000s, as it struggled to safeguard its reputation as the edgiest among competitors. Upon other cable and broadcast channels' rapid adoption of the quality TV formula and after the buzz around HBO's brand-defining flagship series had abated, the company had difficulties in finding the next trendsetting programs to differentiate its brand in the pool of variations on the quality TV model (Leverette et al. 2008a, 6–7; Edgerton 2009, 14–17). It also did not help that this paradigm had a normalizing effect on what counted as taboo (Leverette 2008, 132). In this cultural atmosphere HBO doubled down on its "courting controversy" policy through even more use of violent, sexually explicit, and sexually violent content, most controversially in *Game of Thrones*. Reception of that series problematized HBO's reliance on narratives of gendered violence (Jones 2014; Sepinwall 2014); critics lamented that the channel's pushing-the-envelope strategy tied itself to sexist storytelling traditions. However, critical discourse also noted that *Game of Thrones* endorses the strong female character trope, whose narrative dominance in the program's sixth season affected critical and fan popularity (Marsh 2016; Cuen 2016). These two aspects of the program, coming across as a trade-off—an emphasis on archetypal strong women in exchange for gratuitous nudity and sexual violence—constitute the series' notoriety in popular consciousness as ambiguously negotiating its gender politics (Gjelsvik and Schubart 2016). HBO capitalizes on this ambiguity, mining the cultural anxieties around intensified gender discourses, but its strategies of boundary crossing around the gendered body continue to be familiar from cinema and art history.

TELEVISION'S FEMINIST TRANSGRESSIONS

As shown, in its network era the American television industry constructed its programming's cultural value by drawing on a political rhetoric for which the medium was considered an ideal venue. This logic facilitated discourses of quality and relevance in the 1970s, surrounding the MTM and Tandem sitcoms, respectively. In this period quality TV was primarily associated with liberal TV, not with excessive aesthetics or high production values.

Representational transgression meant locating themes deemed progressive in the era and embedding them in emphatically politicized narrative contexts. In accordance with television's reputation as a verbal rather than a visual medium, transgression was linked to politicized narrative and dialogue. Sitcom narratives in the 1970s (and 1980s)—such as Mary Richards demanding a pay rise in *The Mary Tyler Moore Show*, Rhoda's (Valerie Harper) divorce in *Rhoda*, Archie Bunker's (Carroll O'Connor) jovially old-fashioned racism in *All in the Family*, or liberal feminist Julia Sugarbaker's (Dixie Carter) righteous indignation over social issues in *Designing Women* (1986–1993)—were not simply occasional jokes in otherwise harmless plots; they were essential to narrative structures designed to both represent and initiate public debate.

The foregrounded alliance with women's liberation concerns followed from the industry's discovery of upscale female audiences. The term *quality* initially denoted these audiences rather than the content appealing to their tastes. The notion of political progressiveness as a consequence of the industry's targeting of quality audiences has arguably remained a constitutive element of any quality programming to the present day. However, as Santo (2008, 31) argues, the postnetwork strategy of reinventing the moniker was to highlight the idea of quality *content*, which was originally the critical discourse's creation rather than the industry's. In doubling down on the production of quality content, the postnetwork promotion of quality mobilizes paternalistic traditions of cultural value (authorship discourse, cinematic aesthetics, genre hybridity, serialized narrative, explicit content), treating political progressiveness as intrinsic to this masculinized context while obscuring its feminine-coded origins and their initial functions.

This trajectory is evident in the shift in the relationship between genre and quality. The politically transgressive idea of quality was established in the 1970s liberal feminist, female-led sitcom formula, whose cultural influence contributed to the form's enduring association with potentially feminist expression. But the notion of low cultural value is also part of the sitcom's working mechanism, funneling its potential to upset the status quo into the constraints of its expressive modes. The received wisdom that television—and in particular, the sitcom—is *the* exceptional venue where women's issues can be addressed best brings to the fore the carefully managed boundaries of the spaces open for feminine and feminist transgression: on low-culture television, in low-culture genres. It is no coincidence that the postnetwork ideal of masculinist quality TV has been established within the quality *drama* framework (R. J. Thompson 1997, 17; Feuer 2007); as shown, the emergence of this subcategory is a generic shift between the 1970s and late 1990s from the female-led half-hour comedy toward the male-led hour-long drama.

Thus the notion that television and the sitcom have traditionally been the primary sites on which politically transgressive and especially feminist concerns can be negotiated is due to the conjunction of two factors. One factor is related to the lowly position that television and the sitcom have occupied in cultural consciousness. Thanks to this, the medium had relative freedom to improve its reputation by infusing its most popular form with politically influenced narration. But visually and/or linguistically explicit content was banned from network-era television. This led to the second factor contributing to the political notion of transgression in this time: Because institutional self-censorship foreclosed expressing transgression through explicit content, the quality discourse doubled down on associations with white middle-class respectability (Lentz 2000). Maintaining its strictly regulated expressive norms, television distanced itself from its bad reputation as tasteless entertainment by using strategic associations between TV as feminine object, political progression, and respectability. The institutional self-restriction thereby reemerged not as a limitation but as a political asset, where television shuns profanity to express feminine or feminist transgression. This configuration of the transgressive differentiates the network-era feminist sitcom from the Bakhtinian notion of carnivalesque comedy, which locates political transgression in the excessively corporeal associated with low-culture mass tastes (Rowe Karlyn 1995b). Nonetheless, network-era feminist comedy is still very much "mass TV"; it is not exclusively available or subcultural in its aesthetics and target audiences. Yet it cultivates within its framework an ideal of quality that exploits institutional and cultural constraints by emphatically eliminating physical transgressions, contrasting the notion of politics with them. This facet of network-era feminist TV also reflects the historically ambiguous relationship of feminism with body politics, as demonstrated by the so-called sex wars of modern feminist history and the issue of embodied representations of feminism and feminists to the present day.[13]

13　Lentz's discussion of the sitcom *Maude* (1972–1978) provides another media example for this conflict, here in the openly raced contrast between middle-class housewife Maude's (Bea Arthur) white liberal feminism and her Black

It is partly due to network TV's elimination and regulation of the physically excessive and this elimination's centrality in configuring 1970s feminist quality comedy that later landmark representations of the feminist are concerned with transgressions of the body. Rowe's (1995b) ground-breaking concept of the unruly woman shows that in cultural history, untypical female expressions are always treated as excess, as a breaking of societal rules pertaining to expectations of dominant modes of femininity. Rowe's analysis of cinematic examples and of sitcom star Roseanne Arnold implies that these excesses overstep the boundaries not only of the specific era's mandatory femininities but also, since the 1970s, of its expectations of *feminist politics*. Because second-wave feminism has, since the 1960s, become embedded in popular culture's constructions of gender to varying extents, those aspects of feminism that are most amicable to these constructions become period-specific features of ideal femininities, producing perpetually changing contradictions in gender expectations. Thus Rowe's unruly woman subverts not only an ideal femininity but also those dominant mediatizations of feminism. It is owing to this that Roseanne's feminist unruliness is located in the excessive body and voice. In it converges a subversion of, on the one hand, the rule of slim body, pretty face, soft voice—traditional embodiments of ideal femininity—and, on the other, the sitcom feminism that dominated the 1970s and became the epitome of popular feminism for the period.

Roseanne's unruliness thus defies the policing of the female body, including the policing of its feminism. Although both the 1970s feminist sitcom and Arnold's comedy persona challenge the sexualization of the female body, the 1970s feminist sitcom does this through notions of middle-class purity, in accordance with TV's institutional boundaries and with the image of the independent professional woman popularized by second-wave feminism. The sitcom *Roseanne* (1988–1997) and Arnold's celebrity persona transgress these representational tropes by focalizing the discursively unattractive and working-class female body. This aims to disrupt, in part, the postfeminist femininities of the 1980s "backlash" era (Faludi 1991) but also

---

housekeeper Florida's (Esther Rolle) lack of interest in gender politics. The series construes these ideological differences in relation to the two women's different relationship with body and sexuality as raced subjects (Maude's prudishness versus Florida's sexual excess); their relationship to feminism is predicated on their relationship with their raced sexual selves (Lentz 2000, 69–78).

a feminism construed as middle class and respectably, demurely feminine (Rowe Karlyn 1995b, 54). Following from their own eras' different constructions of femininity and feminism, the 1970s feminist sitcom and Arnold express body politics that, for the 1970s sitcom, operate as an elimination of the female body and, for the comedian, as a naturalization of it (the idea of what real women look like). These strategies are also governed by their respective relationships with expectations of cultural value: The MTM sitcom's discursive purity constitutes an asset for the quality label, whereas *Roseanne* expresses political transgression by forming an alliance with traditions of the low-culture carnivalesque. Rather than striving for a higher position in taste hierarchies, this transgression attaches itself to the lower rungs of popular culture in the centralization of the excessive and excessively behaving female body, expressed through the critically dismissed but popular domestic sitcom form.

Both the emergence of cable drama and the cultural transitions of the 1990s (postfeminism and the mainstreaming of pornography) contributed to a transformation of the meanings of feminist unruliness. Cable's institutional sanctioning of explicit content as part of the artistic transgression of televisual aesthetics endorsed representations of an excessive overstepping of bodily boundaries. This new possibility emerged in a cultural atmosphere that valorized the sexualized female body in contexts of empowerment, consumption, and art. Because postfeminist discourse claims to emblematize political (feminist) progression, its foregrounding of the female body—a popularly available site onto which various social anxieties can be projected—aligns with postnetwork quality TV's valorization of explicit representations of sexuality and violence as subversive, not just artistically but also politically. This combination leads to postfeminist popular culture's heightened contradictions around the female body and also to its contradictory critical readings, especially in the context of quality TV (e.g., Johnson 2007a).

The female-centered postfeminist quality dramedy of the 2000s, targeted at female audiences and epitomized by *Sex and the City*, celebrates the newly found political freedom in expressing female sexuality. As such, it inverts Rowe's notion of unruly feminism, which is excessive in subverting ideals of the acceptable female body on TV, even though in *Roseanne* it is not simply the boundaries of what constitutes an attractive female body that are sent up but the ideal of (sexual) respectability that the 1970s sitcom cultivated. In comparing *Roseanne* and *Sex and the City*, the limitations of visual portrayals of and assigning cultural value to the feminist unruliness that Rowe theorizes become clear. In "mass" TV, Roseanne's feminism involves both bodily excess and unruly behavior (sharp wit, sexual appetite) in low-culture domestic sitcom's confines. In the postfeminist quality dramedy, HBO's freedom of visual transgression does not translate this into *politically* excessive explicit visuals; the bodies onscreen and what they do remain anchored to dominant beauty ideals and to the postfeminist paradigm of a classed (sexual) empowerment, and in this aspect they show a closer relationship with the MTM sitcom's femininities. Unlike the MTM sitcom, however, the quality moniker is not achieved by eliminating the female body as sexual object or subject but by centralizing it, a consequence of the sexually explicit's upward trajectory in cultural hierarchies.

Thus postfeminist quality dramedy exploits both traditions of TV feminism in using possibilities of the explicit: It resembles Roseanne's body politics in focalizing the sexually desiring female body; and its (visual) expressions of sexual liberation are tied to the dictates of postfeminism's narrowly classed, raced, and bodily policed ethos. But postfeminism's linking of sexual liberation and individualized consumption culture constitutes a pivotal difference from earlier TV feminisms; it forecloses an even vaguely political rhetoric around women's roles in the public and professional sphere and structural oppressions because it locates its (post)feminism in the intimate private. McCabe and Akass (2009) argue that leading women of the HBO-type quality drama and of the half-hour dramedy (e.g., *Sex and the City*) convey a "female sexuality and erotic desire [that] has rarely been represented in such complex ways" and that this representation is directly linked to "feminism's 'sex wars'" (308). By exclusively speaking to this particular strand of feminist debate, this characterization's sheer volume and cultural prestige contributes to carrying its importance over into widely accepted understandings of feminism.

Although not striving for an overtly politicized, public feminism like the 1970s feminist sitcom, postfeminist quality dramedy still locates transgression in its political value—that of sexual liberation, which the explicit content means to underline—and this forms the basis of its quality moniker. Because it does not focalize a radical subversion of televisual aesthetics or genres, this subcategory does not produce such a transformation of generic and narrative traditions as the quality drama does. Consequently, American television's alliance with feminist politics remains anchored to the half-hour comedy or dramedy and its narrative traditions. This also keeps the form's relative position in taste hierarchies unchanged, even in an elite, critically acclaimed area of television. Premium cable channel Showtime especially cornered the market on female-targeted quality dramedy with its "ladies with problems" programming brand in the mid-2000s (Lawson 2010; Fallon 2010). In this gendered division of institutional branding policies, the quality category's generic hierarchies retain their fixity, which also presupposes where their transgressive aspects are articulated.

Symptomatically, postfeminist quality TV fits more easily into the institutional and aesthetic traditions of network TV than the masculine prestige drama does. *Sex and the City* has fared well in network syndication, with the raunchiest bits censored, but advertisers have been reportedly reluctant to sponsor *The Sopranos*, causing issues with rebroadcasting the series on network channels (Santo 2008, 36; Simon 2009, 203). In addition, HBO did not capitalize on the trendsetting success of *Sex and the City* by commissioning more similar programming, as could be expected; in fact, one way the cultural importance of the series can be measured is its influence on the emergence of similar programs on *network television* and other cable channels, such as Showtime. In HBO's 1990s–2000s branding philosophy, the half-hour women's comedy or dramedy seems to have had little transgressive value beyond what *Sex and the City* already provided politically and in securing an audience. This category was presumably too connected to mass TV, both in its feminine subject matter and in its generic connotations; masculinist quality drama provided more potential for exploiting those aspects of the aesthetically transgressive that distinguish HBO from regular TV.[14]

CONTEMPORARY FEMINIST QUALITY TELEVISION'S TRANSGRESSIONS

The emergence of a programming strategy in the mid-2000s governed by the combining of quality TV aesthetics and an overtly political feminist rhetoric

---

14 Nygaard (2013) shows that HBO commissioned the series *Girls* to again corner female audiences, who had turned away from the channel in the *eight* years between the end of *Sex and the City* and the premiere of *Girls* in 2012. Her examination of discourses about *Girls* stresses that these are nonetheless embedded in the channel's articulation of quality in paternalistic and masculinist terms.

has to be understood in both the institutional context and the context of postfeminist popular culture. In the cultural work performed by the series discussed in this book, we can trace postnetwork and streaming television's efforts to renegotiate the terms on which it articulates the quality moniker. This trend was exacerbated in the 2010s, especially with the proliferation of the strong female protagonist or "antiheroine" character trope (Buonanno 2017), and partly emerged from a recessionary cultural insistence on female resilience in new economic and political regimes of austerity (Lagerwey et al. 2016). In terms of institutional context, it is crucial that it was network television where this trend of quality shows emerged in the mid- to late 2000s, with shows such as *30 Rock* and *The Good Wife* (Nygaard and Lagerwey 2016). These series navigate ideas of transgression by combining a discursively sophisticated aesthetics that dialogues with quality TV culture with a politicized gender discourse that dialogues with the postfeminist legacy and invokes race, class, and body politics. Although they no doubt respond to a recessionary cultural atmosphere, as mentioned, *30 Rock* is an exception because it debuted two years before the economic crisis and is often credited with facilitating the popularity of female-led political comedy (Chaney 2013; R. White 2018, 69).

Representatively, the pilot episode of *30 Rock* betrays an aspiration to be seen as challenging contemporaneous televisual paradigms of transgression, both in terms of the quality trend and gender politics. In an oft-quoted snippet of dialogue, Liz Lemon describes the NBC variety show of which she is head writer as "It's not HBO. It's TV." This is a retort to stand-up star Tracy's (Tracy Morgan) insistence that he wants to do HBO-style explicit ("raw") comedy on the show—shades of the Carlin stand-up discussed earlier in this chapter. Liz's line of dialogue is the motto to Leverette et al.'s (2008a, 1) introduction to their edited book on HBO, intended to demonstrate the company's cultural relevance and exceptionality.[15] But it also illuminates *30 Rock*'s and, through it, NBC's ambition to stand out against the cable competition by defying its strategy of foregrounding "raw" content. Network shows *30 Rock*, *Parks and Recreation*, and *The Good Wife* all tap into the quality discourse by positioning themselves (con)textually as not only fulfilling the criteria of a quality show but also expanding its possibilities

---

15 In light of this, Leverette's obliviousness to the gender politics of HBO's Carlin stand-up is even more glaring, given the narrative context of *30 Rock*'s HBO joke that headlines Leverette et al.'s book.

by means of a smartness and complexity that challenges the cultural hierarchy between cable and network television. Although not a network show but a streaming program, *Orange Is the New Black* similarly represents for Netflix a challenge to cable television's (especially HBO's) cultural-aesthetic dominance.

The institutional-aesthetic talking-back strategy is linked with a similar talking back to postfeminist television's gender politics in the four series' cultural positioning. The invocation of politicized discourse about gender reminiscent of the network-era feminist sitcom operates in a number of series that also assume the quality signifier, both on cable and on streaming platforms (Netflix, Amazon Prime, Hulu). This has worked as a range of generic-aesthetic recombinations governed by emphatically political transgressions undertaken to stand out in the competition (e.g., *Transparent*, *Top of the Lake*, *Orange Is the New Black*, and *The Handmaid's Tale*). This emphatically political address that speaks to a contemporary reinvigorated and contested popular feminism provides these programs' narrative tensions and, most important, ensures that they will be discussed in the context of quality television. This programming aspires to narrative complexity through the political complexity of contemporary feminisms, channeling its tensions through the narrative-aesthetic models of quality TV.

COMEDIES

2

THE "FEMINIST COMEDY OF DISTINCTION"

GENRE AND GENDER IN THE FEMALE-CENTERED QUALITY SITCOM

GENRE DISTINCTIONS IN THE FEMINIST QUALITY SITCOM

In postmillennial television culture the quality *sitcom* is an especially curious phenomenon. Sitcom theorists account for the form's prominence in American television by its suitability to reflect on the ever-changing social environment, which makes it "an enduring sociodramatic model that has helped 'explain' American society to itself" (Hamamoto 1991, 153). The association between the sitcom's popularity, its ubiquity, and its lowly position in the cultural hierarchy of TV genres is similarly widespread and also suggests that precisely its triviality provides it with the potential to progressively challenge social structures (Mills 2005, 153–54), an argument akin to the Bakhtinian theorization of the medieval carnival's social function as the contained disruption of power relations. Thus the sitcom's ideological power lies in its domesticity, familiarity, and roots in conventional modes of television production and consumption.

Consequently, if quality television is governed by a discursive distancing from television traditions in terms of aesthetics and audience address, then quality comedy's formation involves an especially distinct rupture from genre conventions, considering how deeply the traditional sitcom form is entrenched in American cultural consciousness. Mills (2009) stresses that the ideological motif underlying quality comedy's development is the struggle for cultural distinctions and classed taste hierarchies: "It's hard to argue that newer forms of sitcom are *funnier* than traditional ones; the fact that certain audiences might find them so can then instead be understood as indicative of categorized responses and preferences which are likely to correlate with social distinctions" (134). The departure from original sitcom conventions, however, cannot be as extreme as to render the form unintelligible; the "comedy of distinction," as Mills terms it, is thus the "sitcom repositioning itself in order to protect its future by denying its links to the past" (135). This repositioning is manifested mostly in aesthetic details for Mills; otherwise, the quality comedy exhibits working mechanisms that are quite similar to its predecessors with respect to its narrative and expressive strategies.

If the contemporary quality comedy is characterized by a Bourdieusian cultural distinction (i.e., by a denial of its low cultural legacy), then the comedy series that I analyze exhibit a more ambiguous position in their discursive formulation of quality. Both *30 Rock* and *Parks and Recreation* fit into Mills's concept of the postmillennial quality comedy in aesthetic-generic terms, but their "distinction" becomes complicated by both series' open invocation of a specific historic legacy, namely, the network-era feminist sitcom. This is blatantly so in *30 Rock*'s case; the very premise of the show hinges on the viewers' recognition of its inter- and metatextual nature as a show-within-a-show backstage comedy. The series positioned itself from the beginning as a successor of 1970s feminist sitcom (a much noted example is the musical cue introducing Liz Lemon in the pilot episode, which tweaks *The Mary Tyler Moore Show*'s familiar credit sequence [Mizejewski 2014, 75]) and name-checked most of its prominent earlier representatives throughout its run. Although *Parks* is not this explicit about its lineage, its dominant strategy of modeling story lines after topical political and social events and its social commentary on gender in the workplace comedy framework draw on the female-centered workplace sitcom tradition (R. White 2018, 64).

Two opposing forces operate in the establishment of these two sitcoms' cultural status, then. On the one hand, they use the female-led network comedy heritage as a legitimizing historic reference. On the other, the postmillennial quality comedy aesthetics work as reassurance that the programs represent a departure from earlier eras of comedy and their characteristic gender scripts. This operates most explicitly through the prominent and self-conscious use of satire, which signifies this departure both aesthetically and politically. The productive ambiguity between legitimation and departure hinges on and does not exist without the two series' gender politics; the heightened referentiality that feeds into their comedy of distinction status also reassures that an emphatically politicized, feminist TV tradition is continued. In other words, unlike other comedies that are frequently analyzed as examples of the era's comedy of distinction (e.g., *Arrested Development*, *Curb Your Enthusiasm*, *The Office* [2005–2013], and *Scrubs*), this feminist quality comedy relies just as much on a gendered political heritage for carving out its place in the hierarchy as it does on distinctive aesthetic markers.

This picture becomes further nuanced when we examine these two sitcoms in relation to the immediate predecessor of female-centered quality TV: the millennial postfeminist dramedy trend, epitomized by *Sex and the City*'s global success and its imprint on the female-led comedy or dramedy genre emerging in its wake (R. White 2018, 65). As comedies of distinction, *30 Rock* and *Parks* distance themselves from the postfeminist dramedy more firmly than they do from the 1970s sitcom heritage. Whether the genealogy is admitted or not—for *30 Rock* it is, because *Sex and the City* is a prominent reference throughout—it works both paratextually and textually, not simply as a tradition continued but as a tradition critiqued, even refused. Most obvious here is the postfeminist dramedy's reliance on cinema's romantic comedy as a generic reference, mixed with the melodramatic mode, both of which centralize the domestic arenas of romance and sexuality (Arthurs 2007). Although the romance narrative is part of *30 Rock* and *Parks*' storytelling, it does not feature with such weight here as to determine or alter the programs' generic categorizations—they still foreground comedy, satire, and parody. This generic distinction becomes especially significant when considering that in postnetwork television, the establishment of a feminized quality brand was founded on dramedy, the fusion of domestic melodrama and comedy. That the studied comedies render this categorization inferior to parody and satire speaks to their ambition to be included in the quality brand by way of a different route.

The use of satirical and parodic comedy in *30 Rock* and *Parks* can be considered part of a trend that sees an increasing dominance of satire and parody in American postnetwork television (Imre 2016, 242–43). But this explanation does not account for the gendered significance of using these forms. Satire and parody are considered comedies of higher value than putatively average representatives of the genre. Both King (2002, 93) and Mills (2005, 20) note that this has to do with these forms' presumed closer proximity to "serious" modes of storytelling through their "statements about other forms or social events, . . . while 'simpler' fare, such as romantic or gross-out comedies, are deemed interesting only inasmuch as they somehow entertain the masses" (Mills 2005, 20). The centralization of sexual politics and the corporeal in romantic and gross-out comedies accounts for this classed and gendered cultural disdain—in contrast to satire and parody, which are regarded as more cerebral manifestations of humor and are held in higher esteem. This difference is revealing for the distinction operating between the postfeminist dramedy and the examined comedies. *30 Rock* and *Parks* are closer to these more prestigious categories of comedy, which are embedded in a heritage of masculine-coded modes of expression. The notion of a feminine-coded or women's comedy is historically tied to the romantic and screwball comedy heritage (Rowe 1995a, 1995b); in addition, gender-themed or even feminist satire and parody have no established history in cinema or TV (except for the 1970s female-centered sitcom, which displays some characteristics of satire, but this does not affect its generic labeling). The positioning of *30 Rock* and *Parks* in the realms of satire and parody of *gender relationships* and their discursive categorization as quality (i.e., unique) television on this basis lay bare the lack of such a relationship in comedy history.[1] In light of this (lack of) tradition, both *30 Rock* and *Parks* enact a gender inversion on two fronts: Not only do their premises downplay the domestic romance framework, instead centralizing a satire of the public-professional sphere, but they also heavily rely on another male-coded comedy heritage, the comedian comedy genre, by positioning a female comedy persona at the center of the action.

The central persona in comedian comedy is an "anomalous and privileged figure" (Neale and Krutnik 1990, 105) in conflict with the "real" world by continually breaking its rules and stepping outside its boundaries. This disruptive nature provides fodder for comedy but is also contained by the resolution of the narrative conflict. As such, comedian comedy offers itself for an ideological reading in which "cultural oppositions are at stake—nonconformity, eccentricity, sexual difference, the lack of fit between individual characteristics and desires and institutional norms and requirements" (106–7). Neale and Krutnik also observe that comedian comedies of sexual difference mostly exist in *romantic* comedy's narrative framework, but here the comedian's performance does not feature with such prominence as in

---

1   Female-centered satires of gender became popular on American television in the 2010s, with programs such as *Broad City, Inside Amy Schumer* (2013–2016), and *Unbreakable Kimmy Schmidt*, which is often attributed to the influence of *30 Rock* and *Parks and Recreation* (R. White 2018, 89).

classic, male-led comedian comedies. Rowe (1995a, 45–46) emphasizes that comedian comedy is inherently male-centered in that female performers are missing from its historic canon, which has much to do with the form's centralization of comic performance and comic body at the expense of narrative. Thus the reliance of *30 Rock* and *Parks* on their star performers' comedian comedy in the workplace sitcom and satire frameworks, though not unprecedented, is an anomaly in the canon. And again, its significance for negotiating gender in comedy is especially crucial in light of the *postfeminist* romantic comedy's ideological work.

If romantic comedy is the main vehicle through which comedy negotiates gender inversions, then this also implies that the genre is the main channel through which feminist concepts tend to be inserted into popular narratives. Put bluntly, popular feminism happens mainly by means of the romantic comedy. This especially applies to millennial postfeminist romantic comedy, even though, as its feminist critics stress, postfeminism puts a conservative spin on the form's articulation of gender politics. Here, gender inversions and transgressive rearticulations of female agency give way to the rhetorical dualism of a "dated" feminism and a postfeminist logic as "oppositional forces grappling with each other for authentication" (Bowler 2013, 187).

The feminist quality TV comedy's rejection of the postfeminist romcom or dramedy can thus be read as the form rejecting a historic dependence on the heterosexual romance narrative as the carrier of gender politics. *30 Rock* and *Parks* use this departure partly to ensure a higher place in quality television's hierarchies for their novelty component, combining the female comedian's centrality and the satirical-parodic mode. The fact that this kind of comedy still centralizes gender politics is crucial to its critical evaluations. Both comedies are concerned with emphasizing the female point of view and the ideological struggle between feminism and postfeminism in their narratives while operating in the hybrid genres of ensemble workplace comedy, mockumentary, comedian comedy, and political satire. This also means that the application of historically more prestigious and male-coded forms of comedy does not presuppose its putative masculinization, where the presumed gender inversion fulfills the requirement of symbolic progression. When the comedies centralize *politically motivated* themes about gender within these generic frameworks, this results in simultaneously repositioning the cultural relevance of gender politics, including the postfeminism-feminism dualism, from the domestic and intimate arena toward the public and politicized.

In short, *30 Rock* and *Parks* strive to elevate the position of gender politics and feminism in the hierarchy of television's popular genres and thus in cultural consciousness. That this attempt requires a simultaneous criticism and ridiculing of earlier established forms of narrativizing gender politics highlights the precarious position of this discourse in popular media. Notably, the balancing of the plot and various aesthetic methods that ensure that they are not read as romance but rather as self-conscious distancing throws the supposed feminist intent somewhat into question—it is not a stretch to interpret this distancing as a lampooning of and hostility toward a specifically feminine-coded tradition of popular entertainment, namely, romantic comedy and postfeminist TV dramedy.

"WE DON'T NEED TO PROVE IT TO YOU": *30 ROCK* AS FEMALE-AUTHORED QUALITY COMEDY

That *30 Rock* aspires to be a platform for a self-conscious discussion of gender politics operating in American society and specifically in show business becomes evident from the pilot episode, which also acknowledges the show's own stake in breaking away from associations with the derided traditions of feminine entertainment. The show-within-a-show premise as a narrative device allows for this transparent self-referentiality, which *30 Rock* turns into a license for multithreaded cultural criticism. In one of the first scenes of the pilot, Kenneth, the NBC page, describes the fictional variety show called *The Girlie Show* as "a real ladies' show for ladies" to visitors on the NBC studio tour and thus to the TV audience. In this moment Liz Lemon steps out of the elevator in front of the group, and Kenneth proudly presents her as the show's head writer. Cut to an unimpressed kid releasing a loud burp. The series repeatedly articulates throughout its run that network television generally but especially its female-targeted programming is by definition the opposite of prestigious. In a subsequent scene the newly appointed NBC executive Jack Donaghy (Alec Baldwin) analyzes the show's ratings in this vein to an indignant Liz, but he translates the gendered derision into demographic terms: According to a ratings report, the show's current stars are "popular with women and older gays . . . but you're missing men between eighteen and forty-nine." Liz responds, "I'm not *missing* them. They're just not there." Jack's insistence that this is an issue to be fixed is questioned by a sarcastic Liz: "So your job is, you take things that are already working and you fix them." Television's cultural position as a source of feminine pleasures needs fixing in the quality era, and the show's commentary on the gendered tensions of this process works as an acknowledgment of its own establishment of the quality moniker. Donaghy's energetic entrance into his own office (kicking down a door), upsetting with his hypermasculinity the equilibrium of a hitherto well-functioning feminine space, can be juxtaposed with the program's own production history. Baldwin's attachment to the project and his celebrity persona as an established film actor with a difficult personality contributed to NBC picking up *30 Rock*, and Fey often stresses how vital his presence was for the series' survival (Fey 2011, 172). Indeed, over the years Baldwin's occasional announcements of leaving the production were followed by TV critics' assertions that his presence or absence was closely tied to the fate of the already ratings-challenged program (Carter 2011; Crider 2011). Its male star's old-school masculinity profoundly affects both the fiction and the show's political economy itself, underpinning *30 Rock*'s status in the quality brand. But if the establishment of quality status requires a certain degree of masculinization in the television business, *30 Rock* does it by making this condition its storytelling premise, presented as a central and contentious issue.

Another factor in *30 Rock*'s assessment by TV critics as prestige comedy is its self-referential cultural commentary, in itself hardly a novelty in television. The historic connection with *The Mary Tyler Moore Show* that both the text and the critics reiterate is based partly on the predecessor's similarly self-referential nature, combined with the narrative premise that centralizes a single professional woman on a television program's production team. Self-referentiality and intertextuality played a crucial role in the quality category's design in the 1970s, established when MTM pioneered its new type of sitcom (Feuer 1984a; R. J. Thompson 1997). R. J. Thompson (1997) describes this aptitude for intertextuality as the signature tool of the "quality factory" MTM to assert the artistic superiority of the company's programs (82–83), and he explains the function of intertextual references in prestige drama as a way to secure the aesthetic legitimacy of television culture and history (89). Feuer (1984a) similarly describes cultural legitimation by means of postmodern self-consciousness as part and parcel of MTM's quality brand. She argues that beyond legitimation this tool can also fulfill deconstructive purposes to critique the medium's genres and styles (44), a method whose potential subversiveness is dubious, considering that for its target audiences "presumably it's OK . . . to hate TV" anyway (50).

In these accounts, then, the self-referential history of broadcast quality TV has a double-edged function: It helps assert the exceptionality of a program while insisting that there exists a television tradition that can compete with more prestigious art forms, and the viewer is rewarded for (and by) recognizing this history. With Bianculli (2000) we can call this being "tele-literate." Teleliteracy, then, claims a cultural presence and is awarded some prestige. It is important to note that both Feuer and Thompson describe this feature of the 1970s–1980s quality program as initially used only for rein-forcing audiences' recognition of television as a potentially smart art form; intertextuality was not yet used for political satire and overt institutional self-criticism, because TV was still busy establishing its higher position in culture. According to Feuer (1984b, 52–53), this style was taken beyond mere self-referentiality to satirize television as an institution, but only spo-radically, in programs such as *Buffalo Bill* (1983–1984), and was developed further in cable programming with, for example, *The Larry Sanders Show* (1992–1998) and *Curb Your Enthusiasm*. Further, R. J. Thompson (1997, 50) describes the early MTM program formula of parody and self-mockery as pitting the competence and powerlessness of a protagonist like Mary Richards against the institutional environment's incompetence. In contrast, the satire of *30 Rock* and many other contemporary TV comedies depicts the central character as *not* more competent than those surrounding her. As Feuer (1984b, 43–44) argues, *The Mary Tyler Moore Show* lacks real satirical bite, because this would clash with its aspiration to present an overall sym-pathetic central character; in contrast, *30 Rock* uses Liz Lemon for cultural criticism and satire just as much as any other character around her.

The Mary Tyler Moore Show is thus split between "warmedy" and politi-cal satire as two irreconcilable styles, which has to do with its foregrounded gender politics. Feuer (1984b) theorizes the series' character comedy as the method that carries the progressive (for its time) feminist message by depicting an independent, smart, professional woman exhibiting depth of character and eliciting "empathetic laughter" in the audience (37). As discussed in chapter 1, for Bathrick (1984), this format pushes politics somewhat into the background to defend the primacy of individual charac-ters as the basis for comedy. The mockery of television does not affect this characterization, which is separated from the mocking: Mary Richards is not responsible for the awfulness of the news show and has an uninfluen-tial job at the TV station. In contrast, *30 Rock* treats the "network television as low-cultural form" theme as connected to its gendered nature and to Liz

Lemon's middle-management position, all working toward an overarching political satire. Intertextual satire as a tool ensuring the series' quality status presumes the gendering of this feature; quality aesthetics (intertextuality, satire, and parody) and the protagonist's gendered subjectivity (as creative laborer, avid consumer of mediocre television, and single woman) mutually reinforce each other.

The disparate gendering of workplace comedy further underlines the difference between the blueprint series and the successor. *The Mary Tyler Moore Show* transplants the gender politics of the domestic sitcom by presenting the television studio as a masculine workplace that becomes feminized and familial through Mary's nurturing, accessible presence (Bathrick 1984, 105). *30 Rock*'s pilot presents broadcast television as a medium serving feminine pleasures whose balance becomes brutally disturbed by alpha male Jack's entrance and his insistence on adding the Black movie star Tracy Jordan to the cast of *The Girlie Show* and renaming it *TGS with Tracy Jordan*. The raunchiness of Tracy's comedy act is intended to imbue the fictional sketch show and the workplace family with a raced masculinity. In a further difference with Mary Richards, although Lemon's role in the ensemble dynamic is similarly that of the workplace mother, this is not an implicitly present ideological characteristic (to be noticed by media scholars) but an established trope of ensemble television to be openly mocked by the text and thus informing the satire. The episode "Khonani" makes this explicit: When Liz gets upset with her staff after she notices that they exclude her from their social activities, one of them explains to her, "If this is a family that makes you the mom. And you don't wanna go out drinking with your mom."

Central to the discourse about *30 Rock*'s production history is that Fey conceived it with the intent to explore contemporaneous issues of gender, race, and class. The comic premise stems from the disparate social positions of the ensemble cast, especially of conservative businessman Jack Donaghy, liberal feminist comedy writer Liz Lemon, and Black rags-to-riches comedy star Tracy Jordan. As Fey writes in her memoir *Bossypants*, this setup allows for showcasing their ideological differences "about any topic that came up—race, gender, politics, workplace ethics, money, sex, women's basketball—and they would agree and disagree in endless combinations" (Fey 2011, 170–71). In other words, the narrative tensions that provide the program's episodic conceit are grounded in an issue-based premise. Fey has also stated that the social satire aims to show a multiplicity of perspectives, where Liz's centrality, representing middle-class white femininity and feminism, is counterbalanced with other points of view ("Questions for Tina Fey," 2007).[2] This mission statement evokes contemporary feminist discourses that critique popular feminism for its narrow focus on privileged white womanhood and that champion intersectionality; but the addressing of a variety of points of view also fits with broadcast television's imperative to cater to a broad set of audience tastes and subjectivities. Network quality television typically uses such economic necessity to promote political correctness by subjecting a moral social issue to a variety of discussions in individual episodes (R. J. Thompson 1997, 171–72). 30 Rock links the multiple-points-of-view feature to feminist politics, which informs the quality moniker in overdetermined ways, including the centralization of female subjectivity, the text's frequent dramatizations of gender issues, Fey's star text as cerebral feminist and trailblazer of female authorship in TV comedy (e.g., as the first female head writer on the late night variety show *Saturday Night Live* [1975–]), and, connected to this, a heavily promoted female authorship discourse. Even though the multiple perspectives are filtered through the same parodic and satirical aesthetic, the comedy of Liz Lemon's "failed femininity" and feminism (Mizejewski 2014, 26) exists in a *primus inter pares* position to other perspectives and facilitates the narrative.

The promotion of female authorship is a feature that further establishes 30 Rock's quality credentials on two levels. First, in media discourses it accounts for the program's exceptional nature, speaking to the quality TV brand's requirement of novelty, which here is achieved by the author's gender. This way, by implicitly assuming the masculinism of the quality industry's authorship discourse, 30 Rock is posited as a subversive ("edgy") corrective to that status quo. Second, this femininity of authorship affects the series' position in the history of female-led comedy: Although 30 Rock fashions its relationship to network-era feminist sitcom as a reverent one, the female authorship context helps express critical commentary on the postfeminist dramedy and its reliance on romance narrative. I examine these two aspects in more detail in what follows.

In the first instance, both Fey and media discourses contribute to 30 Rock's dominant understanding as stemming mostly from its singular

---

2   Fey has also stated publicly the ideological influence of the Norman Lear sitcom on *30 Rock*'s issue-based approach and on its preference for contrasting a variety of character perspectives. See https://www.youtube.com/watch?v=YjNXz9HoyC0 (accessed July 24, 2020).

creator's mind. Although Fey also emphasizes in *Bossypants* the contributions of other writers and showrunner Robert Carlock, she often refers to the series as her baby, a phrase offering a juxtaposition between motherhood and creative labor through an array of jokes and puns. For example, Fey's account of *30 Rock*'s production history runs parallel with that of her first daughter's birth: "In September, my daughter was born. (For the record: epidural, vaginal delivery, did not poop on the table.)" (Fey 2011, 172). Several pages later: "In March, the first season of *30 Rock* was complete. (For the record: no epidural, group vaginal delivery, did not poop on the table.)" (194). Motherhood and childrearing are the primary metaphors to relate the experience of being a television producer. Fey even links this to network quality television's reputation as sophisticated but unrecognized entertainment in an affectionate tone.

> *30 Rock* is the perfect symbol for the pro-life movement in America. Here's this little show that no one thought would make it. . . . As the mother of this now five-year-old show, would I still rather have a big, strong *Two and a Half Men* than our sickly little program? No, I would not, because I love my weird little show. (Fey 2011, 194)

Similarly, *Bossypants* dedicates a chapter to relating the story of a busy Saturday on which Fey juggled three major responsibilities: guest starring on *Saturday Night Live*, filming a special scene of *30 Rock* with Oprah Winfrey, and organizing a birthday party for her daughter—and "each of these events was equally important in my life" (Fey 2011, 202). Thus the authorship discourse that is so crucial for establishing the quality reputation of TV programs and that creates a paternalistic understanding around most art forms becomes literally maternalized and thus privatized here, at the same time also feeding into Fey's star persona that itself negotiates a precarious balance between feminist and postfeminist understandings.[3]

---

3 I develop my argument around this negotiation more in chapter 3. On Fey's gendered celebrity, see Mizejewski (2014, 67–75), Lauzen (2014), and Patterson (2012). It is worth noting that Fey habitually discusses motherhood (whether literal or authorly) in a sarcastic tone similar to these quotes, betraying an effort to strip it from sanctimonious associations by highlighting its abject aspects.

As noted, authorship discourse also informs *30 Rock*'s relationship to its direct thematic predecessor, the postfeminist dramedy. *Sex and the City* is a constant reference as a legacy to be parodied, criticized, and overcome, a relationship that influences the whole tone of the series.[4] The single-career-woman-living-in-New-York premise sends up this connection from the outset. The parody works to ideological ends to reassert that this show is about the sexual and romantic explorations of its heroine only insofar as it refuses the expectations of that postfeminist premise. Often confirming in interviews that Liz is a parody of Carrie Bradshaw (Sarah Jessica Parker), Fey describes the major differences between the two characters as those between sex drives[5] and the relationship to work (Brown 2009). The latter helps shift the program's genre toward workplace comedy, and the former affects its tone, highlighting the parodic and satirical rather than the melodramatic. Both media discourses and Fey articulate this characterization method as expressing a more realistic kind of womanhood than that represented by the postfeminist heroine (Brown 2009; Griffin 2010). Here, then, Lemon's disinterest in sexuality, her commitment to work, her obsession with food, and all other exaggerated characteristics that provide the basis for comedy also become points of identification. Griffin (2010) contrasts Liz Lemon with Carrie Bradshaw in this vein: "We wanted to be Carrie; Liz Lemon is who we feel like in comparison. . . . We love her because she's one of us, but we love her even more because she's even grosser, weirder and more awkward than we are." The text offers up this distancing from fantasy toward realism openly: In a scene in the first-season episode "Cleveland," Lemon, her friend Jenna (Jane Krakowski), and Jack's girlfriend Phoebe (Emily Mortimer) chat in a restaurant about boyfriends, and Jenna remarks, "How *Sex and the City* are we? I'm Samantha, you [Phoebe] are Charlotte, and you [Liz] are the lady at home who watches it."

The satirical treatment of *Sex and the City* also moves *30 Rock*'s genre toward comedian comedy, a feature that becomes more prominent after

---

4   Rosie White (2018, 71–73) discusses *30 Rock*'s critique of the postfeminist romantic comedy in detail, applying a queer theory approach. Although this approach also informs my argument on body politics (chapter 4), I find White's argument flawed in a key point: It misidentifies *30 Rock*'s aesthetic as comedy verité, in this way lumping it together with *Parks and Recreations*' mockumentary style. This is a fundamental misreading if the aim is to consider how the two series configure their relationship to quality comedy's aesthetics and gender politics, as will be shown in the comparative analysis of *30 Rock* and *Parks*.

5   See https://www.youtube.com/watch?v=0qjrmTTPBFI (accessed July 24, 2020).

the first season. Fey and showrunner Robert Carlock noted in a panel discussion that they changed the series' tone after season 1 to this effect.[6] During this discussion, Fey first evaluates the female characters' early features as "too typical" of contemporaneous TV, and, tellingly, as a "waste of Jane [Krakowski's] talents" as a *comedian* with a knack for the absurd. Referring to a scene in the season 1 episode "The Baby Show," in which Liz and Jenna talk over a cake about "boys 'n' stuff," Carlock disparagingly comments that the realistically filmed and joke-free scene is "boring and this is not our show, and not what these characters should be doing"—at least as evaluated from the perspective of the ultimately absurd and cartoonesque style of *30 Rock*.

Indeed, although themes and story lines typical of the postfeminist dramedy about single women permeate Lemon's narrative, this becomes a trope to be parodied, in the process aligning the series more with comedian comedy. If the comedian comedy's ideological importance is "a celebration of the individual in opposition to restrictive social or collective institutions" (King 2002, 42) that centralizes an everywoman character who does not fit into the boundaries of these institutions, then Lemon's shifting position as a comic heroine in a multiplicity of narratives reinforces this ideological work both inside and outside the text. The ideological-generic convention opposed in this setup is the postfeminist romance narrative's oppressive dominance for female comedians. The flexibility of comic actions and plots in which Lemon is variously a straight woman, buffoon, comic foil, and so on helps maintain comedian comedy's integration of narrative and comedian: The fictional universe is built around the comedian and not the other way around (i.e., the comic actress is not integrated into a romance narrative), and Fey's comic skills are mined for laughs as motivators of plot. One aspect of this is the romantic heroine's and her narrative's ridicule, and the parody integrates the two (comic performance and romcom conventions) in Lemon's figure.

Such integration is best exemplified by the episode "Stride of Pride," whose Lemon plot is based on a *Sex and the City* parody. Following a recent "sexual awakening," Lemon unsuccessfully tries to find some women at work to have brunch with *Sex and the City* style, namely, to discuss their sex lives over cocktails. The last scene is an explicit reference to the aesthetics of the predecessor. In a setup atypical of *30 Rock*'s usual imagery and tone, Lemon

---

6 See https://www.youtube.com/watch?v=J7wb0SJjJ4Y (accessed September 1, 2016).

is reclining on her bed with coiffed hair and wearing a pink tutu á la Carrie Bradshaw, typing into her MacBook the moral and emotional lesson for each story line of the episode. The image of the computer screen fills the TV screen while we also hear Lemon's uncharacteristically high-pitched voiceover as she is writing down her musings about interpersonal relationships in the style of Carrie's tortuous questions. Her long monologue concludes, "I guess what I'm saying is, I need to modify my Zappos order so please email me back at your earliest convenience." Having finished typing, she closes the computer, falls off the bed with a thud, and the episode ends (Figure 1).

The scene parodies the postfeminist dramedy's trope of offering trite observations about gender relations by means of a protagonist voiceover that pulls each story line into one generalized life lesson. This also entails mimicking and sending up *Sex and the City*'s portrayal of female (feminized) authorship as a privileged site of status in the romance genre. The female comedian is central to the parody in that the parody is structured around her comic performance. This centrality also dialogues with the episode's other story line, in which Tracy questions the funniness of female comedians, claiming that even a monkey in a suit is funnier than any woman. When Lemon and Jenna get back at him by performing a sketch to great success, we see only a montage of this (so whether the sketch is funny or not is irrelevant) accompanied by an extradiegetic song with the following lyrics: "This sketch is hilarious, take it from me / Women are funny, we can all agree: / Carol Burnett, Lucille Ball— / No, we're not gonna do it, it's beneath us all / Cause we don't need to prove it to you." Although *30 Rock* makes great efforts to show that the comedy Fey performs is multifaceted (and "we don't need to prove it to you"), it also has high stakes in a frequent evocative distancing from the melodramatically inclined postfeminist romance that relies less on comedian comedy and more on a conflict- and closure-oriented romance narrative. In short, it aspires to prove that its heroine is funny by positing what she is *not*: a postfeminist romance heroine.

Again, authorship discourse feeds heavily into this shift from romance narrative toward comedian comedy. Fey frequently emphasizes her inclination toward physical comedy in terms that speak to the binary categorizations of female comedians on the pretty/funny axis (Mizejewski 2014). In interviews she expresses this as a disinterest in filming romantic or sex scenes. To an interviewer's suggestion that Lemon is the female Homer Simpson, she replies that a lot of criticism about the comic exaggerations of the character concerns Lemon's unease with sex: "I wanted to write her that way because I didn't want

Figure 1. Liz Lemon (Tina Fey) as Carrie Bradshaw in a *30 Rock* parody of *Sex and the City*.

to film those scenes. I wanted to be able to have a show where I didn't have to be cute and I didn't have to sit on top of anyone in a bra—that was important to me as a writer-performer. I liked it because it was not something I had seen before that."[7] In short, comedian comedy dominates *30 Rock* because of its star

7   https://www.youtube.com/watch?v=0qjrmTTPBFI (accessed October 6, 2020).
    See also Baldwin (2015).

comedian's gendered authorship and influence. In this discourse the series' universe is bent toward the preferences of its author-star, who recognizes that as a female comedy performer, her options to do comedy are closely tied to the postfeminist romance traditions that centralize women primarily as sexual subjects, and she opts to steer away from such narratives and aesthetics by parodying them.

30 Rock's generic establishment as quality comedy thus relies on post-feminist dramedy's parodic and satirical treatment, predicated on the discourse of gendered authorship about its comic star. As Mizejewski (2014) writes, "As a metafiction, television about television, *30 Rock* is especially self-conscious about media representations of women," which become central to "the intense and unusual referentiality" of the series (67). The specific ways in which parody and satire are used have implications for the series' cultural work as ideological criticism, and thus it is important to examine to what extent *30 Rock* can be evaluated as a text expressing a *critique* of its generic predecessor. King (2002) pinpoints the difference between parody and satire as a difference in targets. Parody tends to target aesthetic or formal conventions (King 2002, 107–9), undermining these conventions but also "pay[ing] an effective form of tribute to the originals," because "to become a target of parody is to have achieved a certain status" (112), namely, the status of being culturally relevant. In these terms, *30 Rock*'s treatment of *Sex and the City* can be seen on a par with its treatment of other cinema and television texts. The series lampoons a wide array of media products, where the parody works not just as comic referencing of styles and aesthetics but as a plot template: The conflicts and resolutions are taken from the source text but are incorporated into a different cultural setting, and the comedy stems from this discrepancy. Throughout its run, *30 Rock* worked films, series, and high-culture texts into its narrative fabric, such as *Amadeus* (1985), *Mamma Mia!* (2008), *Harry and the Hendersons* (1987), *Night Court* (1984–1992), *Friends* (1994–2004), *Willy Wonka and the Chocolate Factory* (1971), *The Dark Knight* (2008), and *Macbeth*. These references work similarly to the kind of intertextuality that R. J. Thompson (1997) discusses: The quality TV text establishes its knowingness, thus positioning itself in popular media history, although *30 Rock*'s use of these sources extends name dropping through instances of complete repurposing of plot (e.g., the narrative of the episode "Succession" recycles and parodies the *Amadeus* plot). This type of transparency, then, speaks to the series' intent to pay playful homage, and its aim remains at that level; style and narrative are reappropriated as reassurance that *30 Rock* knows its media history and inserts itself into it. In this feature it is similar to a number of other earlier and contemporaneous programs, such as *Community* (2009–2015).

If satire is "a form of comedy that also widens the scope for social/ political criticism" (King 2002, 94), then satire is not the aim of these homage parodies. However, satire as the aesthetic expression of critiquing social-political circumstances does exist on *30 Rock* in relation to a variety of issues, most prominently relating to feminism, postfeminism, race relations, sexism, corporate capitalism, nation, and show business. But it is mainly in the case of postfeminist dramedy where the series uses parody and satire as an effective mixture, corresponding to King's concept. Overarching aesthetic parody is used for political ends, that is, to satirize the fiction of postfeminist womanhood. In other words, the series mobilizes satire through the parody of a specific televisual form, which speaks to the targeted notion's (post-feminist femininity's) rootedness in media fiction. Its ultimate purpose is to achieve ideological parody and satire as the grounds on which to articulate the female protagonist's comic persona.

The other instance where a similar mixture of parody and satire is prominent is the treatment of broadcast television as low-culture enter-tainment. *30 Rock* is also renowned for its invention of fictional programs to ridicule and criticize broadcast TV's political economy and aesthetics. Some of these shows are only mentioned throughout the series. Others are shown in brief scenes or even provide the premise of whole story lines. They include reality shows, game shows, and scripted series such as *MILF Island*, *Queen of Jordan*, *Are You Smarter than a Dog*, *America's Kidz Got Singing*, *Gals on the Town*, and *Bitch Hunter*; and the female-targeted Lifetime TV movies *A Dog Took My Face and Gave Me a Better Face to Change the World: The Celeste Cunningham Story* and *Kidnapped by Danger: The Avery Jessup Story*. The fact that precisely these two areas, postfeminist womanhood and broadcast television, provide the primary basis for simultaneous parody *and* satire speaks to the overdetermined connection between them: The heroine's establishment as comic figure and the female comedy performer's establishment as author of her comedy hinge on their ideological distancing from a gendered media tradition (postfeminist romance), just as network quality television's configuration hinges on a critical distancing from its immediate surroundings. Gender politics (feminism) and the recognition as quality television are inseparable stakes of representation for *30 Rock*, ultimately determining the program's tone and genre.

"THE COMEDY OF SUPER NICENESS": *PARKS AND RECREATION* AND MOCKUMENTARY AS FEMINIST UTOPIA

Critical reception established a comparative-competitive relationship between *Parks and Recreation* and *30 Rock* throughout their runs because of the shared career background of their central female stars as *Saturday Night Live* alumni and also because of the series' similar genres and gender politics. Rosie White's (2018, 57–90) academic study of female-led sitcoms also grounds its analysis of postnetwork era women's comedy in a comparison of these two shows. Although this discursive connection is an important referent for my own analysis as well, first I want to engage with a similarity that has *not* been at the center of critical focus but is an appropriate starting point to unpack *Parks*' reputation as quality comedy. This concerns an aspect of the series' production history, namely, its tonal rebooting between seasons 1 and 2. This reboot, like *30 Rock*'s, was reportedly the production team's conscious effort to course-correct the show's character (Baysinger 2015). In *30 Rock*'s case the change of tone and pace during the first two seasons was a strategic choice to shake off the air of postfeminist romance in order to develop a comedy that foregrounded absurdist satire, thus elevating its reputation. *Parks* also underwent such a change, and its transformation similarly has to do with the relationship between genre conventions and gendered assumptions, with contextually different results. This difference is rooted in *Parks*' specific production background: The series, from its commissioning, had struggled with the dubious reputation of being a spin-off of the American version of the British mockumentary *The Office* (2001–2003), a copy of a copy; and protagonist Leslie Knope (Amy Poehler) was considered little more than a female Michael Scott (Steve Carrell), the American *Office*'s central character. Consequently, the production team had to find a way out of the predecessor's shadow.

In his dismissive review of the first season of *Parks*, *Variety* critic Brian Lowry (2009) demonstrates why *Parks* was seen as problematically aping the *Office* template(s) and offers insights into which aspects appeared to be in need of revision. For Lowry, not only does the first season "feel . . . like that established program in drag," but it also fails to use the mockumentary format to express something original, which he suggests could be achieved by adding some "political bite." Lowry attributes the failure of *Parks* as quality comedy to two aspects: First, it does not use the mockumentary format for political satire to a required extent (i.e., to make it unique and different from *The Office*); and, second, it does not make us "care about Leslie's quest" (Lowry 2009). These two criticisms are fundamentally interconnected for Lowry, suggesting that a feminized version of *The Office*, being solely a vehicle for Amy Poehler's comic persona, does not carry enough cultural value in itself and that the way to remedy this is to amp up the political commentary aspect. The show's second-season reboot took care of precisely these two perceived issues: the female protagonist's characterization and the lack of political critique.

These two aspects are also the elements of *Parks* that were later credited with its ground-breaking and smart nature ("TV's smartest comedy," according to *Entertainment Weekly* [Frucci 2011]). They also account for the show's cross-sectional position in media commentary that frequently uses *The Office* and *30 Rock* as immediate cultural references and templates for *Parks*. In the following discussion I examine how the amalgamation of these two factors—the mockumentary tradition as political commentary and the female protagonist's character comedy—were adapted to establish *Parks'* quality descriptor, resulting in a "comedy of super niceness" (Paskin 2011) that incorporates popular feminist political satire.

From its inception the mockumentary or comedy verité (Mills 2004) tradition as genre reference determined *Parks'* cultural position in the quality comedy discourse; in addition, the series was co-produced by Greg Daniels, creator of the American *Office*. These connections explain the imperative to remove the copycat label from *Parks'* reputation and to find the novelty element in its concept. Scholarship on mockumentary's cultural work shows that the hybridization of documentary and fictional forms in postnetwork TV is a representative example of attempts to reconfigure the sitcom tradition and create a "comedy of distinction." For Mills (2004), this mixture of the serious (documentary) and the comic (fiction) aims to shake off the stigma of TV comedy as being "mere entertainment," and the British comedy verité does this by reengaging with television's "active social role . . . which sitcom has traditionally been criticized for abandoning" (78). The British *Office* and other mockumentaries use the documentary form for comic intent, where the humor stems from exposing the self-deception and inauthenticity of the camera's observed objects (74). The question of veracity, or rather of the possibility or impossibility of capturing a putative truth, is at the core of mockumentary discourse, and for its analysts (e.g., Mills 2004; Hight 2010; Middleton 2014), this function provides the possibility of social satire designed to elevate it above the level of discursively average comedy. Both Hight and Middleton engage in comparative analyses of the British original and the American remake of *The Office* as blueprints for the form's popularization. They highlight that the Americanization involved a "toning down of the satirical bite of the original" (Hight 2010, 284) through "an affectively charged representation of the workplace as a space of individual and interpersonal happiness and fulfilment" (Middleton 2014, 142). Middleton shows how the British original's aesthetics expose the corporate work environment's "cruel optimism" (Berlant 2011) in the every-man character Tim (Martin Freeman) and his forever deterred fulfillment of fantasies of a better life (Middleton 2014, 147–48). For Middleton, the series is a satire of post-Fordist white-collar work culture, and, as paradigm of "cringe comedy," it uses the faux documentary setup (the blurring between notions of real and unreal) to create an increasing discomfort in the viewer: "We cringe in part because of the feeling that there is nothing we can look away *to*" (147; italics in original).

The *Office*'s cultural value, then, is predicated on its satire of labor relations in twenty-first-century Western societies, conveyed through a comedy of awkwardness that in its bleak worldview and gritty realism is often hard to experience as comedy—Middleton (2014) notes that for Berlant, the series is "situation tragedy" (154). Middleton sees this defining cringe aspect of the British *Office* as its aesthetic and ideological strength, especially compared with the American version. For him, the remake and Michael Scott's "psychologically developed" (156) character, who becomes more and more sympathetic, "alters the effects of the British version" to "defuse the awkwardness and mediate the show's critical potential with conventional forms of narrative pleasure and viewer identification with characters" (160).

Hight (2010, 274–78) further develops the evaluation of mockumentary's satirical potential with his analysis of HBO's *The Comeback* (2005–2014), a comedy considered another pinnacle of self-reflexive and satirical mockumentary. For Hight, this series does to the world of show business, celebrity culture, and popular television formats (the sitcom and the reality show) what the British *Office* does to the corporate work environment. The mockumentary form lays bare the uncomfortable discrepancies between the individual's performance of identity in social spaces and the petty desperation that these performances conceal. The embarrassing and humiliating situations that David Brent (Ricky Gervais) and Valerie Cherish (Lisa Kudrow), the central characters of *The Office* and *The Comeback*, respectively, get themselves into serve as scathing critiques of the social environment. The

Comeback expresses this perhaps even more brutally, because it frequently configures the exposure of Valerie's indignity as *gendered* victimhood in show business, an aspect with which Hight does not engage. While *The Office* exposes Brent as a workplace bully (against whom it offers Tim as a relatable point of identification), Cherish is the victim of the TV industry's systemic bullying, a situation for which she is partly responsible as an aging sitcom actress with delusional hopes of a successful comeback. The cringe, that is, the viewer's urge to look away, comes from slightly different impulses. In Brent's case it is our discomfort with having to follow this horrible man, an affect reinforced by the supporting characters' frequent side glances at the camera, establishing this muted mode of sympathetic connection with the viewer (Mills 2004, 69; Middleton 2014, 150). No such methods are evident in *The Comeback*; the viewer is left alone with her unease and without a sympathetic reference figure to connect with, and this results in Cherish's even deeper isolation—both within the diegesis and between viewer and text—as debased casualty of the Hollywood machinery.

Hight (2010, 278) notes that *The Comeback* was a flop for HBO, never garnering a solid audience base during its initial run, and he attributes this to its relatively rare format in American sitcom conventions. Although this may account partly for its failure, in itself this is hardly a convincing explanation, because at the time of its broadcast, many other experimental—and economically viable—formats and aesthetics were prominent in the quality TV landscape. A more likely explanation of the initial obscurity of *The Comeback* is the series' treatment of the *female* protagonist within the mockumentary format. A program whose cultural work lies in laying bare the repeated and specifically gendered humiliations of its central female star without even a hint of retaliation, let alone any affective connection to the viewer, was not a welcome sight, even in the name of acerbic cultural criticism, for prestige television in the mid-2000s—a time when female-centered programming operated by and large under the imperative of postfeminist empowerment rhetoric.[8]

This examination of the mockumentary context returns me to my point that *Parks'* second-season reboot was determined by factors that lie in a cross-section of American modes of representing identity in the

---

8   With the popularization of female-centered comedy, this trend turned around in the 2010s with such series as *Veep*; HBO's commissioning of a second season of *The Comeback* in 2014 speaks to this cultural shift.

mockumentary sitcom format on the one hand and the expectations of representing *female* identity on the other. Middleton's and Hight's implied critique of the American *Office* for its relative lack of social criticism as it turned into a sentimental story about the workplace family fails to consider the American workplace sitcom tradition into which the British series was transplanted. This tradition, which *The Office* tried to update, has specific female-centered origins. The American *Office*'s novelty aspect was precisely the sharpening of this heritage, and in this context the mockumentary aesthetics do help the program appear more critical of workplace relations than previous fare by exposing the male boss as a slightly racist and sexist buffoon. Leslie Knope's presentation in *Parks*' first season follows a similar path, exposing the middle-management boss as delusional, bureaucratic, racist, and inappropriately enthusiastic about her work in local government.[9] However, this female protagonist's characterization also evokes *The Comeback*'s humiliation techniques in that it has a specifically gendered edge, where Leslie's failures as a civil servant are interdependent with her failures as a single career woman.

If the male boss's (however slightly) critical characterization by means of the mockumentary format ensures the American *Office*'s novelty, that template's feminization was seen as problematic to establishing *Parks*' prestige. Crucially, this was not only because the embarrassment narratives followed the *Office* template too closely in season 1 but also because this method sat uncomfortably with the aspirational rhetoric of female-centered media texts. The first season's humor lies primarily in contrasting Leslie's aspirationalism about public service against the grim reality, and it works to expose the ineffectiveness of public institutions through the ineffectiveness of Leslie's efforts. But this is achieved using humiliation techniques that target her character both in her professional position and in her private life, akin to the postfeminist chick flick's ideological strategies. For instance, she has an imagined romantic history with cynical city planner Mark Brendanawicz (Paul Schneider), a character who inexplicably but tellingly disappears from the series after season 2. This characterization seems to deflect from the political commentary aspect (see Lowry's lament about the lack of "political bite"), a problem that was never really a reference point for the American

---

9   In this perspective the first-season version of Leslie Knope is also more similar to *30 Rock*'s portrayal of Liz Lemon, and to that comedy's cynical humor, than her post-reboot character.

Office for journalists. Dramatizing so-called bigger (political) issues became a priority only after the first season's critical failure; producer Dan Goor highlights that the program's first real "issue" story line occurred precisely in the second season's first episode (Snierson 2013).

The *Office* template's feminization thus carries within itself the potential political critique's gendered individualization and privatization—that is, the story relies too heavily on the career woman's ridiculing—which, as we have similarly seen in the case of *The Comeback*, was an ambiguous and unpopular characterization technique for satirical comedy. The way to turn this around in the second season was to tap into popular feminist themes about women's struggles in the workplace, institutionalized sexism, female solidarity, and successful women as role models. The humor came from contrasting Leslie's feminist aspirationalism, shifted from delusional to justified, with the political critique of American public institutions that inhibit her ambitions. This aspect soon became the ground on which the series was celebrated, witnessed in glowing reviews (Escobedo Shepherd 2015; Trantham 2015; Ryan 2015). However, because the aspirational (or can-do) feminist discourse provides the social criticism's foundation in this new configuration, the series contradictorily ends up endorsing the effectivity of public institutions, accumulated in Leslie's career success. Nonetheless, this still accounts for *Parks'* achievements for critics, at least in terms of quality, if not ratings, implied, for instance, in Alan Sepinwall's (2015a) estimation written at the time of the final episode's broadcasting. Sepinwall's review is especially representative for its associations between the show's cultural value, political utopianism, and rhetoric of female empowerment as both professional achievement and successful maternity: Starting out as "delusional" in her political ambitions, Leslie proved "prophetic" in ending up as a "super woman," "an influential federal official . . . , and as a wife and mom with a small army of adoring friends" (Sepinwall 2015a). Even the program's economic struggle becomes a point of praise: "The show's ability to last seven seasons despite middling-to-awful ratings is a Knope-ian feat in and of itself" (Sepinwall 2015a).[10] Sepinwall concludes, "In the end, it is one of the best comedies TV has ever seen, and one that stands out from so much of the great shows of this new Golden Age of Television because . . . its

---

10   Note that Fey used similar language when discussing *30 Rock*'s consistently low ratings, associating lack of broad popularity with uniqueness, high aesthetic value, and exceptionality.

default philosophy was one of optimism at a time when even the best comedies today tend towards ironic detachment." Sepinwall's last point about the series' joyful tone connects feminist discourses (Leslie as superwoman and maternal figure) with its optimism or "super niceness" (Paskin 2011), configuring optimism as feminist virtue that elevates *Parks*' cultural value.

Sepinwall's celebration also illuminates a prominent difference between *Parks* and mockumentary's earlier iterations: Whereas Lowry (2009) laments the missed opportunity to use mockumentary for real political critique, the praise here, as in virtually all other accounts, barely ever mentions mockumentary as a reference point for the show's quality, or if it is mentioned, it is in a dismissive tone. The disappearance of "cruel" from the series' "optimism" (Berlant 2011) becomes its virtue because it is replaced by a rhetoric of female empowerment, carrying its own mode of social commentary. The mockumentary discourse's significance became concomitantly muted throughout *Parks*' run, including the format's working mechanism that highlights character critique and, through it, a critique of institutions and social and cultural conditions. The mockumentary tradition became a reminder and remnant of the series' rootedness in the quality discourse, a genre signifier of cultural value. Specifically, it was adapted for the utopian optimism that permeates *Parks*' world, originating in the comic heroine's feminist aspirationalism and transforming the whole fictional universe.

Consider a scene in the pilot episode in which Leslie shoos a homeless man (Jon Daly) off a playground slide. The mockumentary format is used here to mock Leslie's work ethic as a pointless effort to change things in small-town America by using a bureaucratic approach. Producer Mike Schur mentions in an interview that the series finale ("One Last Ride") gives us an easy-to-miss glimpse into how that man's life turned out: When Leslie and the gang are asked to do one last Parks and Recreation job to get a broken playground swing fixed, the well-dressed ordinary citizen making this request is played by the same actor who played the homeless man in the pilot. Schur underlines this twist's significance: "I liked the (tacit) implication that somehow Leslie pushing a miserable drunk out of that slide in the cold light of morning was a low point for him, and that he cleaned himself up and turned his life around and was now a productive member of society. That's got a nice Dickensian flavor to it, I think" (Sepinwall 2015b).[11] Although

---

11 Such use of narrative memory as a symptomatic method of quality TV's serialization practices and Schur's use of the word *Dickensian* (also frequently applied

the mocking of public service, local politics, and small-town life and its inhabitants continue to be an important aspect of the series, this mocking becomes framed in an affective mode reinforced by the utopian "niceness" with which Leslie and her team are portrayed[12] and is ultimately embedded in the Obama era's political discourse about patriotic meritocracy. *Entertainment Weekly* critic Jeff Jensen (2015), in his celebratory review of the finale, explicitly stresses the latter: "In Leslie Hope and ragtag band of proximity workplace acquaintances, we are left with a portrait of—to borrow some words our president spoke shortly before *Parks* premiered—'a new spirit of patriotism, of responsibility, where each of us resolves to pitch in and work harder and look after not only ourselves but each other.'"

Thus both the text and its reviews dismiss the political importance of cringe comedy for the show's mockumentary format. The series' cultural work emerges as a political optimism whose significance lies in its perceived uniqueness in contemporary quality television. Willa Paskin's review especially sets up this contrast between cringe comedy and *Parks*.

> This comedy of discomfort, still in its most perfect form in the British version of *The Office*, is such a staple of the Thursday night sitcom experience . . . that when things start to go haywire on *Parks and Recreation*, sometimes we instinctively reach for a pillow, even though *Parks* no longer causes cringing. It has abandoned mining the uncomfortable for laughs, in order to explore the comedic potential of super nice people. If deep down inside, under the endemic disgruntlement of *The Office* or endemic egomania of *30 Rock*, most sitcom characters are

---

to cable dramas such as *The Sopranos* [Newman and Levine 2012] and *The Wire* [Williams 2014]) provide further evidence of the efforts to position *Parks* as quality TV. Thus the two strands of rhetoric around aspirational feminism and quality TV converge in the homeless man's story on *Parks*.

12 *Parks* still uses the cruel comedy aspect in Jerry/Garry/Larry/Terry's (Jim O'Heir) figure, hyperbolically focusing on the cruelty with which the others handle him. However, this is present as a remnant of the mockumentary tradition, here operating only within the diegesis, and is carefully offset with Jerry/Garry/Larry/Terry's happy private life and general bonhomie portrayed in an equally hyperbolic fashion. The character's constant mockery serves to reinforce the "niceness" of the rest of the narrative.

"good people," on *Parks* there's no deep down inside about it. (Paskin 2011)

Paskin's praise, based on *Parks'* differentiation from contemporaneous quality comedies, is itself in contrast with academic literature's positioning of the series, which evaluates it as being on a par with its contemporaries. Similar to Mills (2009), Newman and Levine (2012, 59–79) assess the quality comedy as discursively and textually moving away from the "conservative" sitcom tradition; they classify *Parks* among the type of comedies that operate with this aesthetic and political dissociation. As noted, they consider the historical establishment of cultural hierarchies as influenced by a gendered progress narrative, that is, as "a shift away from the feminized past and toward a more masculinized future" (11). In television comedy's case, this shift works between the old-fashioned, multicamera soundstage sitcom and the new, cinematized single-camera comedy. The latter "is invested with value by differing from a past ideal of television, one associated with the period before convergence. . . . By relegating this kind of show to the past, or to the realm of the juvenile, feminine, or *passé*, the culture of television's legitimation seeks a new identity for the medium" (79).

Because Newman and Levine mention both *Parks* and *30 Rock* as representative examples of this process of cultural legitimation, it would follow that these series and the discourses in which they are embedded perform similar cultural work, including the aspect of defeminization. But as seen, these series' legitimation processes are fundamentally different from other comedies of the convergence era that Newman and Levine also cite, in that the distancing is entangled with a strategic association with the 1970s female-centered MTM sitcom. Yet even though for *30 Rock* this is rooted primarily in the sarcastic evocation of some narrative elements and politics (*The Mary Tyler Moore Show* as the predecessor in its setting, the narrative premise, and the career woman's centralization), for *Parks* the connection is more subtly ideological and involves tone and characterization.

Consider the generic descriptors by critics: "comedy of niceness" (*Parks*) and "warmedy" (the MTM sitcom). For Feuer (1984b) "warmedy" means a foregrounding of empathetic character development for the 1970s independent woman who struggles against the social conventions of her time. As discussed earlier, the quality discourse of the MTM comedy needed a competitive contrast with contemporaneous sitcoms for its establishment, evident in the hierarchical evaluations of the Norman Lear and the MTM sitcom. Evoking a similar dichotomy, *Parks'* critical evaluation often configures it as different from and more progressive than *30 Rock*, as seen in the quote from Paskin. This competitive differentiation—surfacing in a number of reviews—singles out *Parks* on the basis of its feminist optimism, which is atypical of contemporaneous dark quality comedy, and invokes the past, as in a later paragraph of Paskin's (2011) review: "If championing good old fashion [*sic*] niceness makes *Parks* a throwback to a simpler sitcom era, it hasn't made it any less funny." The remark displays a concern with praising the program through an ambiguous negotiation of the past that works as both distancing and legitimation. The production team is similarly keen to emphasize this connection: Poehler's remark at a panel discussion that she sees Leslie and Ron's (Nick Offerman) relationship as akin to that of *The Mary Tyler Moore Show*'s Mary Richards and Lou Grant (Friedlander 2014) is representative. The *Variety* article reporting the comment is titled "*Parks and Recreation*'s Hidden Political Commentary," and it refers to Poehler and Mike Schur's comments about the character dynamic between Leslie and Ron as that between the mom and dad of the workplace family. Schur puts this in political terms: "When people want a dad, they vote Republican, and when they want a mom, they vote Democrat."[13]

Ultimately, then, it is *Parks* and not the American *Office* that can be considered the logical completion of the British *Office*'s Americanization, in that it becomes fitted into the female-centered workplace comedy tradition with its rhetoric of female empowerment. This involves a complete reversal of the "cruel" mockumentary's ideology, but the "old-fashioned"—antiquated, passé, feminine—niceness into which it is transformed retains its quality descriptor by mining contemporary feminist concerns for political satire. The Leslie-Ron dynamic corresponds to the pairing of Jack and Liz on *30 Rock* as gendered social-political commentary, and in both cases this is founded on feminist politics' invocation, at the same time allowing for a discursive connection with a specific chapter of American television's past as legacy. But *Parks'* niceness works to reconcile the warm character comedy of the past with the postmillennial feminist political satire, a reconciliation always treated ambiguously on *30 Rock*. The utopianism in which this reconciliation results overwhelms *Parks* to the extent that by the seventh season it even impacts its genre, creating an actual utopian science fiction witnessed in the three-year time jump and flash-forwards to a utopian future. The

13   https://www.youtube.com/watch?v=TRFyBDEBcdo (accessed July 24, 2020).

connection between Leslie's feminist enthusiasm and American society's general well-being ultimately become indistinguishable and overdetermined; if "feminists love a utopia" (Shapiro Sanders 2007), *Parks* certainly gives us one.

If reviewers praise *Parks'* singularity in its difference from *30 Rock's* mode of social criticism, then this speaks to the ambiguous evaluations of their alliances with contemporaneous popular feminisms and consequently to the debated cultural status of these feminisms. Here the question of post-feminist discourses comes into play, informing the ways in which the two comedies invoke feminism. I address this issue in the next chapter, which also engages with Fey and Poehler's star texts that foreground feminist discourses in their transgressive enactments of women's comedy. Chapter 3 thus also asks how these personas relate to their positioning as comic heroines in sitcoms whose quality descriptors rely on associations with feminism.

3

NEGOTIATING (POST)FEMINISM IN FEMINIST QUALITY COMEDY

GENDER AS POLITICS IN QUALITY COMEDY

As argued, both *30 Rock* and *Parks and Recreation* and their journalistic evaluations attribute great importance to the female protagonists' representational politics. The discursive significance of these gender politics affects the series' genre configurations and modes of comedy, which in turn are brought to bear on their assigned cultural value. Representational politics are of course a pivotal issue for media criticism, often ascribing higher urgency to these politics in cases of media products whose cultural importance seems located in their centralization of socially marginalized identities. In these instances, methods of representation often determine judgments of quality. In postrecessionary discourses about the quality TV moniker, media producers and critics grant special attention to the treatments in television texts of social identities that mark out marginalized communities. Political relevance and appeals to diversity once again become bases on which the TV industry conceives of its prestige products and caters them to target audiences, resembling the state of affairs in the 1970s. Both the trade press and producers acknowledge and circulate the diversity trend as a negotiation of representational progress, aesthetic achievement, and the industry's economic imperatives in the "Peak TV" era to supply novel content compartmentalized by audience fragmentation (VanDerWerff 2015b; Ryan 2016b; Morris and Poniewozik 2016).

The intense attention paid to the politics of representation and the cultural and economic investment in it also explain the debates surrounding the female protagonists of *30 Rock* and *Parks*—two network comedies that garnered media attention for their initially rare method of situating heroines in workplace settings and situations while also mining the female comics' talents outside the romance framework and instead in comedian comedy and satire. For a while, feminist and other TV critics devoted think pieces to the question of whether Liz Lemon or Leslie Knope was the better feminist role model (e.g., Dailey 2010; Brooks Olsen 2015; see also R. White 2018, 67). The verdict in these evaluations usually declared Knope the winner with her unrelenting feminist aspirationalism dismantling institutional barriers; Lemon gradually became seen as failing the feminist promise for which the first few seasons of *30 Rock* supposedly laid the ground because of her portrayal as grotesque and childish (e.g., Holmes 2012). Mizejewski's (2014, 75–85) analysis of Fey and *30 Rock* investigates the backlash the series and its star increasingly suffered by the early 2010s, with one of the critics dubbing the series' questionable gender politics "Liz Lemonism" (Dailey 2010). Mizejewski (2014) notes that these evaluations habitually conflate the fictional character with the comedian and also that "the mixed signals around Fey—the longing for and nervousness about feminism in popular culture—are demonstrated in the high stakes of the looks of this perfect feminist idol, given multiple cultural pressures to picture her as nonthreatening, mainstream, and even glamorous" (84). A similar dynamic is evident in the journalistic fascination with the comparison and contrast of the feminisms operating in *30 Rock* and *Parks* and in the impetus to establish a competitive relationship between the two protagonists based on their narrativized relationship with feminist representation.

Yet although in the Lemon/Fey backlash the star text and fictional character are interdependent for critics, the Lemon versus Knope feminism contest rarely invokes the—by this time widely circulated—friendship narrative between the two comedians.[1] The popular press describes this friendship primarily in terms of cooperation, female solidarity in a male-dominated profession, and an appreciation of different comic talents informing their double act performances (Fox 2015). These accounts do not discuss this in the way they do the fictional characters: through competitive comparisons of their enactments of feminist politics. This avoidance is all the more significant because popular cultural discourses about feminism regularly pit female celebrities against one another based on their articulations, refusals, and presumed disparate understandings of feminism, a

---

1   Elsewhere I discuss the history and characteristics of this friendship narrative (Havas 2017).

discourse that Poehler has been known to criticize (Duberman 2014). This discrepancy, then, speaks to the importance attributed to feminisms enacted *within the quality series*. In other words, competitive evaluations of Fey's and Poehler's feminisms become projected onto their respective programs, bearing the responsibility of progressive representations of women and leaving the interplay between their star texts intact. The feud between the two fictional characters, created entirely in popular journalism but not supported by the two series' promotional strategies or production teams (let alone by the two comedians), signals the perennial struggle in media discourses to control feminism's meanings (Banet-Weiser 2018), which here governs the comparative criticism leveled at the two texts. Equally important, it also demonstrates the postfeminist cultural environment's nervousness about female-centered TV texts that position themselves in the quality discourse for both their aesthetic *and* representational features.

This nervous investment in the programs' gender politics thus speaks to the link between quality television and the postfeminist ethos that operates in women's televisual representations. As discussed in chapter 1, there is an overlapping logic inherent in these two paradigms' development. First, exclusivity in class terms is a constitutive component for both; quality TV's imperative to target upmarket audiences and postfeminism's insistence on an empowerment narrative for privileged white femininities produce the "quality postfeminism" (Negra 2004) that feminist scholars have described and interrogated. Second, if television's cultural strength has historically been configured as an immediacy in thematizing social issues, it primarily does so by individualizing and privatizing them in quality television's serial narrative (see, for instance, Creeber's [2004, 116] interpretation of the millennial soap drama's cultural work). This heritage is particularly suitable for the postfeminist mode of reinscribing the feminist political project onto the private spheres of sexuality and romance, motherhood, choice feminism, and so on. Third, the cultural work and successful integration of both paradigms into cultural consciousness hinges on declaring their respective historic backgrounds as overcome while obscuring their dependence on this legacy for their existence. McRobbie's (2009) description of postfeminism as "feminism taken into account" can be paralleled with HBO's "It's not TV" slogan for the way they both necessarily contain the term they allegedly leave behind.

Considering these features that make the two phenomena such perfect bedfellows, the idea of a feminist quality TV seems a contradiction. This contradiction partly accounts for the uneasy cultural position of *30 Rock* and

Parks, mostly expressed in the debates surrounding their feminisms and located, for instance, in the criticism that a program centralizing privileged white femininities is already suspicious in its appeal to feminist politics. Further, the way in which the comedy of distinction operates for *30 Rock*, meaning an intense preoccupation with its own past and present, also speaks to this unease. Consequently, *30 Rock*'s explicitness about this distinction cannot be interpreted without considering the importance it ascribes to its genderedness (and vice versa), an interdependence rarely analyzed by its popular and academic critics—put bluntly, it is either discussed as a quality series or as a feminist or gendered one. Kenneth's list of "no-no words" presented to Lemon makes explicit how *30 Rock* plays on its own problematic efforts to produce aesthetically superior comedy on network television that centralizes and *politicizes* female subjectivity. The comedy framework capitalizes on these contradictions as a genre operating to both expose and contain the anxieties inherent in cultural phenomena (which in this case means the series' very existence). The fact that feminist quality comedy creates such cultural anxieties signals the precarious position of efforts to politicize issues of gender in putatively nonfeminine subgenres of television.[2]

The contradictory position that *30 Rock* and *Parks* occupy in the quality comedy model as a result of their feminist moniker provides a concept to account for their generic shifts demonstrated in the previous chapter: These shifts in tone were direct consequences of the *female* comedian's centralization, and they resulted in extreme genre hybrids. *30 Rock* thematizes the complexities of (post)feminist womanhood by situating it in an increasingly cartoonesque and cynical satire, expressing its pessimism through over-the-top absurdism—the trait for which TV critics celebrate it as exceptional (the series is an "apocalyptic view of the TV industry" for Emily Nussbaum [2012a]).[3] Although *Parks* obviously uses a different tone, mobilizing an

---

2 This precariousness probably also explains why *30 Rock*, in its zealous name checking of female-centered and other predecessors, avoids referencing *Roseanne*. This series' alignment with working-class feminism in domestic sitcom form and Roseanne Arnold's comedy of excess exclude *Roseanne* from the history of female-centered *quality* comedy.

3 Jeremy Butler (2010), in his analysis of quality comedy's aesthetic-stylistic features, draws up a schema termed "televisual continuum" between the extremes of "stylistically utilitarian" and "stylistically exhibitionistic" comedy. He sees animated series as the ultimate fulfillment of the exhibitionistic style for their capacity to "contain visuals impossible to generate with camera and

optimistic mode of comedy, this leads it similarly outside the realms of discursively realistic genre traditions all the way to utopian science fiction (an especially extreme leap, considering the program's mockumentary and comedy verité origins). The final season's time jump and flash-forwards signal the ultimate and perhaps logical endpoint for articulating an aspirational feminist politics, and these plot devices have been treated by critics, similar to *30 Rock*, as pivotal to the comedy's exceptionalism.

Both *30 Rock* and *Parks* thus narrativize their distinct takes on gender politics in forms that help them stand out in the postnetwork comedy cohort, and, even more noticeably, they both mobilize their respective genre hybrids (absurdist satire and mockumentary/utopian sci-fi) in ways that can be called parabolic. This links them to American fictional television's tradition of focusing on small communities, established within well-defined identity boundaries. But *30 Rock* and *Parks* directly invite an understanding of their narratives as corresponding to events and conditions of a discursive American reality in the parable, allegory, or morality tale frameworks. In both sitcoms the trope of the small workplace community standing in for American society operates as a politicized space where contained experiments with gender, race, and class relations are carried out.

For instance, the *30 Rock* episode "Believe in the Stars" metatextually uses Tracy and Jenna's characters as "the" Black star and "the" woman star of the fictional variety show to satirize the journalistic question of who has it worse in America, Black men or women (the corresponding social event at the time of the episode's broadcast was Hillary Clinton and Barack Obama's competition during the 2008 Democratic presidential primaries). When the two start a social experiment to prove their points by dressing up as the other (i.e., a white woman and a Black man), not only does the story make its own function as social parable explicit, but it also turns into a whistle stop tour of what demographics the main characters represent, or what they think they represent (e.g., Jack considers Kenneth not a white man but "socioeconomically speaking, an inner-city Latina"). Liz invites Oprah Winfrey, whom she thinks she met earlier on a plane, to mediate. The denouement in which it is a chirpy Black teenage girl named Pam (Raven

---

actors" (216) and places *30 Rock* close to this end of the spectrum. In this light, *30 Rock*'s frequent descriptions as cartoonesque and Liz Lemon's comparisons with Homer Simpson reveal its discursive associations with "extremely" stylized television, even in the quality television context.

Goodwin) who arrives instead of Oprah, not only lampoons Liz's unwitting racism (she mistook Pam for Oprah while on a sedative) but also satirizes how discourses about race and gender ignore nonwhite femininities, unless they are mobilized to "fix" the perceived issues of more visible social groups. (At the episode's end, Liz praises Pam's mediating skills to Jack, and he advises her to "be a white man. Take credit.") The parable makes statements about each character's social standing, using them as representatives of their culturally defined social groups. The premise and narrative strategy are a result of efforts to integrate contemporary feminism's identity politics into quality comedy, producing the hyperbolically metafictional, cartoonesque, self-obsessed, absurd, apocalyptic comedy for which *30 Rock* is known. Put another way, the intense scrutiny of gender and identity politics appears to call for the frantic, sarcastic style, which is mandated with carrying the meanings it struggles to articulate.

Similarly, in *Parks* the municipal government setting functions as an insulated environment corresponding to representative groups of American society and as a site of labor relations where, like the cultural industries in *30 Rock*, a visible area of American society can be observed in operation, offset here with this community's provinciality (R. White 2018, 82). For Jeffrey Sconce (2009) this provinciality effects a derisive mode of comedy, but his description applies largely to the first season and loses its relevance once the tonal shift takes place and overwrites the narrative. The extent to which *Parks* distances itself after season 2 from this "condescending" (Sconce 2009) humor hinges on its alliance with feminist satire, a strategy that at the same time ensures that the narrative no longer represents only a provincial and ridiculed type of government and its gender relations but also applies to broader social-political conditions. For instance, the episode "Filibuster" takes its main plot from national political events, namely, Texan Democratic senator Wendy Davis's headline-making 11-hour-long filibuster in 2013 to block the Texas state senate from voting on a bill aimed at restricting abortion rights in the state. The episode satirizes the misogyny of the Pawnee City Council when Leslie Knope similarly attempts to block a vote, sporting a pair of roller skates that allude to Davis's infamous pink sneakers. This episode also integrates into this plot a controversial voter ID law proposed in Texas in 2011, considered by its critics as discriminatory against low-income and minority voters. The proposed bill that Leslie filibusters in *Parks* would revoke voting rights from non-Pawnee citizens and is tailored against Eagletonians (a more affluent town previously merged with Pawnee), who oppose Leslie's council membership. The story thus turns into a dilemma for Leslie between a democratic, morally right choice (blocking the vote on an undemocratic bill) and one that would benefit her career (letting Eagletonians lose their voting rights to save her seat). *Parks* frequently presents such dilemmas as central to Leslie's politics, complicating the meanings of her feminist ambition and energy. The convolutedly politicized plot comes to dominate the series in a way that is both predicated on specific feminist concerns and identity politics (of the feminist as political figure) and also determines the insulated lab experiment nature of its meaning making, culminating in the series finale's utopian vision.

In sum, the exceptional, extreme tonal characteristics of *30 Rock* and *Parks* in narrating their female protagonists' stories cannot be divorced from the (post)feminist cultural context in which these stories are articulated. Both series function as—in their times—isolated efforts to integrate a public (as opposed to privatized) idea of gender politics with quality television's aesthetic and representational features, and this choice leads them to non-realist territories of genre and modes of comedy. In the following section I examine in more detail how this works in each comedy.

THE AMBIGUITY OF (POST)FEMINISM IN *30 ROCK*

The pilot episode of *30 Rock*, as discussed, makes explicit claims about the relationship between network television's cultural status as a feminized source of viewing pleasures and the ways that masculinized ideals of value become integrated into this, thereby foregrounding the relevance of gender in quality TV discourse. The pilot also makes clear that its primary perspective will be that of the single career woman figure as both target audience and producer of network TV's derided content. Ensuring that the viewer understands what kind of femininity Liz represents, the pilot has Jack describe her in a condescending minilecture, a quote that has ever since functioned as Lemon's sleight-of-hand profile for critics. To Liz's remark "I don't cook much," Donaghy replies, "Sure, I got you. New York third-wave feminist, college-educated, single-and-pretending-to-be-happy-about-it, overscheduled, undersexed, you buy any magazine that says 'healthy body image' on the cover, and every two years you take up knitting for . . . a week?" We get a handy user manual here for Liz's character, as conveyed by the conservative older male boss. The description is a recognizable type of womanhood originating in second-wave feminism's popular image, a staple of postfeminist media culture: the self-absorbed, self-described feminist successor of the urban empowered career girl, an image popularized by *Sex and the City* and its ilk. Nussbaum's (2012a) praise of Lemon and Fey, defending them against the backlash, treats this monologue as "nailing" Liz "on sight." Rebecca Traister (2010) also uses this quote to defend Fey against the backlash, arguing that her self-deprecating comedy involves lampooning her own star text in relation to popular feminism. Mizejewski's (2014) academic analysis refers to the "third-wave feminist" moniker to demonstrate that Lemon functions both as a caricature of the "sourpuss" workaholic feminist and as a criticism of corporate culture's institutionalized sexism (66).

Although these assessments usefully point out how *30 Rock* articulates Lemon's social identity, its understanding is incomplete without considering the next lines of dialogue. To an inquiry about how he came up with such a "dead-on" reading of Liz, Jack replies, "Years and years of market research." This implies that reading Lemon as a prime example of postfeminist and third-wave feminist womanhood follows from the television executive's experience with studying audiences and/as consumers—Jack's job title is Vice President of East Coast Television and Microwave Oven Programming. The dialogue connects Lemon's "dead-on" description to corporate capitalism's strategies of establishing and catering to a society of consumers (the series often mocks and explains corporate terminology, such as vertical integration), of which the postfeminist or feminist single woman is a prominent representative. Lemon not only is a caricature of this woman but is also conceived as a construct of the capitalist culture industries. Thus the series admits at its beginning that if Lemon is to be read as *the* postfeminist or failed feminist woman, then she is created by and through the culture industries; she is media fiction. Whether Jack "nails" Liz's character or not is not the concern of this dialogue but rather the blurring of identity that it causes: Liz can simultaneously function as a potential (though progressively failing) role model—that is, as an example of a strong female protagonist trope—and as a caricature of (post)feminist womanhood (explaining why her critics feel let down by her portrayal in later seasons). Third, she functions as an open admission that even this caricature of the postfeminist woman is a creation of American consumer culture. *30 Rock* makes clear its struggle here with its embeddedness in postfeminism by the character's overdetermined nature, and it makes this struggle the program's starting point. In this, the female protagonist's treatment as a transparent and shifting figure—also always inevitably projected onto Fey's star text as her comic alter ego—betrays an effort to comment on the portrayal it produces. As I will show, Fey's already established reputation as an observer of gender and other social relations also feeds into this interpretation of social commentary accumulated in Lemon's figure.

Linda Mizejewski's (2014) analysis of *30 Rock* and Fey offers insight into the intricacies of the series' thick web of commentary on the relationship between the media industries, corporate capitalism, nation, identity, and body politics. As discussed, race relations and the ambiguous dynamic of feminism and postfeminism take a prominent place in the satirical treatment of these categories. Mizejewski's key argument is that the series is hardly a straightforward feminist text, precisely because of its observational character: "*30 Rock* is not a feminist text but rather one that explores the unruly ways feminist ideals actually play out in institutions and in popular culture" (26–27). Interrogating the development of Fey's comedian persona as a brainy satirist of gender relations, which had led to her reputation as a feminist, Mizejewski also engages with how this persona became complicated in its "cover girl" iteration once Fey garnered overnight popularity and media interest during the 2008 presidential campaign with her impersonations of Republican vice-presidential candidate Sarah Palin. Mizejewski's overview of Fey's comedy and star text emphasizes that both involve a consistent and wide-ranging mode of observational humor. She describes this facet of Fey's comedy as the defining feature of her career, with *Mean Girls* (the 2004 film whose script she wrote) being praised by critics as a "sociological" take on "girl world" or with her Weekend Update news anchor persona on *Saturday Night Live* as a no-nonsense feminist making acidic jokes about institutionalized sexism and misogyny. Mizejewski considers Fey's pre-*30 Rock* comedy significant because it discusses gender in a way that positions the comedian as an outsider to the social relations on which she comments—even to her own celebrity.

Indeed, Fey's persona as more of a writer-observer rather than an actor-performer of gender relations has been part of her celebrity from the beginnings of her career. An early article profile has Amy Poehler describe her thus: "She's not the first girl to belly-flop into the pool at the pool party. She watches everybody else's flops and then writes a play about it" (Heffernan 2003). But if the strength of Fey's comedy is rooted in its observational humor, then this becomes ambiguously interpreted as feminist once her own star text is the target by means of Lemon's satirical, sarcastic portrayal. Mizejewski's reluctance to saddle *30 Rock* with the feminist moniker is linked to the series' sarcastic tone, concentrated into Lemon's (Fey's alter ego's) position in the show's fiction.

> Far from claiming *30 Rock* as a feminist text, my primary argument here is that it does a different kind of cultural work than expected in representing a feminist TV writer complicit in profit-driven, sexist, mainstream media and in exploring the messy ways feminist ideals play out in institutions and popular culture. . . . Significantly, Liz Lemon is a liminal figure in relation to corporate and cultural power as well as to feminism, and *30 Rock*'s comedy draws from both corporate and feminist politics. (Mizejewski 2014, 77)

Liminality and outsiderness in relation to feminism describe both comedian and fictional character for Mizejewski; it is precisely the scrutinizing take on Lemon and feminism that precludes classifying the series as feminist television. Paradoxically, then, the trait through which Fey's popular image was established as Hollywood's token feminist, namely, the position of outsider-observer and astute satirist of gender relations, works against this moniker when the object of scrutiny becomes the cultural state of affairs of feminism and postfeminism projected onto the token feminist comedian's fictional alter ego.

If *30 Rock* is problematic in the way it can or cannot be declared a straightforward feminist text for its critics, then this is due to Liz's portrayal as a representative, consumer, and producer of images of postfeminist womanhood, also always carrying the extratextual understanding that she is Fey's fictional version. As shown, the series not only acknowledges this portrayal but also foregrounds it as a premise to be interrogated and lampooned. Feminist or not, in this feature the series nonetheless evokes feminist theorists' critique of postfeminism's rootedness in neoliberal ideologies of individualist consumerism. McRobbie (2009, 2011) scrutinizes how neoliberal governments, colluding with popular media, assign to affluent young women a key social role as ideal subjects of what she terms "the new sexual contract." She discusses this as an ethos that ties women's economic power to the "freedom to consume," fueling the expansion of the fashion-beauty industry under the aegis of consumer citizenship, and discouraging political participation (McRobbie 2011, 182). As Gill and Scharff suggest, "Neoliberalism is always already gendered, and . . . women are constructed as its ideal subjects" (quoted in Wilkes 2015, 26).

Lemon's portrayal and the intricate matrix of workplace and domestic relations in *30 Rock* insist that neoliberal postfeminist capitalism and media culture are "already gendered" and target female or feminized subjects. Further, it satirizes the individualization politics inherent in this paradigm, evidenced in the constant clashes between Liz's uninformed and entitled social consciousness feminism and her environment's efforts to stifle her politics. Mizejewski (2014) offers a detailed analysis of the episode "Brooklyn Without Limits" that (like many others) thematizes this tension, noting that, although the series satirizes "both feminist hypocrisy and postfeminist bourgeois angst," there is also "a privileged, middle-class politics looming under the surface of *30 Rock*'s comedy as its perimeter in imagining social change" (84). The episode sends up Liz's social consciousness as she proudly buys a pair of jeans from a company that she thinks is an independent fair trade business and not part of a multinational corporation, until Jack enlightens her that it is owned by Halliburton and exploits Vietnamese workers. Because a major draw for Liz was that this pair of jeans was the only kind in which her backside has ever looked attractive and she now has to return to unflattering clothes that accommodate her politics, the episode narrativizes the conflict between a (secretly self-centered) feminist consciousness and corporate capitalism, projected onto Lemon's body. Mizejewski posits that, although this story line is sharp and quite dark in mocking both Liz's political consciousness and Jack's defense of global capitalism, it also unwittingly exposes its own blind spots regarding its treatment of feminist politics because it "does not acknowledge . . . the limitations of Liz's liberalism." It centralizes "a personal choice about her looks, money, and commodities" instead of actual political activism against corporations, thus "accept[ing] personal power as the only viable kind of agency" (85).

For Mizejewski, this individualization of social issues is the real "Liz Lemonism," that is, the fault in *30 Rock*'s gender politics. However, if Lemon is a caricature of the ideal subject of postfeminist and neoliberal cultural politics, as proposed in the pilot episode, then the episode's and the program's insistence that the uninformed liberal feminist inevitably buys into the rhetoric of self-work and a shortsighted concern with commodities makes perfect sense. Importantly, the series' trajectory stresses the process in which Liz increasingly conflates the political with the personal, gradually shortchanging her bleeding-heart, issue-oriented feminist intentions for individual concerns. A three-episode arc at the beginning of season 2 scrutinizes this process at length, interpreting it as a struggle between Liz and her environment. This semiserialized plot revolves around Jenna's body issues: During the show's summer hiatus, she gained enough weight to be deemed unpresentable on television, a conflict lampooning the media industry's sexist treatment of female performers. "She needs to lose thirty pounds or gain sixty. Anything in between has no place in television," says the slightly overweight Jack ("Seinfeld Vision"). The next episode deals with the weight gain's consequences for Jenna's celebrity and with Liz and Jack's opinions on this, representing the liberal feminist and the sexist capitalist stances, respectively ("Jack Gets in the Game"). Liz initially insists that they ignore Jenna's changed body and continue to treat her as the show's resident pretty girl. As she consoles Jenna, Jack interjects, and the massaging of Jenna's self-esteem turns into an "issue" debate between the two leads.

> Liz: How come men can be heavy and be respected, like James Gandolfini or Fat Albert? You know it's a double standard, and America needs to get over its body image madness.
>
> Jack: Oh, come on, what are we, back in college, freshman year? Let's go to the common room and talk about apartheid.
>
> Liz: Well, OK. I'm sorry if I care about making the world a better place.
>
> Jack: You should be. It's a complete waste of time and prevents you from dealing with THIS *(gestures at Lemon's body)*.
>
> Liz: Excuse me, what about THIS do I have to deal with?
>
> Jack: How's your love life going?
>
> Liz: I . . . believe that love comes to you when you're not looking for it.
>
> Jack: Did you return that wedding dress that you bought?
>
> Liz: I'm gonna sell it online but my Internet is being weird.
>
> Jack: How about the furniture for your home office. Have you even set that up yet? *(A smash cut shows a stack of unopened cardboard boxes in Lemon's apartment.)*

Liz: I'm not making excuses Jack but THIS *(gestures at her body)* is taken care of. *(Yelps and touches her cheek.)* Nerds! I missed a dentist appointment this morning!

The scene sets up the issues around which the comedy about the ridiculed "fat" female body revolves: Although voicing the obvious feminist stance, articulated as sociocultural concern by Liz, it also shows that her feminism is easily steered off course by corporate capitalism's local representative into a personal, self-absorbed identity politics. Crucially, Jack's manipulative change of subject from the issue's social relevance to Liz's own romantic and private life culminates in a punch line that locates Liz's body as the main problem. However, the symbolic body centralized here is not the "THIS" that both Liz and Jack emphatically gesture toward. Shifting from the sexualized connotation inscribed onto the female body (love life, marriage), the scene locates the comedy in the unsexy notion of Liz's toothache. The scene follows a trajectory that starts with verbalizing the feminist concerns at stake, which is highjacked by the power-that-be into the language of postfeminism, which the comedy again thwarts such that the focus on the female body lands on the discrepancy between Liz's sexual(ized) and comically disintegrating body.

A later scene reprises the same arc in which Liz's hyperbolic interest in Jenna's body image problem as a feminist issue becomes ridiculed and turned back against her as rooted in her unhappy personal life, culminating in the physical comedy of Liz's failing body. Jenna and Liz decide to ignore the weight issue: Jenna out of vanity and Liz to prove the feminist point, still adamant that the TV industry needs a lesson in social consciousness. A male voice distracts them again as staff writer Frank (Judah Friedlander) enters and suggests a "fat Jenna" character with the catchphrase "Me want food." Lemon refuses.

Liz: We are gonna dare America to change their own attitudes about body image.

Frank: Why do you have to make everything into an issue? Don't you have things to do with your own life?

Liz: At least I don't live with my mum. *(Yelps, touches her cheek.)*

Frank: Hey, my mum is cool.

Liz: I got my life together, OK? (*A tooth falls out of her mouth.*)

In repeating the joke of the earlier scene, the narrative presents Liz not simply as an already "failed feminist" but as a template of the uninformed one on whom the postfeminist capitalist project has been doing its work. Still at the beginning of Jack's mentorship—a central theme of the series—Liz here retains her interest in "making the world a better place," a mantra later replaced, through Jack's influence, with "Get out there and get yours" ("Kidney Now!"). If Liz "constantly compromis[es] her ideals as the cost of working for a national network, becoming 'schooled and seduced' into sleazy network thinking" (Mizejewski 2014, 76), then this process prominently entails gradually abandoning the feminist project as her ideal. Fey's observational comedy at work uses the spaces and communities of privilege not to inherently confirm a postfeminist ethos but to lay bare its working mechanisms. Traister (2010) argues that the Fey backlash signals an uneasy relationship between feminism and comedy, noting that Fey "is a professional comedian" and "not a professional feminist." Mizejewski's academic examination, as noted, is also reluctant to link the series' cultural work to feminism, following a similar logic in which a comedy *about* feminism and postfeminism forecloses using the descriptor.

Entangled in this uneasy connection between comedy and feminism is the metatextual authorship discourse about Fey as producer and performer of quality comedy, intensified by using the Lemon figure as a fictional doppelgänger. In comedian comedy history the idea that the comic persona is a thinly veiled alter ego of the comedian is a familiar staple, which in television merges organically with the establishment of quality comedy. Prominent TV comedies regularly built their worlds around this alter ego in both the network and postnetwork eras, in some cases using this transparency to create metacomedy about the television business (e.g., *Curb Your Enthusiasm* and *The Comeback*), their titles often bearing the comedian's first or last name. The authorship discourse surrounding quality drama, which is concerned with explaining the TV text with the discursive author's personality and art (Martin 2013), has in this way been prominent in television comedy history as well, regardless of its assigned cultural value. And although comedian-comedy-type sitcoms about and by a comic performer have primarily been a male domain (Mills 2005), there have been instances of female-centered metatextual comedian comedies on television, for example, *Roseanne, Ellen* (1994–1998), *Cybill* (1995–1998), and *Fat Actress* (2005). These programs' cultural significance revolves around the extent to which they upset the gendered codes of decorum for the female performer as the subject and object of humor. *30 Rock* combines these distinct traditions: It uses the female-comic-performer-as-alter-ego trope as a metatextual comedy about the TV industry. But in casting the female performer as the *writer* of comedy and with Fey's initial star persona being that of the comedy writer, as opposed to the performer, it blends the parallel traditions of male comedian comedy as the revered definition of authorship (Jerry Seinfeld, Larry David, Louis C.K.) and female-centered comedian comedy that has until recently been understood as outside the quality discourse and/or about the female *performer* (Roseanne Arnold, Ellen DeGeneres, Kirstie Alley, or Lisa Kudrow).

The metacomedy about television, female authorship, and feminism through which *30 Rock* inserts itself into the quality discourse is as such unprecedented and creates multiple issues, which the series perpetually negotiates. Fey's author persona as writer-performer-producer of her own comedy writer alter ego seems to be an impossible sign in this discourse—and part of this impossibility is the comedy's concentration on feminism and postfeminism as its dominant object of satire.

Fey's next project after *30 Rock*, the Netflix comedy *Unbreakable Kimmy Schmidt*, lacked both the comic alter ego aspect and an overarching meta-satire of feminism, with Fey being mainly involved in a writer-producer capacity. Perhaps not coincidentally, *Unbreakable* has been more unequivocally embraced by critics as feminist text. This suggests that a centralized mockery of feminism and postfeminism in Fey's comedy is tied to *her* self-centralization as a comic performer, invoking the common wisdom that women's comedy relies on self-deprecation (Mills 2005, 112), a point dominant for analysts of Fey's humor. Female comedians' uses and abuses of conventions of self-mockery to lay bare unequal gender relations have been an object of scrutiny for feminist scholars (Rowe Karlyn 1995b; Arthurs 1999). Fey's discursively authored comedy in *30 Rock* resists a stable positioning in this context, an instability that results from its centralization of feminist politics as channeled through the female comedian's self-mockery and as agent of the quality status. Feminizing articulations of her author persona, like the use of maternity shown in the previous chapter, work to mitigate the cultural unease that this instability causes.

I offer these considerations not to take a stand on the question of *30 Rock* and Fey's feminism or postfeminism. Rather, my concern has been to show that both text and comedian consistently keep querying discursive assumptions about the popular cultural presence of feminism and postfeminism. Because this strategic instability of meanings is so prominent in the series and in Fey's star text and because both betray an intent to politicize these meanings in the quality comedy's expressive modes, *30 Rock*'s significance for popular feminism is best located as presaging the (pessimistically envisaged) postmillennial rebooting of feminist discourses, intensified in postrecessionary media culture. Banet-Weiser (2018) shows how this renewed interest in feminist politics also continues to involve popular culture's efforts to allocate narrowed-down meanings to the term. For Banet-Weiser this phenomenon misappropriates feminism's project of "ambiguity," its concern with interrogating and denaturalizing assumptions about gender and about its own meanings through sustained debate. As my discussion of *30 Rock* and of Fey's writer-performer persona shows, one thing (perhaps the only thing) that can be stated about both with absolute certainty is that they trade in this ambiguity.

PARKS AND RECREATION AND ASPIRATIONAL (POST)FEMINISM

At the same time as Fey's popular reputation shifted from arbiter of feminism to questionable ally because of *30 Rock*'s cultural work and her growing name recognition, Amy Poehler's celebrity narrative traveled in almost the opposite direction: The series designed as her first central TV role also established her feminist image. The two comics' different creative backgrounds partly account for this disparate route: Fey's persona as writer-author determined her evaluations from the beginning of her career, whereas Poehler was not associated with authorship in such a capacity. She first garnered renown as a versatile sketch performer on *Saturday Night Live*, a role dominating her early celebrity. As her star-making vehicle, *Parks and Recreation* articulated this versatility of performance as a feminist trait, mobilized in both the career woman's political empowerment narrative and the series' satire of institutions. I showed earlier how the feminist aspect eventually governs *Parks*' genre and reverses the mockumentary's cultural work, envisaging a utopian aspirational feminism to the degree that it steers the realist fiction toward actual utopian science fiction.

Performance is a key term for comedy scholarship, especially in the context of examining how the mockumentary or comedy verité form upsets its conventions to produce quality comedy (Mills 2004; E. Thompson 2007;

Hight 2010; Middleton 2014). For sitcom theorists the form tradition-ally foregrounds comic performance to distinguish it from more serious and putatively realistic forms. Mills (2004) writes, "'Sitcom naturalism' is based on audiences 'suspending disbelief in return for pleasure,' in which the laughter track, the theatrical shooting style and the displayed perfor-mance clearly demonstrate sitcom's artificial status and its clear, precise, single-minded aim: to make you laugh" (67). However, the mockumentary aesthetic hybridizing factual and fictive forms questions both documen-tary's claim to authenticity, "whose veracity rests on the assumption that there is a *lack* of performance" (73), and the tenability of traditional sit-com's "displayed" performance style (72–74) by exposing the inauthenticity of both kinds of performance. As I will show, *Parks* reverses this process, even while retaining mockumentary's formal aesthetics, a trajectory rooted in mobilizing a politicized and openly employed feminist rhetoric for the establishment of the series' quality moniker.

The extent to which feminist intent overturns mockumentary's efforts to ridicule fake performances (of the self and of traditional comedy) can be demonstrated in the difference between the ways *Parks* uses Poehler's comic talent and, for instance, the British *Office*'s or *The Comeback*'s com-mentary on comedy performance by David Brent's and Valerie Cherish's "displayed" performances. *The Office* and *The Comeback* use cringe comedy, displaying their characters' stupidity and self-delusion, which extend to their own erroneous perception of their environment's appreciation of their humorous performances—the viewer is invited to "laugh . . . at and not with" them (Mills 2004, 73). At the same time, Ricky Gervais's and Lisa Kudrow's performances of this self-delusion are not "displayed," at least not in tradi-tional sitcom terms. *Parks* gradually inverts this strategy. Although Leslie's self-deception is similarly a source of comedy in the first season, the pro-gram increasingly foregrounds Poehler's comic skills without the effect of a diegetic inauthenticity. The difference surfaces clearly in the repeatedly used method of jump-cut monologues, which are the series' signature feature and which first appears in the pilot. In this sequence we see a montage of Leslie asking Ron in different ways to allow her to form a committee. The scene was reportedly not prewritten (Raymond 2013), signaling that Poehler's improvisational talents were strategically incorporated into the program's aesthetic. At the same time, the frequent use of jump cuts is explained as coin-cidentally emerging; the editor of the episode "The Reporter" was apparently unable to decide what to cut from a scene involving a series of Poehler's improvisations and ended up keeping all of them, leading to the jump-cut solution (Raymond 2013). These montages simultaneously invite us to not just laugh at Leslie's diegetic delusional enthusiasm but also to appreciate, extradiegetically, Poehler's improvisational talent. The improvisational feel is in accordance with mockumentary's aesthetic tradition and becomes a dominant feature of *Parks*; even more important, it is frequently used as a commentary on gender relations.

For instance, one of the most celebrated jump cuts occurs in the episode "The Hunting Trip," in which Leslie takes the blame for accidentally shooting Ron in the back of the head on a hunting trip. She gives a statement to a park ranger whose attitude betrays a sexist assumption about the accident's circumstances. Through a combination of Poehler's performance and the jump-cut technique, we first register Leslie's growing exasperation at the ranger's patronizing demand for an explanation and then her resolve to get out of the situation by performing a series of "typical" feminine responses with which he feels more comfortable, ditching her real voice and her non-gendered explanation. Leslie's utterances become increasingly ridiculous and turn into a satirical parody of patriarchal notions of womanhood through Poehler's exaggerated performance in the jump-cut montage. The improvised bits—including "I cared too much, I guess," "I was thinking with my lady parts," "I thought there was gonna be chocolate," "I'm wearing a new bra, and it closes in the front, so it popped open and it threw me off," "All I wanna do is have babies," "I'm just, like, going through a thing right now," "This would not happen if I had a penis," "I'm good at tolerating pain, I'm bad at math, and I'm stupid," and so on—telegraph the ridiculousness of the ranger's sexism. Performance works on two levels: within the diegesis, with Leslie acting out a series of supposedly inauthentic femininities for the ranger's benefit, simultaneously reaffirming her own authentic feminist self in the contrast; and as Poehler's displayed comic performance. Thus performance is not meant to expose the protagonist's delusion (as with Brent or Cherish) but a supporting character's sexist self-delusion and representation of paternalistic male authority (whereas in *The Office* or *The Comeback* supporting characters are used to signal the protagonist's ridiculousness). This scene is included in *Vulture*'s list of the program's best jump-cut montages, ranking second (Raymond 2013), with an introduction that lauds it for an authentic or "subtle" feminism, articulated through the mockumentary's method of exposing the contradictions in documentary's claims to authenticity. The political feminist intent here overwrites mockumentary's ideological intent, and the presumed authenticity of feminism is reconfirmed through Leslie's own authenticity as an aspirational feminist public figure. This authenticity emerges in contrast to her environment's (the ranger's) consistent efforts to sabotage it: We laugh with her at him, not at her. Displaying the female comedian's skilled performance establishes this ideological reversal of aesthetic tools.

During its run, critics celebrated both the program's and Leslie's putatively authentic feminism as markers of a quality series that pedagogically problematizes gender relations. Unlike in *30 Rock* and Fey's case, media reception reconciled the issue of discrepancy or similarity between fictional character and comedian, because Poehler's celebrity was increasingly governed by a performance of a straightforward, argumentative, and optimistic feminism. Poehler's various confirmations of a feminist attitude, her affiliation with feminist organizations, and her founding of the website Smart Girls at the Party, an "empowering" platform for teenage girls (Kleeman 2014), supported this perception. Similarly, her autobiography *Yes Please* (Poehler 2014) betrays an effort to participate in contemporary discourses about an aspirational, optimistic feminism, in its rhetoric echoing the series' and the fictional character's assertive yet accessible feminist reputation. The animated Pixar film *Inside Out* (2015) also capitalized on this by casting Poehler as the voice of the personified emotion Joy. These articulations of her star text in relation to popular feminism were considerably easier to make sense of in popular media discourses than Fey's less directly mediated and strategically problematic, problematizing gender politics.

Yet Poehler and the series' promotion of an aspirational feminism, foregrounding optimism, pugnacious female ambition, self-work, and solidarity, also open themselves up to criticisms of a blindness to class and racial privilege. Indeed, just as her memoir/advice book has been embraced as feminist (Rodriguez 2014) and as complicating the messages of career advice books for women such as Sheryl Sandberg's *Lean In* (Sandberg 2013; for a comparative criticism, see Yabroff 2014), it has also been accused of ignoring social inequalities. Rodrigues (2014) writes, "The white-lady memoir, as informed by white liberal feminism, is complicit in a stagnant form of popularized non-politics that emphasizes non-confrontation, positivity, and individualism." Diane Negra's (2014) academic account similarly shows this to be a dominant feature of postrecessionary female celebrity memoirs, including Fey's *Bossypants*. For both critics these books are unacknowledged allies to recessionary postfeminist corporate culture and, ultimately, a "neo-patriarchal" genre (Negra 2014, 284).

Although Negra's assessment of celebrity memoirs does not include *Yes Please*, its position parallels Rodrigues's criticism of the book. Debates around this literature demonstrate once again the inevitably problematic nature of claims to a feminist politics in a postfeminist cultural environment. What Yabroff (2014) sees as Poehler's resistance to Sandberg-type feminine careerism, instead promoting female solidarity and individualism as summarized in the book's recurring mantra "Good for you, not for me," Rodrigues refuses as a sign of postfeminist privilege for neglecting unequal social, political, and economic circumstances. Such issues around the choice feminism of *Yes Please* loom large for *Parks and Recreation*, yet the series has not been subject to such critical treatment by feminists as Poehler's book. Framed in the competitive comparison with Fey and *30 Rock*, the program has been overwhelmingly embraced as *the* signature feminist TV text of the early 2010s.

A crucial element of the program's celebration as feminist quality TV in its reception is its portrayal of local government's institutional sexism as a hurdle the heroine needs to overcome. A structuralist summary of the series confirms this: The overarching narrative frames feminist aspirationalism as motivation for the protagonist's quest, whereas different iterations of the antifeminist social environment represent the villain; the heroine has her community of helpers, and she occasionally suffers failures in her mission, which is, as stated in the pilot, to become the first female president. That Leslie's ambition is initially presented as delusional but later as justified reaffirms the shift in the storytelling technique toward this grand narrative. This narrative structure, mobilizing quality TV's serialization techniques (Creeber 2004), finds sustained tension between realism (mockumentary aesthetics and stories of Leslie's failures) and fantasy and utopia. The series' ending leaves open the question that the pilot episode posed and that the grand narrative has at stake: We never find out whether Leslie becomes president. The story thus preserves this tension between realism and utopia even for the denouement, but the intense focus on this question (by withholding information) shows the significance attributed to utopia, here equated with a female presidency, itself signaling in American cultural imagination the ultimate realization of women's subversion of patriarchal public institutions. The ultimate utopia is left ambiguous to draw attention to its political significance.

The grand narrative of the quest for utopia in the quality television framework, providing viewing satisfaction simultaneously from narrative resolution and ambiguity, aligns itself with some strands of feminist theory. Lisa Shapiro Sanders's (2007) position on the potential of utopian thinking in debates about feminism's multiple iterations is instructive. She defends second-wave feminism's utopianism against arguments that see it as dated and static in its historically universalizing and essentialist tendencies (3–4). Instead, she locates utopia's usefulness for contemporary feminism in "the productive expression and negotiation of conflict . . . envisioning social change that emphasizes the transformative over the perfected vision" (12).

Because fictional narratives are prominent grounds on which cultural conflicts are affectively negotiated and because television's narrative economy accommodates presenting such conflicts without necessarily resolving them, we can see the series as enacting a feminist utopianism similar to Shapiro Sanders's concept. The collaborative negotiation she calls for is useful for interpreting the textual features of both *Parks* and *30 Rock* and also the intense media promotion of Fey and Poehler's friendship. Further, both series position themselves in a reverential relation to feminist predecessors (the "utopian past" [Shapiro Sanders 2007], that is, the MTM era female-led sitcom), and both comedians are celebrated as successors of network-era female comedians, thus contradicting quality comedy's initiative of denying the past and postfeminism's generationalist tendencies. But the two comedies trade in different invocations of gender politics and feminism, stemming from the female leads' disparate creative backgrounds and star texts affecting the programs' narrative and generic traits. *30 Rock* satirizes the postmillennial reality of a feminism-influenced and privileged urban environment in an increasingly *sur*real and cartoonesque tone,[4] whereas *Parks* imagines an idealized feminism's triumph on both a rural and a national political level. In this sense it overturns the apocalyptic scenario that *30 Rock* presents while situating this fantasy in a form (mockumentary) known for its play with aesthetic codes of realism. For the two programs, then, the putative reality and fantasy of feminism are in reverse connection with the putative realism and fantasy of genre and aesthetics: *30 Rock* creates a "reality" of feminism

---

4 The series plays with the idea of feminist utopia in its epilogue though: Set in a distant, cartoonesque future, the last episode ends on an exchange of dialogue between immortal NBC chairman Kenneth and Liz's great-great-granddaughter, a Black writer who pitches and sells Liz Lemon's life story to him ("Last Lunch"). The sitcom we watched was the product of a utopian, intersectional feminist future.

in a nonrealist aesthetic, whereas *Parks* presents a "fantasy" of feminism in a realist aesthetic. Questions about whether these disparate approaches are in conflict and which is more progressive are turned into crucial issues at stake in their evaluations in (feminist) popular reception; yet Fey and Poehler's carefully publicized friendship narrative and their frequent pairing as a comic double act struggle to neutralize these.

Both the comedies' and the comedians' cultural positions are formed, then, in resistances to popular reception's imperative for monolithic and competitive appraisals of feminism, itself entangled in debates about ambiguity, cultural difference, and negotiation of conflict. In the analysis of these cultural struggles of the two series, I frequently referred to the issue of the female comedian's embodied performance; indeed, the question of the female *body*'s involvement in comedy and in parodies of femininity carries heightened stakes for judgments over the programs' achievements. I investigate this relationship in the next chapter.

4

BODY POLITICS AND THE QUALITY COMEDY

WOMEN'S PHYSICAL COMEDY AND THE QUALITY SITCOM

The structuring concept of Mizejewski's (2014) book about contemporary female comedians is encapsulated in its title, *Pretty/Funny*: Women's comedy is rooted and evaluated in the comedian's relationship to her body as sexual and sexualized object. For Bridget Boyle (2015) the female body is involved in a gendered visual performance even "before the gag." This performance stems from two kinds of associations: the maternal body (too "sacred" to be funny) and the "performance of beauty" (80–83). The second association echoes Mizejewski's argument that the cultural paradigm bluntly described as "you are either pretty or funny" governs women's culturally sanctioned relationship to humor and that women's comedy tends to be borne out of the pretty/funny paradigm's transgressive treatment. This dynamic harks back to various other beliefs about femininity as constructed in the hierarchal opposition of male and female; Mizejewski also briefly refers to the mind-body dichotomy, but the virgin-whore duality similarly signals women's fixedness to an (extreme lack or excess of) physical-as-sexual existence. Rowe's (1995b) influential work shows why comedy is a favored site to transgress these paradigms, given that one of its functions is to release cultural anxieties about human physicality. That women's presence is similarly pronounced in other "body" genres, such as horror or pornography, speaks to the cultural significance of the female body as a sexual sign (Williams 1991), but the unfunny imperatives of these forms explain why female protagonists have historically been more crucial to them than to comedy.

Mills (2005) states, "In comedy, the body becomes vital to performance and characters are often constructed so as to be aware of their own physicality" (86). This accounts for female performers' more pronounced presence in forms that rely on an emphasized physical performance and that are consequently seen as less valuable forms in cultural hierarchies. Comedy's transgressive and empowering possibilities for socially powerless groups stem from its low cultural status as a genre foregrounding physical performance. Further, comedy's signifying strength comes from an assumed common knowledge of social stereotypes, whether confirming or upsetting them; as such, women's displayed comic performance inevitably invites special attention to its relation to sexuality (82).

Nonetheless, as histories of physical comedy, specifically, slapstick, attest, the genre has developed both on film and television by centralizing male comedians (Boyle 2013). For slapstick theorists the (male) body's inscription with specific meanings in its confrontations with the outside world has existentialist connotations, expressing the struggle between the body and the spirit, a thought originating in Christianity. Alan Dale (2000) writes that "slapstick is a fundamental, universal, and eternal response to the fact that life is physical. The word 'existential' sounds too tony for slapstick but indicates its prevalence in our experience" (11). Boyle (2013) calls this notion of the comic everyman's universality "the neutral fallacy." Critiquing Dale's (2000) definition of the slapstick gag as a "physical assault on, or collapse of, the hero's dignity" (3), Boyle (2013) retorts that "this hypothesis presumes that 'dignity' can be located and fixed outside of gender, which feminist theory contests" (91). Indeed, in Dale's (2000) discussion, slapstick's everyman is gendered only in the ways in which his exasperation over the body-mind split includes a failed connection to his love interest (14). Both Dale and Alex Clayton (2007) explain women's historic marginalization in comedy as rooted in the conflict between the hero's lack of dignity and women's cultural position. If the slapstick body signifies a "comic dualism" (Clayton 2007, 146) as "at once an object within the world . . . and a subject acting on the world," then the undignified moves and physical assaults involved (clumsiness, acrobatic contortions) are at odds with "the dominant ideal of female beauty in patriarchal society" (146). In short, the extreme physicality that dominates slapstick seems unfit to express humor when its subject or object is the fragile, precious female body (148).

Slapstick theorists regularly note this tension around women's physical comedy, also praising the few female slapstick comedians for the ways they subvert this. If the slapstick hero is a "martyr" of his physical constraints (Dale 2000, 15), then the slapstick heroine's martyrdom is located in her

sexuality, a notion that also explains why female comedians have traditionally been most visible in romantic and screwball comedies. Because the
female performer is already located in a specific physical (sexual) existence,
her comedy forecloses expressing the existential, universal conundrum of
the body-mind dualism that the male comic's body offers. Rather, her comedy signals a struggle against her inferior position as a sexualized object, and
women's comedy is often evaluated by how successfully it does this. Accounts
of film history often cite Katharine Hepburn's screwball comedies as high
points of this effort. Clayton's (2007) description of the star's slapstick in
Bringing Up Baby (1938) emphasizes how *ostensible* her physical indignities are: "While her numerous accidents in the film . . . all result from a
certain misplaced confidence, the film is less interested in scoffing at such
assurance as it is in savouring her response to the mishap" (149). Clayton
contextualizes Hepburn's performance paradoxically in an empowering
desirability that stems from upsetting gender norms, admiring "the attrac-
tively androgynous qualities of her physicality" (150) (see also Dale's [2000]
praise of Hepburn's "blend [of] slapstick and sexual charisma" [129]).
Hepburn's slapstick reinforces the film's battle-of-the-sexes narrative; her
excessive activity makes clear who is in charge between the male and female
leads, and the film is generally read as overthrowing patriarchal masculinity
in the romance context (Rowe Karlyn 1995b, 147–56; King 2002, 52–55).

Hepburn's case exemplifies how women's slapstick emerges from the
female performer's conflicted relationship to sexual connotations, and its
execution is, especially after second-wave feminism, interpreted on the basis
of its political (liberating) potential from this oppressive heritage of sexualization. Boyle (2013, 2015) finds this a "double bind" of women's (physical)
comedy: The imperative to be funny is in conflict with the imperative to
be politically transgressive, or, as she extrapolates, to be taken "seriously."
Boyle maintains that the two projects, (physical) comedy and feminism, are
conflicted, because "paradoxically, assigning a serious, counter-patriarchal
function to female-authored comedy means that the female comic never
really takes herself seriously as a comedian" (Boyle 2015, 86). The pretty/
funny dilemma translates for her into feminist/funny.

Although Boyle's concept is flawed in its unexamined, assumed bond
between seriousness and putatively disembodied politics, it demonstrates
that the stakes involved in women's physical comedy are tethered to the
politics of representation, guiding its evaluations. Male comedians' release
of aggressive impulses connected to so-called existential and universal

struggles in the slapstick canon translates in feminized forms into a struggle that remains within the physical sphere. Here the conflict is not about the body-mind split but about how that body is to be read: sexual or beyond. The double bind that Boyle describes might then be replaced with a question contextualized in the female body's location in comedy's political possibilities: Can women's physical comedy be anything other than political, and can that politics ever be outside the physical-as-sexual context? Karnick and Jenkins (1995) emphasize the ideological paradox inherent in these possibilities: On the one hand, comedy allows for the "exhilarating release from social control, as a source of transgressive pleasure," but on the other hand, it can also work as a confirmation of a "cultural community's most fundamental beliefs and values, directing its scorn against outsiders and nonconformists who threaten this basic order" (270). The comic female body is entangled in these opposing forces, and the reading of its display (often regardless of the female comic's intentions) is frequently conflicted among disparate social communities. In short, the displayed comic female body is always inevitably political because of its conflicted inferior-yet-superior (e.g., in its maternity) cultural position.

Discussions of the putatively paradoxical notion of serious or political comedy involving the female body evoke theorizations of satire. Boyle's opposition between feminism and physical comedy can be juxtaposed with comedy theory's statements about the uneasy relationship between satire and physical comedy or slapstick. Dale (2000) writes that "problems . . . arise when people try to take a work of slapstick seriously: they usually attempt to 'elevate' it by praising it either as satire, which often seems overstated or wrong, or for its pathos, which is often enough right but which is to praise a comedy for the moments when it ceases to be comic" (17). To foreshadow my argument, these two impossibilities for Dale aptly describe the basis on which *30 Rock* and *Parks and Recreation* have been included in the quality comedy canon. "Low" comedy and serious political intentions make strange bedfellows for King and Mills as well, as discussed earlier regarding the cultural hierarchies operating between satire and the romantic or "body" comedy, implying that only one can dominate in comedy.

If slapstick eclipses satire's political intentions, then the reverse might also be true, and this is clear in quality comedy's case. More generally, because quality television is often praised as intellectual entertainment, it might be expected that it excludes physicality for the sake of aesthetic and/or political sophistication. But television's institutional specificities complicate this statement, as examined in chapter 1: HBO's establishment as not-TV involved a calculated valorization of explicit content coupled with artistic motivations, positioned against putatively regular TV. For quality comedy this strategy is not so straightforward; whether on cable or network television, critics treat the distancing from the sitcom tradition partly in terms of foregrounded verbal and cerebral humor. Hypothetically, mobilizing explicitness and the corporeal akin to cable drama could result in carnivalesque modes of comedy. But in the instances of comedy that capitalize on cable's sanctioning of explicit content, this usually means excessive uses of profanities, as seen in *Curb Your Enthusiasm* (McCabe and Akass 2007b, 62–63) or *Veep*. These are not "body" comedies, that is, comedies celebrated not for a transgressive treatment of physical comedy but for their use of profane verbal humor, improvisation, authored mockumentary, and political-cultural satire.

The comedy of distinction's efforts to break away from the sitcom tradition's reputation as low comedy involve the latter's physical associations. *Sex and the City* could provide an exception to this distancing from physical comedy, were its cultural work not located in a combination of political transgression around female sexuality and verbal wit regarding its frivolous subject matter. As such, it uses the female body as transgressive for its politics but not as a source of humor itself. This practice of the series tethers the female body to the pretty/funny dilemma of postfeminist times: The sexually liberated female body cannot be funny-ridiculous, or else it will not satisfy the parallel imperative of glamour and desirability anchored to its political transgression (Winch 2013, 79). *Sex and the City*'s genre hybrid between comedy and melodrama excludes *comic* female physicality for the sake of politically infused sexual and romantic angst.

If physicality is not a preferred source of humor in the comedy of distinction, then it inevitably presents difficulties for women's physical comedy. Because women's physical comedy is so entangled in political meanings and because these meanings link it to low comedy, few quality TV comedies are premised on a central female character's physical comedy. As discussed, attempts such as *Fat Actress* or *The Comeback* were unsuccessful, even though both series mobilized metatextual discourses about female celebrity, authorship, and comedy performance and thus were hypothetically linked enough to the quality discourse. *Fat Actress*, Kirstie Alley's metacomedy about her struggles in Hollywood after her weight gain, fared worse of the two, canceled after seven episodes and unanimously panned by critics; on the other hand, *The Comeback* was praised as a misunderstood gem and after some years was recommissioned. These comedies' relative failures are connected to their mobilization of female physicality as the source of the character's indignity, but the humiliations suffered differ in the types of physical appearance mobilized and how they are interpreted in the quality discourse.

The Comeback critiques the entertainment business's sexism through the plights of the aging but otherwise recognizably Hollywood-attractive sitcom actress. The physical comedy's emphasis on the discrepancy between performance and authenticity effects a sufficiently sophisticated cultural commentary for quality comedy. In contrast, *Fat Actress* could not be any blunter in stating that its cultural commentary revolves around Alley's discursive fatness, telegraphed in the title. Indeed, critics dismissed the series as a missed opportunity to expose Hollywood's mistreatment of not conventionally attractive actresses, instead relying on an overabundance of visual jokes about Alley's body (Shales 2005). Its failure as quality TV amounted to not linking the fat female body enough to political representation. Further, if the initial reluctance with which *The Comeback* was received can be attributed partly to Cherish's victim status as a deluded has-been, then *Fat Actress* cannot be accused of such treatment of its female protagonist. Fictional Kirstie is portrayed as aware of and blunt about her reputation in show business as a fat actress, and the program is premised on her struggles with this position without mobilizing the mockumentary framework. Consequently, the discrepancies between the authentic and performed self and the resulting indignities are not highlighted to the extent that they are in *The Comeback*. Victimhood does not gain such significance here, owing to the prominence of body jokes couched in the female protagonist's relative self-awareness and Alley's discursive authorship. Alley the performer seems to wallow in excessively joking about Alley the comic persona's fat body, hardly inviting interpretations of gendered victimhood. This trait inhibits the comedy from becoming quality in its politics and aesthetics. *Fat Actress*'s economic and critical failure seems to be rooted in its relative refusal to be political about the fat female body, foregrounding instead the "funny" of its central meaning.

The differences between *The Comeback* and *Fat Actress* illuminate a further aspect of women's physical comedy, namely, the discursive link of its politics to cultural inscriptions of female bodies' anatomical "types." As Arthurs and Grimshaw (1999) argue, the female body is the "disciplined body": Women's relationships to their bodies' cultural constraints throw into relief "questions concerning female agency, motivation, and pleasure" (10). The political implications of women's physical comedy are thus inseparable from traditions of policing the female body, a notion especially fraught with tensions in postfeminist culture, where empowerment rhetoric is predicated on visual representability. Historically, specific norms governing women's bodily presentation come to bear on evaluations of women's physical comedy, and the most prominent of these norms revolves around the fat-skinny body dualism, transposed onto the excess-restraint or the undisciplined-disciplined body dualism. The politics of women's physical comedy are infused with the meanings of these contrastingly configured bodies, but this is not always acknowledged in critical evaluations. For instance, Mills (2005) frames *Roseanne*'s politics in contrast to Lucille Ball's comedy, concluding, "It is arguable that Roseanne's refusal to be laughed at for her body, no matter how unconventional that body is, may in fact be a more radical gesture than Ball's unruly physicality" (117–18). Mills evaluates the two comedians' feminist radicalism without considering the different cultural readings attached to the two discursive types of female bodies in question, which no doubt influence the avenues of transgression open to them. For Lucille Ball's "disciplined" middle-class body, this unruliness may surface in excessive acrobatics (similar to Katharine Hepburn's slapstick); but for Arnold, whose body is already labeled undisciplined, the comedy's unruliness can be found in strategically turning the attention away from her corporeal presence and toward verbal wit.

Jane Arthurs (1999) offers a useful concept to account for this discrepancy, drawing on Mary Russo's (1995) influential work on the female grotesque. Arthurs differentiates between two dominant extremes of female grotesques in modern comedy. The first is the "monstrous and lacking" body, marginalized for its low-class fatness; Arthurs calls this the "'stunted' body who transgresses in her being . . . the passive repository of all that is denied by the sleek and prosperous bourgeois" (Arthurs 1999, 143). Her example is British stand-up comedian Jo Brand, but Roseanne or Melissa McCarthy's film persona also mobilize this type of female grotesque by complicating it with verbal wit and (sexual) agency (Meeuf 2016). On the other end of the spectrum are bodies that are not excessive in their being but become so by denying the limits of femininity associated with them, "embracing the ambivalent possibilities of carnival through masculinization" (Arthurs 1999, 143). These are the active, "stunt*ing*" bodies of acrobatic slapstick performers, who might be conventionally attractive but express female agency by foregrounding funny physicality. This classification shows that the issue of perceived anatomical body type can drive female comedians in different directions to express political subversion.

The female comedians central to *30 Rock* and *Parks* no doubt fit into Arthurs's second category, as both are treated in media reception as attractive actresses transgressing the boundaries that govern readings of their displayed bodies. As I will show, however, the two programs' physical comedies move in different directions because of the discussed shifts in comic tone and genre prominent in their production histories. These shifts in emphasis originate in refusing to develop comedy in the postfeminist romance category; instead, the comedies foreground satire and workplace narratives, and they strive to create quality through the female comics' thwarting of expectations of humor around sexual desirability and agency. Fey increasingly engages the unruly female grotesque as a source of comedy, whereas Poehler goes in a different direction with *Parks'* cerebral humor and earnestness around feminist concerns. Both of these strategies are embedded in a rhetoric of feminist transgression, but, as shown, it is Fey's comedy that became caught up in controversy about its questionable feminism. This had to do with quality comedy's unease with bodily comedy in general and intensified with the complex problems that the *female* comic's authored physical comedy poses. Moreover, Fey's celebrity was already associated with a feminist mode of cerebral, verbal comedy, reconciled in popular journalism with a postfeminist cover girl image. Consequently, the female grotesque's increased prominence in *30 Rock* caused anxieties in popular reception, coming to bear on the program's reputation both as quality and feminist entertainment. *Parks* solved the dilemma of Poehler's physical comedy by gradually removing it from the series' cultural work or by reserving it for the expression of a discursively authentic feminist subjectivity. Transgression here operates as the refusal to offer the female body as an area of cultural contestations over its meanings. *30 Rock*, on the other hand, takes a deep dive into these contestations, occasionally even tapping into the conundrum of whether and how the comic female body can be read as political outside the sexual spectrum.

THE FEMALE GROTESQUE IN *30 ROCK*

As discussed, Liz Lemon's "failed femininity" (Mizejewski 2014, 26) or parody of postfeminist femininity is promoted as the female comic's authorly choice to avoid sexualizing the heroine. However, Mizejewski posits that, though voicing cultural struggles about sexual politics, *30 Rock* otherwise does not use much physical comedy. She notes this when summarizing the episode "Mamma Mia," in which Liz gets to appear on a magazine cover only in a grotesque ("funny") pose instead of a glamorous one: "Neither Tina Fey nor her character Liz Lemon is generally associated with bawdy, grotesque comedy, but the cover-girl episode of *30 Rock* strongly suggests that for both of them, gender expectations about being pretty are rich comic material" (75). Here, I want to challenge this assessment by demonstrating that both Fey and Lemon *did* become gradually associated with a grotesque and physical parody of femininity, and this episode realizes this perhaps the most metatextually. Further, this trajectory is a characteristic of the generic and tonal shifts taking place in the series' second season. *30 Rock*'s physical comedy around the female lead greatly increased concomitant with its growing reliance on the absurdist satire of postfeminist dramedy. The humor mobilizes tropes of the female grotesque; recurring jokes (both verbal and physical) involve virtually every aspect of Liz's obtrusively abject female body, from bowel movements, menstruation, vomiting, hairiness, and sweat to markers of the conventionally unattractive and/or aging body, such as large buttocks, bad skin, and wrinkles.

Debates in the feminist blog culture over the consequences of Lemon's increasing grotesqueness for women's representation demonstrate how prominent this feature became in *30 Rock*. I discussed earlier how this debate also set up a discursive competition between the ideal feminisms of *30 Rock* and *Parks*. Prominent in these discussions is that they position *30 Rock*'s physical comedy, specifically, Lemon's grotesque femininity, as a source of the missed feminist opportunity that *Parks* supposedly achieves. Consider such blog titles as "The Incredible Shrinking Liz Lemon: From Woman to Little Girl" (Holmes 2012) or "A Leslie Knope in a World Full of Liz Lemons" (Brooks Olsen 2015). Lemon's character trajectory corrupts quality comedy's reputation as grown-up and intelligent entertainment in a medium otherwise considered infantile, a reputation involving Fey's author image as a "to-be-taken-seriously" female comedian (Mizejewski 2014, 11). Further, Mizejewski notes that feminist critics' disappointment with the series' gender politics has to do with a perceived incongruity between Lemon's visual portrayal as a "frumpy feminist" and the fact that "*30 Rock* does little to disguise Tina Fey's attractiveness" (83).

Two interdependent themes emerge from the criticisms of the program's treatment of Fey's physical comedy. First and predictably, both feminist criticism and the quality comedy discourse continue to be territories fraught with anxieties about the female comic's body in relation to its political meanings and cultural value. This is also evident in Boyle's (2015) concerns about blending a putatively serious feminism with the comic's imperative to be funny, or in the collective critical refusal of Kirstie Alley's comedy of fatness that eludes being sufficiently political and sophisticated. Second, in Lemon/Fey the attractive female comedian's treatment of desirability becomes questioned based on the discursive reality of her body: The pretty comedian looks suspect for using physical comedy to express unruly ugliness, a suspiciousness doubled with the dubious satire of a *feminist* subjectivity. Boyle (2015) argues that such treatments play into patriarchal beliefs: "When the female physical comedian self-consciously highlights putative flaws in her appearance for comic effect, . . . she reifies a singular, restrictive concept of gender performance" (87). Similarly, when Lemon's hyperbolic grotesqueness is inscribed onto Fey's attractive body, for her feminist critics this precludes the possibility of an authentic feminism and becomes retrograde in its misguided self-deprecation.[1] As Sady Doyle (2010) writes:

---

1   This Fey/Lemon tension evokes romantic comedy's trope of the attractive (female) performer playing an ugly duckling who gets a makeover, revealing her (and the star's) "real" self. Because makeover discourse is already prominent in Fey's star text (see Mizejewski 2014, 72–74), signaling cultural anxieties about women's cerebral humor, it is mobilized frequently for explaining the perceived Fey/Lemon discrepancy—as a reverse makeover. This surfaces in Fey's oft-repeated statements that, although she can be dolled up to pose on magazine covers, she secretly prefers to play awkward nerds who better represent her authentic self (Fey 2011, 5–6). Further, flashback scenes in *30 Rock* that show Liz in unflattering wigs and clothes are regularly explained as reflecting Fey's pre-makeover look. Ugliness is thus here constructed not as a physical feature but as a cultural status to negotiate the Fey/Lemon tension. If Fey is considered a real feminist in some media discourses, this evaluation relies on her star text's constant reminder of a pre-makeover identity.

The character of Liz Lemon is played by beautiful, successful, smart, funny, apparently happy person Tina Fey, and is meant to be unattractive, only semi-successful, smart, funny, and unhappy. It's interesting that "smart" and "funny" get to stay in the picture, as long as the looks, the success, and the happiness are toned down; it tells you something about who you're allowed to like.

The characteristic for which Lemon became a celebrated point of identification in her early media reception, namely, her "deeply flawed" (Doyle 2010) femininity, is recognized in the backlash years by critics as becoming too exaggerated to be authentic to feminism.

Because the backlash revolves so much around both the fictional character's and the comedian's desirability and anatomical features, it can also be considered according to Arthurs's concept. The two distinct categories of female grotesque invite radical possibilities for female comedians to upset cultural expectations. For the stunted female body, marginalized for her passive fatness or ugliness, this unruliness can surface by presenting an actively desiring female subjectivity combined with critical wit. The opposite, the stunting body, resists the imperative of bodily decorum by upsetting the meanings inscribed onto her conventionally feminine appearance. Arthurs's example for the stunting body is the monstrous and "witch-like" Patsy (Joanna Lumley) of *Absolutely Fabulous* (1992–2012), a much-examined character for British theorists of gender in comedy, whose unruliness was influenced by Lumley's preexisting star text "as the epitome of upper-class, classical beauty" (Arthurs 1999, 146).

If the two types characterize the female grotesque of contemporary media, then Lemon and Fey pose a problem for their allocation in this matrix, which might account for the intense controversy around their feminist potential. Nominally, Fey the postfeminist cover girl is incongruous with Liz the ugly and frumpy feminist with the large buttocks, pigeon-toed walk, and nasty eating habits. If the stunting physical comedian expresses feminist unruliness by combining an enhanced version of femininity with an accelerated masculinity of behavior, then Liz hardly fits this mold. Her visual portrayal and her environment's constant appraisals of her as already masculine and ugly position her in the stunted category, a passive (albeit middle and not lower class) female grotesque, "transgress[ing] in her being" (Arthurs 1999, 143). Portrayals in later seasons demonstrate how Lemon increasingly becomes the carnivalesque grotesque spectacle that Rowe describes in relation to the unruly woman. She transgresses precisely those pollution taboos that the carnivalesque female body upsets in her being and behavior; apart from her eating habits, which provide recurring visual and verbal gags, many of the cringe elements of 30 Rock emanate from jokes about her bowel movements. She gets diarrhea on a date with her handsome neighbor Drew (Jon Hamm) and becomes exposed to him when she is found sitting on the toilet while a foul smell wafts from her direction ("St. Valentine's Day"). She gets food poisoning from a dodgy sandwich on a road trip and is repeatedly shown hugging the toilet ("Stone Mountain"). The episode "Reaganing" includes a snippet of Lemon casually sharing with Jack this anecdote: "And I'd been on the toilet so long my legs had fallen asleep, so when I tried to stand, I just fell into my throw-up." Jokes about her menstruation are a similar constant in later seasons (e.g., "Standards and Practices"), and these and numerous other frequently referenced aspects of her leaky, abject female body, be it bad breath, sweating, flatulence, or hairiness, are usually framed in Jack's abhorrence. With Rowe, we can read Liz's female body as a manifestation of the "lower stratum," or Bakhtinian grotesque: "Where the classical body privileges its 'upper stratum' (the head, the eyes, the faculties of reason), the grotesque body is the body in its 'lower stratum' (the eating, drinking, defecating, copulating body)" (Rowe 1995b, 33). Mizejewski (2014) similarly references the Bakhtinian concept in her analysis of the "Mamma Mia" episode, which culminates in Liz posing on a magazine cover squatting over a toilet and pretending to give birth to a rubber chicken (75).

But for Rowe and Arthurs the liminal physicality of the grotesque female figure combines copiousness with *sexual* appetite, and these traits especially provide her with a feminist potential (Rowe 1995b, 48–49). The idea of an out-of-control sexual appetite is notably reversed and replaced with an out-of-control lack of sexual desire in Liz. The "Reaganing" episode mines the potential for grotesque comedy in this lack-as-excess. A therapeutic discussion between the two leads reveals that Lemon's disinterest in sexuality comes from a traumatic childhood memory, shown in flashback with Fey in a bizarre preadolescent girl costume: She once fell over on her way to the toilet, wearing roller skates, with her underwear down, while grabbing a Tom Jones poster, and was found in this pose by an aunt.

Another point in the grotesque, uncontrollable comic woman's theorization is her excessive speech, as a "failure to control the mouth" (Rowe 1995b, 37).

Here, Lemon fits the concept: Her mouthiness is another constant of the series, both literally in the screwball exchanges with Jack and, more symbolically, deriving from her social status as a comedy writer and from her portrayal as a loud defender of rigidly defined values. This aspect of the character discursively connects Lemon to Fey's own cultural status as a comedy writer and stern observer of gender relations, which contributes to the program's cultural position as female-centered *quality*—sophisticated, cerebral—text. The carnivalesque female mouth is a repository of both physical and intellectual connotations, but in this concept these connotations are "never innocent when attached to the *female* mouth"; they suggest "an intrinsic relation among female fatness, female garrulousness, and female sexuality" (37). Lemon's position does not fit this description fully (anatomically, and in its relation to sexuality), and this discrepancy accounts for the intense debates in feminist receptions of *30 Rock*, discussed earlier in relation to Fey's star persona as negotiating the ideal of the postfeminist celebrity body.

Fey's explanations of Lemon's excessive disinterest in sexuality and her use of physical comedy to oppose sexual desirability as empowerment for the female comedy author position the fictional figure in the second type of Arthurs's female grotesque, the stunting female body. This body transcends its preferred readings as primarily a sexually desirable object by demonstrating its other possibilities. However, for it to make sense, this mode of grotesque needs performed desirability as a reference point, as in Hepburn's star text or Patsy Stone's parody of hyperfemininity as masquerade. Lemon's portrayal upsets this imperative because the text positions her body (only extratextually coded as desirable) simultaneously as a stunted female grotesque. Such an ambiguity regarding Lemon's status as a female grotesque is an overdetermined result of the series' and its star's position in discourses about quality TV and postfeminist desirability. If she is portrayed as the stunted female grotesque, liminal in the overemphasis on her abject bodily functions, then this is articulated as a resistance to the postfeminist codes of sexual agency, itself a contested notion in Fey's author and cover girl image. The comedy of the stunted female grotesque is determined by the extent to which its purpose is to refuse the imperative of sexual desirability: Both the lack of sexual appetite and the excess of literal appetite become exaggerated features of comedy, and their precise meaning—empowering or humiliating—is a constant source of tensions.

If Liz as stunted female grotesque emerges as a result of a stunting, actively chosen mode of female transgression—that is, she is frumpy and sloppy because she/Fey resists abiding by the rules of postfeminist femininity—then this is a problematic trajectory because of Fey's celebrity as a cerebral feminist-*cum*-postfeminist cover girl. Indeed, the frumpiness and jokes about the feminist woman's body significantly multiplied on the series following Fey's increased exposure in popular media, causing critics to lament that the figure of Liz had become a pathetic caricature of her former portrayal. Thus the communicated empowerment in Fey's authorly choice to play Lemon against postfeminist womanhood and to develop *30 Rock* as a rejection of romance in generic terms was received less as empowerment and more as retrograde humiliation. The structuring paradox in this tension is that in Fey's communication, creating physical comedy about the female subject that is not rooted in sexual desirability is an act of self-liberation (so supposedly feminist and authorly); but this is an impossible notion because the text is so strongly associated with intellectual, cerebral feminist politics and comedy, starting with the fact that the heroine is constructed as a witty parody of popular feminism.

Yet Lemon's grotesque portrayal still strives to be interpreted as empowerment for the failed feminine and feminist character, echoing paratextual discourses about Fey's agency as a female comedy author. This portrayal is linked to the program's quality features, namely, its complex narrative and joke structures. Lemon's portrayal, as a parody of postfeminist femininity in her grotesque, unfeminine, and sexless womanhood, is carefully offset by a confirmation of agency and her explicit rejection of the romance narrative, a characteristic also prominent in the text's constant metatextual refusal of a Jack-Liz romance. In the most overt instances, as indeed in the "Mamma Mia" episode, Lemon initiates many of these gross performances of unfeminine femininity, and they often function as both culmination and resolution of plot. In the episode "Black Light Attack!" Lemon lets her mustache, nicknamed Tom Selleck, grow out to help Jenna compensate for her anxieties about aging. The scene in which she presents Tom to the world showcases both Liz's subjectivity and the staff's horror as she walks down the corridor in slow motion. The mustache itself is more of a Frida Kahlo than a Selleck, signaling a more realistic image of female facial hair as opposed to comic exaggeration, but the upheaval it causes *is* hyperbolically comic precisely because of the mustache's realness. Lemon has a blast being hairy while publicly eating, drinking (milk, no less), and laughing with a full and open mouth at a male writer who retches at her sight. The scene is counterpointed with a shocked Jack, who looks on in the background, in the midst of a scheme that involves convincing an employee that he is in love with Lemon. Lemon's unruly excess as female agency is counterbalanced with and does not work without an exaggeration of her environment's disgust at it; the comedy emerges from this contrast.

Other examples abound. In "The Tuxedo Begins" Lemon dresses up as a cartoonesque mixture of a bag lady and Heath Ledger's Joker character from *The Dark Knight*, spending the whole episode in the costume to prove a point to Jack about the miseries of urban living, again reveling in the performance of repulsive female physicality. In "Apollo, Apollo" Lemon permits Jenna to show to the staff embarrassing footage of her in a 1990s TV advertisement for a phone sex line; here, her colleagues' rowdy amusement is countered with Liz's stoic observations. In response to the raucous laughter following a close-up image of her and another woman trying to sexily eat a greasy slice of pizza, she comments, "I remember that girl. She cried all day." These instances show Lemon as reveling in or at least owning up to her environment's revulsion over her gross bodily performance, be it a Chaplinesque waddle because of bunion surgery ("Aunt Phatso vs. Jack Donaghy"), countless awkward dancing scenes (e.g., "Flu Shot," "Retreat to Move Forward," "Black Light Attack!" "Dance Like Nobody's Watching"), and any instance of hearty eating. Whether throwaway joke or narrative twist, this active acceptance of her unfeminine body reads as a calculated resistance to the eroticized context in which postfeminist womanhood is commonly articulated (sexual as empowered). This notion of resistance resonates with the extratextual trajectory of Fey's growing popularity and her star text's parallel sexualization. It throws an ambiguous light on popular media's production of meaning around the female celebrity body by contrasting the pretty/funny body.

The episode "The Tuxedo Begins" merits further examination for how it uses Fey's physical comedy in the quality comedy context and also because this episode often serves as shorthand for Fey's preference to play "ugly" for comedy at the expense of glamour (Ess 2013). I finish this discussion with a detailed analysis of the episode to demonstrate the complexities of the program's body politics. The main plot involves a Jack-Liz debate on yet another sociocultural issue, starting with Liz lamenting her fellow city dwellers' inconsiderate behaviors in public places. Jack suffers a mental crisis after getting mugged at the beginning of the episode, and the duo's disagreement revolves around how urban living can be possible in a city marked by decay and overpopulation. Jack insists that his mugging was a sign of class war and proposes to "save" the city and protect the elite by running for mayor. Liz is at first exasperated with people who ignore rules of common decency, but an epiphany makes her leave behind her strict ethics, and she instead vows to outperform her fellow citizens in selfishness. This decision is the rationale for her crazy costume change that becomes increasingly outlandish and positions her as a cartoon villain.

Early in the episode Liz dresses up as a homely old lady in a sketch to fill in for Jenna, who refuses to look ugly and old. This scenario reaffirms that Liz lacks feminine vanity while also living in a happy heterosexual relationship: "Maybe I should wear this home," she says studying herself in the mirror. "Show Chris what he will be looking at in forty years. Looser skin, same underwear." When she notices that the costume—combined with a horrid cough, the smell emanating from her gym bag, and her yelling nonsense at people—provides her with more space on the subway, she decides that the only way to survive in the city is "to sink down into the filth." Thus ensues her increasingly grotesque turn into the unhinged bag lady and, as the plot becomes more clearly a *Dark Knight* parody, into Ledger's Joker (Figure 2). "Sinking down into the filth" then unites the carnivalesque woman's monstrosity and the (male) cartoon villain's amorality: the abject body and the abject intellect. The Jack-Liz debate recreates the film's opposition between the morose superhero and the crazy clown supervillain, similarly configured as a fight for the city's "soul." However, it is only Liz for whom this involves a bizarre costume change; for Jack, wearing a tuxedo throughout the episode suffices to perform the role of privileged masculinity in crisis and to satirize this trend in television and cinema.

Liz's comic costume transformation into the menacing clown's iconic version can in its first stage be interpreted in terms of the female clown who, as Mizejewski (2014) summarizes, is a marginal figure in traditions of the grotesque carnivalesque because of her associations with the "witch, spinster, or hag" (21). If the classic male clown represents potentially sympathetic nonnormativity in his resistance to authority that can also be mobilized in the romance narrative, then the female equivalent, the ugly crone, is harder to reconcile as a sympathetic point of identification because of her noncompliance with normative codes of femininity. Liz's first transformation as a smelly old woman cruising the subway and the streets of Manhattan fits with this tradition and also with the series' consistent jokes about Liz as an old and ugly spinster. Wearing a crone clown costume seems to logically fulfill Liz's overarching portrayal. Further, the carnivalesque nature of this female

Figure 2. Liz Lemon (Tina Fey) as a bag lady in a parody of Heath Ledger's Joker in the "Tuxedo Begins" episode of *30 Rock*.

unruliness is completed with other sensory aspects of her abject body, a repository of dirt and leakiness: She blows her nose, has the ugly cough throughout, eats boiled eggs while laughing maniacally, and the gym bag stuffed with smelly gym clothes becomes her signature weapon. But the crazy hag visually turns into the Joker, and the Liz-as-spinster gag begins to function as a Joker parody in the plot's overall metatextual paralleling of the film's serious themes. If the hag costume visualizes Liz's cultural status, then her turning into the Joker in this intellectualized plot overrides the female clown's low-culture feminine abjectness. The Joker already functions as a receptacle of overdetermined meanings, partly confirmed in the film. Not least, these include his readings in queer theory as a "stereotype of gay and transgender panic" (Bishop 2015). The Joker is already a satire, albeit a menacing one, of (hetero)sexuality: His villainy represents a constant threat to Batman's multiply coded übermasculinity, an aspect that became his manifest trait as a supervillain (gay innuendo, drag) in the Batman comics since the 1980s (e.g., *Arkham Asylum* [Morrison and McKean 1989]), to which the film briefly alludes as well.

The woman-as-hag-as-Joker connotation throws into relief the traditions of both the problematic female clown and the menacing male clown in Fey's performance of the female grotesque. On the one hand, melting the hag into the Joker works toward liberating the female clown figure from connotations that tether her to the physically monstrous *female* other context. The intellectualizing plot, which revolves around a discursively universal, non-gendered issue of community values and class, struggles to position the hag in this context and not in a primarily feminine-coded one. In addition, the Batman satire helps to interpret the plot as a comedy of distinction in which the female grotesque plays a pivotal role. On the other hand, she still remains the monstrous other in the debate, and when the hag turns into the Joker, she also turns into a figure onto whom a nexus of gender and sexuality transgressions have historically been inscribed. This modifies the presumed liberation from the monstrous female other—in that she melds with the monstrous male other. Although the episode strives to express a new kind of unruliness for the female grotesque by inserting her into an intellectualized plot and thus shedding the hag's meaning as *gendered* other, it also underlines the figure's modes of upsetting gender binaries.

Masculinization is a key issue for the female grotesque as performance, and the gendered ambivalence it expresses accounts for its popularity in camp culture. Arthurs notes in relation to *Absolutely Fabulous*'s Patsy that the character's parody of hyperfemininity and hedonism became appropriated for drag performances, a trajectory that eventually allowed for her popular readings as "really a man in drag" (later confirmed on the program as well). For Arthurs (1999), this reading reduces the female grotesque's radicalism, because it reduces her transgressive ambivalence to a definitive "clue to her identity and behavior" (160–61). In Lumley/Patsy, "we have a woman playing a woman who can be appropriated as 'really' a man" (148), eclipsing the original reading as that of a woman playing an authentically unruly woman. In contrast, Fey playing a woman who performs abject femininity as the hag, who transforms organically into a fictional man associated with upsetting gender norms (masculinity and heterosexuality), results in accelerating the anarchic potential in the female grotesque's ambivalence instead of tying it down. The hag's metamorphosis into the Joker does not fix her meaning as "really a man" but rather upsets *his* menacing meanings. Just as the whole episode mocks the Batman franchise's po-faced masculinity, so the Joker parody says, "He is really an old hag," performed by a woman (Liz) enacting a version of abject femininity (the hag). Because this episode never explicitly admits the allegory (unlike most others), this interpretation, however obvious, remains dependent on the viewer's recognition. Further, Liz's Joker costume and makeup keep their ambivalence visually such that the "Joker" could still be read as a crazy old woman with smudged makeup. Textually Liz remains the hag and the Joker impersonation happens only metatextually, even though the allegory function overtakes the episode without much remaining realism.

The episode's busy connotations and allegories are all inscribed onto the female grotesque, the performance of which initiates both the overdetermined codes of quality comedy and the ambiguous treatment of gender. They strive to confirm that the glamorous female comedian can perform grotesque femininity in a way that occludes the pretty/funny problem (because the "issue" allegory overrides the hag performance's associations), and the resulting chain of codes blurs expectations about gender, whether as performance or identity. The episode then ends up undermining comedy tropes about femininity and heterosexuality at the same time as it appears to overcome this whole gendered tradition in favor of intellectual quality comedy.

That the story line is ambiguous about overcoming or, on the contrary, centralizing physical comedy as being about femininity and heteronormativity is further nuanced in the episode's B plot, revolving around Jenna and her female impersonator boyfriend, Paul (Will Forte). This relationship's serialized arc mocks the hedonism associated with celebrity culture and at the same time exemplifies discursively edgy and progressive portrayals of sexual relations. Functioning to humanize Jenna's cartoonishly self-centered character, her love story with Paul is shown as an obvious match because his biggest success as a drag performer is his Jenna impersonation. The progressive attack on heteronormativity is then rooted in Jenna's extreme vanity; her ideal partner is herself, or at least a man looking like herself, simultaneously upsetting and reaffirming codes of heteronormativity. Further, a recurring joke about the couple is their decadent sex life (a comic take on *Sex and the City*'s Samantha [Kim Catrall]), which is disturbed in "The Tuxedo Begins" by the threat of settling into normalcy as one night they accidentally fall asleep without having sex. Instead of accepting this as a common trajectory of a settled relationship, they decide to interpret it as a new sex game dubbed "normalling." When they realize that their everyday activities are not a new kink but "couples' stuff," they agree to break up so both can go on a "sexual walkabout." This story line unfolds parallel to Liz and Jack's, in the wrap-up showing a diegetic connection between the two. As that other plot is resolved by Jack/Bruce Wayne throwing Liz/the hag/the Joker into a pile of garbage on the street, followed by them agreeing on the moral of the story, Paul and Jenna observe from a distance. To Paul's comment "Reminds me of us," Jenna reminisces, "I'll never forget the first time you dressed up like an old lady and I threw you into some garbage."

Thus this couple's progressive-coded love story informs the A plot's tacit commentary on the ambiguity of gender roles (plus it continues to mock the idea of a Jack-Liz romance) but in excessively sexual terms to counterbalance the excess of Liz's lack of sexual appetite and the female comic's simultaneous desexualization. This continued duality is evident in the ending, which also serves as closure to *The Dark Knight* parody because it juxtaposes the film's sinister aesthetic with Jenna's comic hypersexuality. The camera slowly pans away from Jenna to reveal the dark Manhattan skyline (Paul has just run off in a pink wig and without underwear to find new sexual partners), and the episode's signature score lampooning the Batman franchise's agitated string music returns to underline the connection with the film. Quality comedy's smartness is again expressed with a voiceover, as in the "Stride of Pride" episode (a *Sex and the City* parody), providing the punch line to the joke set up by the stylistic imitation. This time the monologue voice is Jenna's (she "authors" this scene), who muses on the dark city's image thus: "New York City. Villains and heroes. The one percent and the ninety-nine. Eight million people in this crazy beautiful city, and I, Jenna Maroney, am going to go to town on every last one of them."

ABANDONING PHYSICAL COMEDY IN *PARKS AND RECREATION*

I demonstrated earlier that the positioning of *Parks and Recreation* in quality comedy involved a paratextual association with the 1970s female-centered comedy or "warmedy." Willa Paskin's (2011) review is especially direct about this connection, praising the program's old-fashioned nature. For her, this means that *Parks* lacks the cringe moments so characteristic of today's celebrated smart comedies, or in her term, "comedies of discomfort." Her analysis also shows that if cringe is replaced by niceness on *Parks*, then this is an excess, or repetitiveness, of that niceness in character development: "Has a sitcom ever had so many characters that are variations on 'sweet, kind person'? The driven sweet, kind Leslie; the goofy sweet, kind Andy; the grounded sweet, kind Ann; the guarded sweet, kind Ben; and Ron, whose mustache only hides the sweet, kind guy lurking underneath." The most hyperbolic expression of that niceness is Chris Traeger (Rob Lowe), who functions as the program's self-reflexive commentary on its own excessive reliance on optimism as storytelling strategy.

Parks' hyperbolic sweetness is coupled with a toning down of physical comedy around the comic heroine and a foregrounding of her aspirational feminist politics. As mentioned earlier, the humor of humiliation is projected onto the buffoon character Jerry/Garry/Larry/Terry, who is even denied his own name; and he is also the figure most frequently involved in slapstick gags of incompetence, clumsiness, and the leaky and large comic body. The episode "Halloween Surprise" plays both his uncontrollable body and his environment's cruelness to excess: When he has a heart attack triggered by Leslie and her friend Ann's (Rashida Jones) prank, the colleagues' genuine worry for him is mixed with ridicule because the attack is accompanied by his explosive flatulence, occasioning jokes about the "fart attack." That this portrayal works as strategic counterbalancing of the program's overt niceness is demonstrated in scenes where Jerry/Garry/Larry/Terry is seen in his (overly nice) family circle: In the episode "Jerry's Retirement" Leslie is shocked to realize that in his own house not only is he surrounded by adoring family members, but he is also physically and intellectually adroit. When the series admits that its figure of discomfort and humiliation, Jerry/Garry/Larry/Terry, is a necessary function of workplace comedy (because he is positioned as such only in the workplace setting, one of American sitcom tradition's central locations), it also associates with this function an emphasis on *physical* cringe comedy. Put another way, this "comedy of superniceness" presupposes moving physical comedy to its fringes in favor of intellectual, verbal comedy at the same time as it removes the cringe aspect. But such a shift in humor toward niceness is apparently a little too old-fashioned without a tongue-in-cheek reference to more "cynical" (Paskin's term) modes of humor, hence the featuring of Jerry/Garry/Larry/Terry as the eternal butt of slapstick jokes.

As noted, *Parks* links the toning down of physical comedy around the female heroine, including the female grotesque, to a progressive feminist politics. Leslie's affective portrayal after the first season as fully deserving the political goals to which she aspires presupposes her visual portrayal as the intellectualized female body, meaning a negation of that body as sexual object and, simultaneously, as central comic object. Because Poehler's star text was never imbricated in discourses similar to Fey's (cover girl, makeover narrative, female authorship), nor did the series foreground her body as spectacle in the way that *30 Rock* did Fey's, no such struggles around the pretty/funny dilemma were overtly present in the series' narratives and in its media reception.

However, the question of the comic female body does feature in *Parks'* portrayal of Leslie, through the series' struggles to configure its novel take on the mockumentary-style workplace comedy. The course correction between seasons 1 and 2 from mockumentary's comedy of discomfort toward "niceness" also involved a recalibration of physical comedy around the heroine. The first season based much of its humor on Leslie's over-the-top enthusiasm and its inappropriateness, and many of these gags were structured around Poehler's physical comedy. This also evokes the postfeminist chick flick's use of slapstick, in which physical humiliations of the heroine tend to establish a link between physical, professional, and romantic incompetence. One of the most prominent of such gags occurs in the pilot, in a scene in which, during an inspection, Leslie falls into a pit she intends to turn into a park. Her blind delusion is evidenced in the monologue just seconds before the fall, as she describes her comically oversized plans for the future park: "Imagine a shiny new playground, with a jungle gym and swings, pool, tennis courts, volleyball courts, racquetball courts, basketball court, regulation football field. We could put an amphitheater over there with Shakespeare in the Park." As she tries to descend into the pit for a photo opportunity, her slip and fall are captured in mockumentary's aesthetic (long shot, whip pan, zoom-in, blurry image), enhancing the contrast between her head-in-the-clouds attitude and reality. Crucially, this contrast is articulated in slapstick comedy terms, that is, between her high-flying ambition and her clumsy comic body drawing her down, awkwardly contorting, rolling, and tumbling to finally stop at the literal and metaphorical bottom (see Figure 3).

Leslie's body *could* be theorized here as the slapstick body in scholars' terms, that is, as body-as-machine (a recurring description of Buster Keaton's or Charlie Chaplin's physical comedy; see Clayton 2007, 91–94), struggling in its rigidity with the laws of nature and thereby expressing the fundamental

Figure 3. Leslie Knope's (Amy Poehler) slapstick body in *Parks and Recreation*.

contrast between body and mind. Yet, if "the slapstick hero's skill at deploying his paradoxically acrobatic clumsiness is central to his status as an Everyman" (Dale 2000, 14), then Leslie's fall, however clearly an attempt to follow a comedy tradition, is caught up in ambiguous meanings and is only semisuccessful in achieving this effect. This is because the slapstick *female* body offers other iconographic connotations, with the butt and spread-eagled legs pointing to the sky in a tight skirt, and, after stopping at the bottom, lying limply on her back in the dirt with one shoe missing. Whether associated with sexual vulgarity or victimhood, this sequence shows why the efforts to highlight Poehler's physical comedy in the context of mockumentary's cringe tradition were subsequently abandoned. These efforts showcase the female slapstick body in the male-centered tradition of that body as struggling and failing against its environment; but the feminized inscriptions are hardly reconcilable with the putatively genderless and universal body-as-machine or body-versus-environment meanings, instead resonating with issues of gender representation. The narrative context that positions Leslie's social identity as a post-second-wave female career politician, expressed in her outfit (gray skirt suit), amounts to ridiculing *this* figure. As discussed, women's slapstick mainly exists in romantic comedy and, in that, as a body that triumphs even in its clumsiness. This triumph follows from discursively preserving desirability (Hepburn) and/or from the acrobatic skill celebrated both for its physicality and the politics it represents (consider Lucille Ball's housewife appropriating public spaces).

Developed in sketch comedy traditions, Poehler's comic persona during her tenure on *Saturday Night Live* was mainly understood in terms of physical comedy skills akin to Ball's comedy. For instance, her popular recurring character Kaitlin, a hyperactive and chatty girl wearing pink Minnie Mouse pajamas, glasses, and braces, makes use of Poehler's energetic and cheerful persona in its physicality, the humor stemming from the discrepancy between this attitude and her tiny frame. Displaying an out-of-control possession of stage space (running and jumping around, climbing on furniture), the performance also involves a similarly out-of-control vocal expression: Her signature gag is to repeatedly shout "Rick-Rick-Rick" at her stepfather, the contrastingly laid-back, quiet, and large Rick (Horatio Santz), and to bombard the weekly host with a chain of absurd questions. As a small, pre-adolescent girl, Kaitlin is also an effort to make use of Poehler's comic body type by desexualizing it. Here, the female grotesque mobilized is that of the stunting body in Arthurs's (1999) term: In Kaitlin, Poehler's comic body as spectacle "transgress[es] the norms of femininity by denying the limits of [her] female bod[y], embracing the ambivalent possibilities of carnival through masculinization" (143). In Kaitlin's case masculinization amounts to defeminization, that is, to ridding the body of markers of adult femininity.

If Poehler's pre-*Parks* physical comedy is that of the stunting female grotesque transgressing feminine decorum, then positioning it in cringe mockumentary's aesthetics causes a discrepancy of ideological meanings. The first season offers several instances in which the female politician's masculinization results in her humiliation rather than empowerment. This comes eminently to the fore in the episode "The Banquet," in which Leslie attempts to join the "boys' club" of politics by showing up at an event sporting a tuxedo and a short, masculine haircut. The humor stems from her misplaced pride in this seemingly feminist act, contrasted with her obliviousness to everyone's amusement and Ann's embarrassment as they are mistaken for a lesbian couple. Although cross-dressing can be considered a transgressive act of the stunting female grotesque, Leslie's inability to read the cultural inscriptions on her own chosen bodily display undermines such ideological subversions. Mockumentary's cultural work operates here in its original meaning, that is, by revealing a conflict between social performance of self and actual self. However, though this method works in such comedies as the British *Office* to expose a universal (Western) condition of labor relations, here the satire is aimed at the state of a feminist womanhood in the workplace setting, lampooned in its bodily expression. Leslie reads her attire as empowered or empowering (failing to notice the loaded meanings of "masculine"), whereas her environment, and supposedly the viewer, reads it as butch lesbian or cross-dresser. The humor relies on a supposition that not only are these identities encoded in fashion choices but they also present comic incongruities. However, because the program, being Poehler's star vehicle, was reportedly developed to express political progression in women's portrayals, such meanings were abandoned in the long term, including getting rid of the feminist career woman's mockery in her physical display.

In later seasons the show abandoned strategies that would ridicule Leslie's feminist aspirationalism and reconfigured Poehler's comic physicality and performance of the female grotesque, including associations of the single career woman. This abandonment of ridicule corresponds to the postfeminist chick flick's gradual decline in American cinema by the late 2000s (Negra 2020) and to the discussed popularization of feminist rhetoric in public discourses. In this, the series followed a different trajectory from *30 Rock*'s, eventually relinquishing grotesque femininity as a central narrative element. At the same time as Poehler's physical comedy was diminished, it was increasingly replaced with mobilizing her skill at vocal work and impersonation—Rowe's unruly woman is mainly present here as the out-of-control female mouth. This characteristic overlaps with Liz Lemon and *30 Rock* in that verbal sparring dominates the working woman's portrayal and plays an important part in constructing quality comedy. The rebooted second season's first episode ("Pawnee Zoo," also the first with an "issue" story line) opens with a scene at the office in which Leslie raps the full third verse of the 1980s hip-hop song "Parents Just Don't Understand." This scene makes up the whole of the cold open and has no narrative significance. Its only function is to set the new season's mood and to display Poehler's mock-rapping skills without any double-edged commentary on Leslie's performance of self in mockumentary fashion, instead painting her as playfully, sympathetically silly. Leslie's rapping even gets genuine applause from her colleagues, which would have been out of place in the first season's character relations. The discussed jump-cut scene in "The Hunting Trip" similarly makes use of Poehler's vocal imitation skills, the displayed performance confirming Leslie's supposedly authentic feminism. Leslie/Poehler's vocal skills are also showcased in other episodes, such as "Park Safety" or "Ron & Jammy," in which she impersonates in jump cuts Ron's ex-wife Tammy Two (Megan Mullally).

The series' remaining physical comedy is rearranged not only to neutralize gendered connotations but also to replace contempt among workplace colleagues with genuine comradeship. The comedy abandons workplace satire in the ways that Hight (2010) and Middleton (2014) lament in the Americanization of the British *Office*: It configures the workplace "as a space of individual and interpersonal happiness and fulfilment" (Middleton 2014, 142). Still, comedy of discomfort rooted in incompetence is not completely abandoned; a scene in the episode "The Comeback Kid" offers an example. Producer Mike Schur describes the scene in question as an uncharacteristic and "physically uncomfortable scenario" around which the whole episode was written (E. Adams 2012). Its plot revolves around Leslie's public announcement of entering the race for city council. Because of a shoestring budget and her colleagues' mistakes, the event goes massively wrong: They book an ice hockey rink for the venue; the podium, built by Ron, is too small and lacks stairs; the campaign banner shows an enlarged quarter of Leslie's face; and only the first few seconds of the entrance music (Gloria Estefan's "Get on Your Feet") play on a loop as Leslie and the entourage enter the rink. Because her assistant was also unable to secure a carpet that goes all the way to the podium, the gang continue the rest of the way tiptoeing on the ice in a long slip-and-fall slapstick sequence. This scene, the episode's narrative highlight, has been praised as one of the best executed gags of the series, both mining the slapstick potential gradually to its limits and also functioning as character development: The gang, shuffling and slipping toward the stage, struggles to keep *Leslie* on her feet, with Ron eventually dropping to all fours to serve as a step for her to climb up, or rather for the others to shove her onto the stage (Figure 4).

Figure 4. The ensemble cast of *Parks and Recreation* performing group slap-stick comedy.

The workplace ensemble's collective struggle toward a common goal is literalized as physical comedy here, emphasizing that this is all in service of realizing Leslie's political dream. Mockumentary's satire of incompetence is reversed on affective terms: The first season's character dynamic in which everyone mocked Leslie as incompetent and inappropriate is here distributed evenly among the group, because the whole collective is at fault for the disaster. The scene exploits the genre's contrasting of disingenuous public performance and a discursive reality as they try to smile and wave their way to the stage; the rally audience functions as incredulous witnesses to the group's failure. But the event, however disastrous, happens only because of Leslie's popularity among the team, and *this* results in the physical comedy gradually enveloping all of them. The comedy trope of "ragtag group of misfits prevail by helping one another" (Heisler 2012) overturns the mockumentary's ideological work such that it celebrates workplace incompetence and inappropriateness if mobilized to help the feminist woman achieve her goals.

The female protagonist is still much involved in physical comedy, but her role changes. As seen in Figure 4, her arrival on the stage ends in her lying limply on her back to regroup; this position can be contrasted with the one in Figure 3 (Leslie lying at the bottom of the pit). Although in both instances the camera angle and the long shot correspond to mockumentary's relationship to its objects—that is, literally and symbolically looking down on them and observing them from the distance—the implications are different: In the earlier example, the point of view is that of Leslie's colleagues making fun of her; in the second, it is that of the rally audience watching the bundle of doubled-over bodies of the same colleagues, holding Leslie up and doing their pratfalls. Leslie's misery is not just her own, and the camera does not gender her physicality in the way that the pit scene does. Contrasted with the pilot's visual and narrative treatment that singles Leslie out from her environment, comradeship is here reinforced mockingly and affectively at the same time. Schur comments that this scene's group arrangement visually resembles the Iwo Jima Memorial, with Leslie being the human flag that the others are trying to raise (see Figure 4), encapsulating the comedy's operation both as group slapstick and as a relationship to its own ideology (E. Adams 2012).

The set piece nature of the physical comedy in "The Comeback Kid" is not just an expression of cooperation; its singularity also illuminates the series' otherwise muted reliance on slapstick. Indeed, if physical comedy is mobilized around the female heroine, it is to underline Leslie's enthusiasm, couched in some form of cooperation and affective relationship. It also mostly involves dancing and dress-up. In the "Filibuster" episode Leslie's silly 1990s roller skater garb lightens the political theme, and earlier in the episode she and boyfriend Ben (Adam Scott) perform a dance routine in their costumes. In "The Comeback Kid" she attempts to break-dance in her camera confessional to celebrate reentering the race; in "Halloween Surprise" she and Ann start dancing enthusiastically after she decides to buy a house; in "The Fight" Leslie and Ron's conflict is resolved by her dancing to and reinventing the lyrics of Billy Joel's "We Didn't Start the Fire," culminating in the pair's reconciliatory rendition of the song. Although these examples reinforce Leslie's energy and comic relatability to counterbalance the ideologically argumentative plot about the feminist politician, they also stand out as incidental to the program's larger narrative trajectory. The body politics accompanying this narrative push gendered slapstick into the background to construct the female politician as a primarily intellectual subjectivity, a characterization that also dominates the series' humor as supposedly sophisticated entertainment.

Parks, then, mobilizes a different mode of comedy from *30 Rock*'s to express women's comic performance and imagery. Although both series are concerned with narrativizing a politicized resistance to the pretty/funny dilemma that dominates discourses about women's comedy, Fey's sitcom centralizes the female comic's body in self-referential narratives to showcase its possibilities and boundaries, and *Parks* strategically abandons it to articulate a rhetoric of respectability politics. This strategy affects the program's tone not only in its reliance on verbal and political comedy but also, gradually toward its sixth and seventh seasons, in its mixture of comedy and melodrama. The discursive niceness and empathetic character treatment of *Parks*, somewhat similar to *The Mary Tyler Moore Show*, eventually effects an affective tone with muted irony, best exemplified in the Leslie-Ben romance but also evident in portrayals of friendship. Mills (2005, 85) notes that comedy usually avoids openly emotional characterization methods, as psychological realism is more consistent with drama and soap opera's modes of expression. These forms enhance the audience's emotional involvement by using a shooting style that entails the frequent use of close-ups, a less preferred shot in comedy. Mills demonstrates how *Friends* (1994–2004) balanced comedy and melodrama in a way that illuminates the difference between comic *performance* and (melo)dramatic *acting*, the former requiring a degree of emotional detachment and the latter empathetic involvement.

Parks frequently exhibits a similar mixture of modalities in later seasons. The shooting style adapts to this shift, reducing the mockumentary's visual vocabulary that expresses observational distance (long shots, shaky cam). A scene at the end of the episode "Smallest Park," where Leslie and Ben make a pivotal decision about their relationship, abandons comedy for the sake of affective narration; the dialogue accordingly contains only a few jokes and turns serious by its finish. The camera gradually zooms in on the actors' faces to capture emotions and reactions, concerned with establishing this as a moment of serious or realistic sentiment. In this, the remnants of the mockumentary aesthetic (handheld camera, blurry image, refocusing) are used against their original ideological intent: As the camera aims to catch genuine behaviors and emotions, the style returns to a premockumentary state that in these instances could be called documentarism. As this scene demonstrates, such modalities are mostly present in the romance narrative and in other intimate relationships, such as friendship and solidarity. The discursively progressive political narrative appears to presume a partial return to comedy forms (the warmedy) and aesthetic methods (documentarism) associated with earlier cultural periods.

The increasing sincerity of generic and stylistic strategies corresponds, then, to an earnestness about feminist politics on *Parks*, evoking Boyle's (2015) concept that women's (physical) comedy and the intent to express feminist transgression are uneasily reconciled. This is an operative sentiment for *Parks*, effecting its celebratory comparison with *30 Rock* in media reception as more progressive in its portrayal of women and women's comedy. A great deal of that critical judgment is rooted in *Parks'* emphasized turn away from women's *physical* comedy and from the practice of cringe slapstick. Because *Parks* expresses female unruliness through foregrounded intellectual and political narratives around the career woman, the occasional physical comedy is mostly present in service of the narrative's feminist-coded intentions.

CODA: NEGOTIATING THE POLITICS AND AESTHETICS OF WOMEN'S PHYSICAL COMEDY

As discursively feminist and quality television, body politics are pivotal for *30 Rock* and *Parks and Recreation*; both the configuration of aesthetic and ideological meanings and their critical appraisals hinge on them. A similar ideological intent nevertheless leads the two comedies in dissimilar directions in their use of physical comedy and in exploring the question of female experience in public spaces. The issue of physical comedy and slapstick looms large for critics' evaluations of the series' feminism and quality. In *30 Rock* the abundance of Liz's physical comedy in later seasons was argued to have undermined a convincingly progressive feminist rhetoric. As shown, Fey's physical comedy is pivotal to the plotting, resulting in constant negotiations across intellectually, aesthetically "complex" (Mittell 2015a) narratives, a mobilization of feminist concerns, and the ideological tensions already inherent in women's physical comedy. Efforts to focus on the heroine's idiosyncratic physical comedy, precisely because of the differing imperatives of these paradigms, account for both the text's noticeable struggles to offset them and critics' unease.

Representative of this problem is the episode "The Natural Order" and its mixed critical reception for a backward treatment of gender and race politics (West 2009). The episode rehashes an already dramatized "issue" narrative around the different ways women and Black men are treated in the workplace. In this iteration Liz and Tracy feud over who gets undue preferential treatment based on gender and race, occasioning another exercise in a social experiment with the opposing parties forcing the other to accept what it means to have full equality. This leads to Tracy being expected to behave like a professional adult and not a spoiled TV star (so in his case race and celebrity discourses collide) and Liz to be treated as literally "one of the guys." She is forced to participate in masculine-coded activities, such as changing a heavy water bottle and going to a strip club with the male writers. Reviewers lamented the episode's illogical politics that conflated equality with uniformity, again illuminating how the series' quality features are associated with its identity politics, thanks to its own appeal to these as narrative foundations. Yet the political plot allows the series to foreground another set-piece physical comedy from Fey: When Tracy challenges Lemon to replace the empty water bottle without help in the name of equality, this culminates in a prolonged slapstick gag of the "(wo)man against inanimate object" kind in a mostly dialogue-free sequence. Lemon's minute-long battle with the bottle, splashing water everywhere and repeatedly missing the cooler's opening, fully exploits the opportunity to showcase the slapstick comedian's skill at interacting with her physical environment.

If Poehler somersaulting downhill in the pit scenario amounted to the contradictory use of the comic female body for its visual execution and narrative function, ineffectual in achieving putatively acceptable slapstick for women, then the Lemon-versus-water-bottle scene works better in positioning itself in the genre's iconography.[2] As such, it is a clear example of the program's efforts to make women's physical comedy attainable in a discursively nongendered tradition—yet it achieves this by positioning it within a heavily politicized plot around gender and race. The episode's political clumsiness and this scene's set-piece position (stopping the storytelling around the halfway mark in favor of fully playing out the incident) suggest that the political plot is subordinated to the physical comedy and not vice versa; in other words, the political plot is an excuse for Fey to display her slapstick skills.

The method of emphasizing Fey's body comedy in a way that reinforces the quality comedy's aesthetic sophistication is a recurring strategy on *30 Rock*. The episodes "Sandwich Day" and "Jackie Jormp-Jump" are memorable in their overdetermined combination of displayed comic performance and stylization. Both use a long-take sequence of Fey's medium close-up (their length fairly unconventional on American network television) to forward the narrative as played out on the actor's face, effecting a comic schtick. In "Sandwich Day" Liz/Fey eats a whole sandwich in one go (and take) to get through airport security. In "Jackie Jormp-Jump" the minute-long close-up tells the story of a day when Lemon hangs out with a group of rich socialite women and indulges in their activities (spa, plastic surgeon's office, sushi restaurant) without noticing the passage of time (Figure 5). The story plays out fully on Liz's face and in her monologue, isolated from its environment and moved into an imaginary space that the viewer's recognition fills with realistic context, helped by color-coded background and props. This gimmick foregrounds Fey's facial performance and separates it from the rest of the diegetic space, reinforcing aesthetic singularity in the filming method.

---

2   The slapstick gag of person versus water bottle is a recycled one. For example, the sitcoms *Ellen* (1994–1998, "The Hand That Robs the Cradle") and *Joey* (2004–2006, "Joey and the Critic") both executed it. For these series the scene is purely a sitcom gimmick characteristic of multicamera TV comedy, that is, an insulated gag to display comic performance, and is not integrated into the plot. In contrast, *30 Rock* both embeds the sequence in quality comedy's convoluted plotting and inflates it: Much longer than in these earlier examples, it is played more to its limits through repetition and extended interaction between diegetic space and body.

Figure 5. Liz Lemon's (Tina Fey) facial expressions presented as sophisticated comedy in *30 Rock*.

These sequences use close-ups against the conventions of melodrama and soap opera, as discussed by Mills, mining the comic possibilities of the human face instead of seeking emotional involvement—again demonstrating the different aesthetic strategies between *30 Rock* and *Parks* that stem from their different relationships to the question of how feminist politics and the female body can be mobilized in the quality comedy. *30 Rock*'s facial comedy examples work similarly to the full-body slapstick sequence in "The Natural Order" in that they negotiate between narrative and show-stopping comic performance. But the critical failure of the political story arc in "The Natural Order" points to the contradictions that female-led quality comedy is caught up in, from a perspective directly opposed to *Parks*': If *30 Rock* strives to be progressive in constructing physical comedy that strategically overcomes the sexual connotations of the female body and the sexual and feminist politics in which it is inevitably entangled, it relies on an overdetermined politicizing of plot around gender to achieve this. In contrast, an emphasized political motivation causes *Parks* to ditch women's physical comedy almost altogether, even though its central comedian's star text emerged on *Saturday Night Live* as a discursively transgressive foregrounding of physical comedy.

Ultimately, the two comedians' preexisting star texts, including their differing involvement in discourses about feminist entertainment, women's physical comedy, and female authorship, come to bear on the ways that their respective sitcoms articulate feminist politics in the comedy of distinction. *Parks* tempers Poehler's earlier bodily comedy as stunting female grotesque in favor of earnest and intellectual feminist politics, effecting shifts in the series' generic signifier (mockumentary) and modalities (comic versus [melo]dramatic). This indicates more generally the cultural unease with narrativizing women's political and identity struggles in the comedy framework. That this unease is linked with tensions around the female body's representability in comic forms surfaces in the way that feminist rhetoric on *Parks* seems to necessitate the neglect of Poehler's physical comedy. *30 Rock* contrastingly insists on the possibility of a successful melding of these and in the process is constantly at pains to secure its position simultaneously in the quality cohort (aesthetic innovation) and as feminist television (politicized plotting), both of which are thoroughly upset by the intensity with which the series promotes Fey's physical comedy.

DRAMAS

5

CULTURAL STATUS AND GENRE IN THE FEMALE-CENTERED PRESTIGE DRAMA

DISCOURSES OF GENRE AND REPRESENTATION IN FEMINIST QUALITY DRAMA

While comedy's cultural position and its sanctioned cultural transgressions allow for a relatively prominent female presence and authorship, drama is a more complicated area to negotiate this. Feminism's influence on television has primarily meant a relative abundance of women-centered sitcoms (Dow 1996; Rabinovitz 1999; Lagerwey et al. 2016), and according to the industry truism, female performers have a better chance for a successful career in half-hour comic forms than in hour-long dramas. Similarly, comedy provides more opportunities to foreground female authorship; the comic female performer and writer is a prominent figure in postmillennial American television. This trend mobilizes the comic alter ego trope of comedy traditions (Roseanne, Kirstie, Cybill, Ellen, Fey/Lemon, Cherish/Kudrow, Amy Schumer, Lena Dunham/Hanna Horvath, Mindy Kaling, the double act of Abbi and Ilana in *Broad City*), where comic meaning emerges from the perpetual interplay between fictional character and discursive author. This mode of comedy is rooted in stand-up traditions and provides fertile ground for centralizing gender politics through the inexhaustible tension between performance and authorship and between notions of enacted and real self (Gilbert 2004). This relationship and its rootedness in embodied performance can explain why quality comedy has been a more welcoming form for female-centered narratives and authorship than quality drama. In quality drama, performance (embodied presence) and authorship are rarely intertwined in discourses about modes of expression and cultural value. The notion of the author-mastermind emerges here as an intellectual but not embodied presence; it is located outside or above the text and within para-textual, critical, and industry discourses (Newman and Levine 2012, 38–58).

The issue of women's representation in television and cinema has predominantly revolved around screen presence (the idea of women in front of the camera), corresponding to women's traditional location in cultural history. Consequently, the idea of female authorship as a purely intellectual presence (behind the camera) has been a much thornier issue in debates about gender in dramatic forms (Tasker 1998, 201–3). Accounts of the masculinism of postnetwork quality drama stress that this extends beyond the text's aesthetic features and involves celebrating the male author-genius, complicating television's previous status as an unauthored and feminine medium (Newman and Levine 2012; Martin 2013; Bigsby 2013; Lotz 2014). Quality drama's accelerated masculinization, including authorship discourses borrowed from film and art history, accounts for the contradiction that the medium, previously derided as feminine, evidently struggles in its prestigious formats to reconcile female presence, understood both as female talent in front of and behind the camera and as feminine-coded cultural meanings.

Although female authorship and centralized female subjectivity have always been scarce and problematic in American television drama (as *Cagney and Lacey*'s tortuous production history attests, as recorded in detail by Julie D'Acci [1994]), it is in the current context of putatively nontelevisual and masculine-coded quality TV that this historic difficulty surfaces with especially high stakes. The discursive tension became more pronounced with the emergence of postmillennial feminist quality TV. For instance, *The Huffington Post*'s Zeba Blay (2015) illustrates "how feminist TV became the new normal" as programming that focused on "difficult men" in millennial quality TV became overshadowed by series with "complex female leads," attributing foregrounded female subjectivities in fictional programming to feminism. Blay cites programs with different formats and institutional backgrounds as influenced by this trend, highlighting the upsurge in *quantity* in prestige programming across the board. Blay celebrates progressive representational politics of race and body image and the attendant media dispute over television's responsibility for representational realism. *The Atlantic*'s Kevin O'Keeffe (2014) also describes "TV's renaissance for strong women" as a matter of representational diversity, citing *How to Get Away with Murder*'s (2014–2020) protagonist Annalise Keating (Viola Davis) as a prominent example of progressive transgression both as racial diversity and as a portrayal of an "unlikable" leading female character.[1] O'Keeffe's description of Keating as "a Walter White among women" links together gendered categories of prestigious television and anchors existing hierarchal positions and favored avenues of emulation. However, he sees a crucial imbalance in these representational trends, chalked up to institutional context: Network television seems more accommodating to the strong female character than cable because of network TV's broader audience reach and targeting of women viewers: "Cable has become a boys' club, and network TV is the true land of women" (O'Keeffe 2014). Both Blay and O'Keeffe describe these representational shifts as emerging in the early 2010s, the "only outlier" being Alicia Florrick (Julianna Margulies) of *The Good Wife* with her few years of head start (O'Keeffe 2014).

---

1 Blay (2015) discusses as the epitome of transgressive portrayal a scene in which tough lawyer Keating removes her wig, fake eyelashes, and makeup to dramatic music ("Let's Get to Scooping"). Similar to Blay, publicity discourses herald the scene as "one of *the* most revealing moments on television" (https://www.youtube.com/watch?v=l-vyiXsOvxA, accessed September 20, 2020). Within the context of representational transgression as quality TV, it is notable that this portrayal's link to highbrow drama's depiction of complex male characters revolves around getting rid of markers of glamorous Black femininity and thus around an *embodied* tension between public performance (masquerade) and supposedly genuine Black womanhood. The trope of a woman removing her wig and makeup in front of a mirror is in TV's and cinema's visual vocabulary linked to female duplicitousness and monstrosity, characteristics associated with villainous female protagonists' desire to gain social power. Although here it signifies a cleansing process, the mise-en-scène evokes Glenn Close's Marquise de Merteuil in *Dangerous Liaisons* (1988) removing her makeup in shame, but Kimberly Shaw (Marcia Cross) dramatically removing her wig in *Melrose Place* (1992–1999) or Tilda Swinton's Karen Crowder and her anxious ritual of donning the lawyer outfit in *Michael Clayton* (2007) also come to mind. However, in discourses about the complex and racially coded female character, this trope expresses authenticity and relatability, inscribed onto the Black female body and encapsulated in her (removal of) accoutrements of femininity, thus shifting the trope's original associations. The narrative still involves female duplicitousness, but if it is positioned as the monstrousness of a power-hungry woman, it becomes justifiable as complexity or reality of character, of which this scene operates as key signifier.

Feminist academics contextualize such representational changes in the recessionary culture's broader socioeconomic background. Diane Negra (2015) argues that, although American quality TV has until recently been understood as masculinized TV, the increased prominence of strong female characters in series such as *Orange Is the New Black*, *Homeland*, or *The Good Wife* provides narrative-affective frameworks for making sense of economic precarity, channeling female anger and a "negotiated/situational morality." Negra describes these (anti)heroines as "troubled by forces that are shown to be systemic and social" and thus "[the programs'] importance lies in the critiques they can generate of our current affective marketplace" (see also Leonard 2018, 171–84). Kathleen McHugh's examination of *Orange* and *Top of the Lake* expresses similar views. McHugh (2015) sees these series as landmarks of feminist quality TV, specifically as feminist interventions in the postfeminist representational paradigm because they "share deep structural concerns with power, inequality, and gender-based violence" (18). The respective production contexts and authorship discourses signal feminist politics for McHugh, also accounting for the series' singular aesthetic-narrative traits; in short, their political motivation produces their superior aesthetic and cultural value.

If TV critics interpret this supposed feminist turn as a breakthrough in women's portrayals on postnetwork, postrecession quality television, then this notion of success corresponds to a broader understanding of the recession's impact on gendered narratives of success and crisis. Negra and Tasker (2014b) stress that these popular cultural narratives ascribe an imbalance in the recession's impact on men and women, contrasting dramatizations of troubled masculinities with narratives around female (economic) success. Similarly, Suzanne Leonard (2014a) interprets the emergence of female-centered TV dramas such as *The Good Wife* as media representations where "women routinely serve as symbols of financial vitality," contrasted with "male insignificance" in the workplace (51).

Although these works situate media texts in the postrecessionary *economic* context of female success and male crisis, the dualism corresponds to the logic inherent in popular writings on representational trends of gender in quality television, evidenced in the cited think pieces. The journalistic accounts interpret the programs' increasing engagement with social critiques of women's oppression and gendered adversity as female-centered television overthrowing expired masculinity-in-crisis narratives (without describing these female-centered programs as, for instance, femininity in crisis or troubled womanhood). Thus they translate the thematic trends that feminist academics locate in popular texts into terms of industry trends. Fictional portrayals of female precarity and institutional oppression become a success story for women's representation and for feminism in critical evaluations of quality television's gender dynamics. The progress attributed to this trend revolves around character complexity as a key marker of both quality and gender representation: Quality here means feminist intervention effecting that female protagonists become more complex, more morally ambiguous, and more diverse than before, recycling the terms on which highbrow quality drama articulates complex masculinities. Yet, although character complexity is the buzzword habitually used to measure the significance of both of these gendered subjectivities, such shared attributes perform different cultural work: The complex female character, regardless of narrative context, stands for feminist success and the legitimation of female subjectivity (*strong* female characters), whereas her male counterpart's ambiguous morality mediates anxieties about *fragile* patriarchal masculinities.

Although journalistic and academic discourses about gendered quality TV tend to revolve around character complexity and thematic concerns, the differences drawn as masculinity in crisis versus female regrouping say little about the complex relationships between such characterizations and traditional television forms or tropes of aesthetic-narrative complexity. Female-centered (melo)dramatic storytelling is nothing new in American television, and a significant body of scholarship exists around the topic. Amanda Lotz's *Redesigning Women* (2006) examines the unprecedented increase of female-led TV dramas around the millennium, advocating for a review of existing analytical tools by considering television's institutional and economic shifts in the examination of this trend. Attributing the period's upsurge in female-centered programming to accelerated audience fragmentation and cable television's increased dominance, Lotz contends that the prevalence of female-targeted cable channels such as Lifetime or Oxygen in this period organically led to the ubiquity of fictional content incorporating so-called "women's issues" storytelling. Lotz's approach centralizes genre features, accounting for her book's structure around types of dramatic forms. She views the workplace drama as the form in which diachronic shifts in women's representation are clearest, because of the form's prominent position in American TV drama history and the discursive importance of women's depiction outside the home and in workplace narratives (Lotz 2006, 144–64). Her examination of the Lifetime series *Strong*

Medicine (2000–2006; a medical drama) and *The Division* (2001–2004; a cop drama) emphasizes that *Strong Medicine*'s episodic format is better suited for incisive dramatizations of women's issues, because it concentrates on patients and women's health issues using disease-of-the-week storytelling, than *The Division*'s serialized narration focusing on characters' individualized melodrama. *Strong Medicine* "educat[es] viewers through fictional storytelling" (151) and is "feminist in nature, providing a service for women beyond narrative entertainment" (153), whereas *The Division* "offers little innovation, tells few original stories, and mainly provides a different version of the cop series by exploring interpersonal relationships among officers more than the work they perform" (155).

Thus Lotz evaluates the programs' alignment with feminist concerns by considering how they are incorporated into television's narrative forms (episodic versus serialized). The question of cultural value—that is, these examples' relationship to discourses of postnetwork quality television—is not addressed, although Lotz briefly notes that the series' innovation is due to the niche audience focus, relatively low cultural status, and limited budget. This cultural position stands in obvious contrast to that of cable programmers producing high-production-value original content. Lifetime's reputation as a female-targeted channel that modernized the "women's weepies" in the TV movie subgenre is an easy target for parodies in U.S. culture (not least on *30 Rock*) precisely for its feminine-coded aesthetics and storytelling. Further, the importance that Lotz ascribes to *episodic* storytelling for incorporating feminist material is at odds with quality drama's valorization of high-concept serialization and raises the question of how female-led quality drama negotiates these gendered hierarchies of storytelling.

In Lotz's account also reverberates a received belief about the hierarchical positioning of genres. For cultural critics drama is the ultimately desired form to fulfill the obligation of progressive female representation as peak innovation in gendered storytelling. As argued earlier, this distinction goes back to the disparate cultural positions of serious versus funny storytelling, where serious plots are understood as more genuine representations and comedies as comparatively distorted reflections of reality (Mills 2005, 22). The historic scarcity of women protagonists in highbrow dramatic forms speaks to the polarized cultural value of drama and comedy (Rowe Karlyn 1995a), which sees drama as a more genuine mode of storytelling. Comedy's discursive distance from a dignified realism is similarly true for female-targeted melodrama with its associations with over-the-top pathos, gendered victimization, and physically excessive audience (over)identification (Williams 1991; 2014, 107–36). If these genres are further removed from the putative realism of representation than drama, then the gender disparities among them follow from ascribing a similar, hierarchal dynamic between the representability of male and female subjectivities: Female experience is portrayed as further removed from realism, again confirming the feminist adage that patriarchal culture normalizes male or masculinized experience.

Academic and journalistic accounts demanding or celebrating more female presence in prestigious dramatic forms are always at risk of reproducing this logic of value hierarchy; carving out a female space in the higher echelons of artistic representation runs the risk of reinforcing such hierarchies in pursuit of a relative proximity to representational realism. When Bridget Boyle (2015) critiques the "feminist comedy" phenomenon, her concern is that feminism as a serious or direct political effort is hard to reconcile with the genre's aesthetic intentions, implicitly assuming that discursively serious representation is closer to reality than comedy. Likewise, Lotz's repeated use of phrases such as "educating" audiences when discussing the increase in "women's issues" themes in TV drama links this concern with the real and serious. This link motivates popular and academic critical evaluations of the narrativization of feminist concerns in television, also inscribed onto character development. The pursuit of a putatively real representation effects ideals of cultural value for female-centered drama that are markedly different from the male-centered quality drama's signifiers. In addition, it creates the much discussed divide between prestige dramas along gendered lines, as the two articles by Blay and O'Keeffe exemplify.

Realism has a special resonance for television's representational trends. Thornham and Purvis (2005) summarize this as rooted in "television's ubiquitous sense of 'nowness'" and its appeal to realism and as an imperative to organize the "disorder of reality" into "recognizable, meaningful and safe" forms (66). Television's inherent feminization (the "fluidity" and "formlessness" of mass culture) is meshed with the medium's understanding as a unique purveyor of a narrativized reality in cultural consciousness, contrasted with masculine-coded cinema's "more coherent, structured—and prestigious—narratives" (66). These contrasting characteristics also apply to the hierarchies that exist among television forms: "Those forms of television which have sought to identify themselves as 'serious,' as concerned with 'quality,' as producing 'difficult knowledge' rather than 'easy entertainment,' have sought on the one hand to identify themselves with realism and on the other to distance themselves from the general 'flow' of 'television itself,' with its 'trivializing' tendencies'" (67). Postmillennial female-led television drama strives to occupy precisely this cultural space. For instance, the "difficult knowledge" that the vision of a Black woman removing her wig and makeup in *How to Get Away with Murder* produces as "serious" entertainment and as a heightened "quality" of realism emerges by appropriating the terms on which television's putatively genuine and masculine-coded realism has historically operated. Meanwhile, the "difficult knowledge" produced by masculine-coded highbrow drama involves the pursuit of an aesthetic-narrative singularity associated with cinema. But quality drama's much-praised aesthetic superiority is caught up in a contradiction: The cinematic aesthetic and self-contained narrative of high-concept dramas depart from previous prestige television's discursive alignment with a narrativized political realism. It is now female-led quality programs whose cultural value is predicated on alignment with representational realism and political "nowness," producing their own gendered distancing from "the general flow" of "television itself." Thus the historic gendered differentiation as described by Thornham and Purvis continues to exist in quality drama culture, even in the discursive praise of feminist quality drama.

Prestige drama, then, continues to yield distinct aesthetic and political markers that are influenced by a gendered address. This is governed by television's historic amicability to representing a putative reality, as opposed to cinema's investment in creating fantasy. The academic debate about television's "aesthetic turn" (Lury 2016) is similarly divided along an ideological line governed by the dualism of aesthetic and political analysis. Scholars arguing for the legitimacy of aesthetic evaluation (e.g., Dasgupta 2012; Mittell 2015a; Nannicelli 2016; Logan 2016) bemoan the dominance of political approaches in television studies and consider them a methodological obstacle (Logan 2016). As a dominant strand of political analysis, feminist scholarship centralizes questions of representation as a potential aspect of cultural value. Although this has also started to investigate how female-centered programming negotiates masculine-coded quality TV culture (Lagerwey et al. 2016; Nygaard and Lagerwey 2016), the two academic discourses rarely overlap.

An exception to this divide is Amanda Lotz's work, which has separately studied both the female-led drama's millennial popularity in *Redesigning Women* (2006) and the prestige male-led drama's representation of masculinities in *Cable Guys* (2014), which also considers prestige cable television's aesthetics. As discussed, Lotz's approach champions a progress narrative inscribed onto both the examined texts' presumed feminism and, in *Cable Guys*, the high cultural value they supposedly represent. In *Cable Guys* Lotz posits that these texts signify a departure on television not just aesthetically but in their progressive alignment with feminism *as* male-centered television (as such, she understands the masculinity-in-crisis trope as feminist).[2] This stance is directly opposed to scholars who are skeptical of quality TV, such as Newman and Levine (2012). Their engagement with classed and gendered processes in the legitimation of "cinematic" quality TV is a useful critique of the quality trend, but it leaves open the question of quality television's existing and historically influential invocations of feminism. Such a simultaneous consideration of these approaches is rare in scholarship (for exceptions, see T. C. Miller [2016] and Nygaard and Lagerwey [2016]). Although much has been written about how the male-centered quality drama repurposes storytelling traditions of television's derided female-targeted forms, especially the soap opera and melodrama, the academic and journalistic focus on female-centered drama has not yet engaged much with how this trend relates to the masculine-coded quality drama, the current paragon of the prestigious televisual aesthetic.

The Good Wife and *Orange Is the New Black* are well suited for examining television's alignment of masculine-coded aesthetic value with a discursive feminism, because media reception hails both programs as quality and feminist entertainment. In academia the feminist entertainment perspective dominates; that is, with the quality status taken for granted, scholars tend to examine the texts' politics. This is also true for Jason Mittell's short study of *The Good Wife*, demonstrating how the series' "progressive" gender politics affects its "complex" storytelling (Mittell 2015a, 258–59). Media discourses similarly position the programs as highbrow drama's female-oriented pioneering offshoots. O'Keeffe (2014) sees *The Good Wife* as a precursor of the strong female character trope and of the narrative emphasis on female experience in prestige drama. Broadcast on CBS, the network long associated with procedural crime franchises targeted at older audiences, the program was considered exceptional at its 2009 debut for both its focus on a female lead and its serialized political narrative (Flint 2013), and it is still

---

2 Jason Mittell, in *Complex TV* (2015a), argues similarly, positing that the aesthetic complexity of contemporary quality TV involves a political complexity of gender relations (see chapter 6).

regarded as CBS's flagship entry into the prestige drama category (Adalian 2016; Goldberg 2016). As will be shown, the promotional campaigns for *Orange Is the New Black* highlighted both its aesthetic singularity and its concentration on diverse womanhood to establish Netflix's reputation as a prime platform for female-targeted and female-centered quality content. Although other series after *Orange* mobilized similar marketing strategies on Netflix, *Orange* continues to be seen as the company's first flagship series targeting female audiences.

Beyond programming context and promotional strategies, *The Good Wife* and *Orange* also help us understand how the negotiation of two discursively irreconcilable features—masculine-coded quality TV's stylistic features and female-led drama's politics—redefines the aesthetic-narrative terms on which postmillennial television appeals to cultural value, supported by reception and industry discourses. As a prelude to the individual analyses, I provide here an overview of a shared characteristic of the two series that is used to reconcile the feminist and quality monikers: The programs mobilize a notion of marginalized female subjectivities as a key component of their inception and cultural positioning. This use emerges in three aspects: (1) themes and characterization techniques presented as novelty traits of the quality series, (2) stylistic-generic markers resulting from this thematic focus, and (3) the programs' positioning in their respective institutional environments as problematically categorizable in the quality cohort.

As a thematic device, the centralization of marginalized female experiences works as a key dramatic tension reproducible for television's storytelling practices. Both series are known for novel storytelling modes by focusing on subjectivities typically excluded from prime-time narration. *The Good Wife* unusually centralizes the wife in the scenario of the high-profile politician's sex scandal, and the wife figure also allows the series to intertwine this serialized political plot with the legal procedural's episodic structure. Alicia's position as an underdog (both as a politician's wife and as an attorney reentering the workforce) allows for a narrative mobility between the husband's world of high-profile politics and the legal workplace environment's case-of-the-week plotting with its more typically televisual narrative, underlining the gendered traditions of television storytelling through centralized female subjectivity. *Orange* similarly focuses on marginalized female identities, using this theme to complicate points of identification: The series' premise, in which the young, privileged, self-centered white hipster Piper Chapman (Taylor Schilling) goes to prison for a relatively minor offense, is a springboard to contrast the postfeminist woman's perspective with those of the other(ed) inmates at Litchfield Penitentiary. Upsetting the fish-out-of-water story conventions is the program's and its promotion's hook, to the extent that the centralizing of marginalized femininities, associated with realism, becomes the basis on which critics celebrate its novelty. For *New York Post* critic Robert Rorke (2014), *Orange* is a "TV revolution for women" because it has changed "our notions of what kind of actresses we saw on TV."

Second, the two programs integrate the theme of marginalized womanhood with the requirements of aesthetic exceptionalism that the quality brand advocates. For *The Good Wife* the portrayal of the underdog female lawyer who at the same time represents the scorned wife figure in political sex scandals expresses a departure from characterizations that such female roles arguably invite, rooted in melodrama's aesthetic-narrative traditions. Much has been made of Julianna Margulies's portrayal of Alicia Florrick as an opaque, sphinx-like figure resisting gendered martyrdom and scrutiny, and this also speaks to the program's aesthetic efforts. Suzanne Leonard (2014b) argues that this characterization works as a resistance to the media frenzy over political sex scandals through Alicia's silence "as a strategy of power rather than compliance," offering a "feminist stance" (14). The strong female protagonist's characterization as a stoic and calculatedly undecipherable figure, problematizing the relationship between marginalized subjectivity and silence, corresponds to the series' aesthetics, which are hailed as sophisticated and subtle. Because of its blending of serialized and episodic narratives, coupled with a clinical visual style and performances stressing characters' "unknowability," Emily Nussbaum (2014) heralds *The Good Wife* for its cynical and critical take on "pretty much every institution under capitalism," even though it started out "much like an empowerment procedural for the ladies, a 'Lean In' fairy tale about a strong woman who would find her way" (110). Nussbaum demonstrates how the series uses the strong female character, defined by her resistant silence, to overwrite a specifically feminine-coded mode of storytelling and aesthetics to appeal to more prestigious trends of televisual narration and ideologies.

For *Orange* the theme of marginalized femininities means an affiliation with realism as aesthetics and ideology, helping the program express cultural value as politically motivated narrative-aesthetic complexity. McHugh's (2015) praise of the series' feminism highlights the realist, documentarist style of its title sequence, a dynamic montage of real-life female prisoners' "multi-ethnic" (20) faces in extreme close-ups. She finds the sequence unusual in its refusal to present a linear associative structure typical of opening credits, instead highlighting reversibility and "seriality without direction or progress, a fitting structure for its prison setting" (21). Linking the diversity of the collage of faces to realist aesthetics, McHugh concludes that the documentarism, a unique stylistic choice, exposes the "privileged demographic" of Netflix subscribers to the reality of incarcerated women's subjectivity and experiences (21–22). The documentarism that, as McHugh argues, underlines the series' feminist credentials is also what lands it in the quality cohort for journalists—"a TV revolution for women" for Rorke. Alan Sepinwall (2013) remarks that "not since *The Wire* has there been a show that's been this large and great a showcase for obscure actors of color." Because *The Wire* is regarded as a pinnacle of quality television for using documentarist aesthetics and representational diversity for social and political commentary, the comparison appreciates *Orange* as superior television for a similar racial politics and realism.

But the mobilization of marginalization as a narrative tool in *The Good Wife* and *Orange* yields dissimilar configurations of the quality aesthetic, influenced by institutional and generic environments. For *The Good Wife* the inscrutability of Alicia's face and character, boosted by the text's polished, symmetric aesthetic choices, indicates a critical view on American politics, law, and expectations of female morality. For Leonard (2014b) the resulting moral ambiguity stems from the series' refusal to judge Alicia's character in the context of her sex life. The fact that the series stresses Alicia's sexuality as the most debated and politicized arena also aligns with broadcast television's own negotiations of self-censorship and wide audience targeting, a negotiation that feeds into underlying discourses about the cable versus network TV dualism. Contrastingly, where *The Good Wife* refuses insight into the thoughts and sex life of a political wife dissected by media coverage, *Orange* advocates revelatory insight into lives (including sex lives) so far rendered invisible in popular media, corresponding to Netflix's self-promotion as a challenger to the masculinist sexual explicitness of reigning cable aesthetics. This contrast between the two series surfaces in McHugh's (2015) article, which uses *The Good Wife* as a counterpoint to *Orange*'s laudable feminism-as-realism-as-quality, critiquing the "lush *mise-en-scène*" (22), the chic costuming, and the relative lack of diversity as accounting for *The Good Wife*'s failure to become feminist (as opposed to postfeminist) quality TV. I return to this point later, but for now it demonstrates that the two programs' focus on specifically marginalized femininities accounts for the aesthetic superiority to which they aspire: These womanhoods' position in the media landscape and the two shows' programming backgrounds in relation to cable television determine the different manners in which these aesthetics emerge.

Visual renditions of female faces reveal the two shows' different focus on mobilizing a certain feminist politics. In *The Good Wife* fictional character Alicia's or Kalinda Sharma's (Archie Panjabi) Kabuki-mask face (also implying the face's coalescence with makeup and masquerade) is in obvious contrast to the multiplicity of real and nameless paratextual faces in *Orange*'s title sequence, framed "up-close-and-personal" (McHugh 2015, 21) and without makeup, showing every wrinkle and blemish (Figures 6 and 7). Yet these strategic associations of female faces with certain kinds of female subjectivities and feminist struggles, however disparate they seem, logically follow from these series' institutional, cultural, and generic environments, influencing the manners in which they articulate the theme of women's marginalization and overcoming thereof.

Programming and industry backgrounds are the third area in which the notion of marginalization (or rather marginality here) emerges. This has less to do with creative choices and more with discursive negotiation processes of positioning the two series as quality television. The production history of both programs is marked by mediated struggles over categorizing them as female-centered quality dramas in relation to both the male-led quality drama and the female-centered dramedy. This struggle surfaced clearly in annual awards circuit discussions, as the trade press saw both series as perennially overlooked in prestigious television award competitions, such as the Emmys and the Golden Globes. Journalists attribute this undervaluation to the series' respective liminal positions in programming contexts: In *Orange*'s case this is expressed in genre terms, and in *The Good Wife*'s case, in terms of institutional background associated with cultural value. When *The Good Wife* is lauded as quality television, this is often formulated as a virtue *despite* the network environment (Goodman 2013). Yet precisely this environment was understood to forever preclude *The Good Wife* from entering the big league of cable quality by winning the industry's most coveted awards, such as Outstanding Drama Series, at the Emmys (Hinckley 2014; Travers 2014; Idato 2014), a verdict that speaks to the discursive dualism of cable and network television's associated value hierarchies. I discuss this issue in more detail later; for now I want to highlight that *The Good Wife*'s murky position in its programming context ("straddling the line between ambitious cable fare and network series" [Lowry 2015]) accounts for its

Figure 6. The Kabuki-mask faces of Alicia Florrick (Julianna Margulies) and Kalinda Sharma (Archie Panjabi) in *The Good Wife*.

reputation as marginalized quality television, surfacing most visibly as a disadvantage in the awards circuit. This liminal position follows from the program's female-centered storytelling and feminism rhetoric: The theme of marginalized female experience propels its lauded quality aesthetic and narrative. *The Good Wife*'s modes of expressing this theme earn their reputation as sophisticated television by turning the constraints of broadcast TV into a virtue, as shown in Nussbaum's (2014) appraisal of the series as

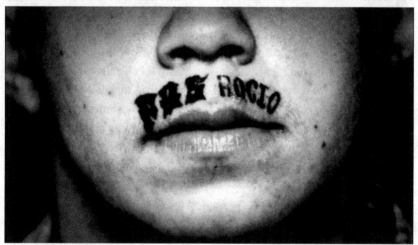

Figure 7. "Real" female faces in *Orange Is the New Black*'s opening credits.

a critique of institutions in the guise of an "empowerment procedural for the ladies."

The issue of marginalization affecting a program's cultural cachet emerges for *Orange* around the question of genre. During its run the program was variably described as comedy, drama, and dramedy. Feeding into this uncertainty was series creator Jenji Kohan's previous work. As creator of the Showtime program *Weeds*, a representative of the channel's cultivated female-led programming, Kohan was associated with half-hour comedy-drama production. The issue of genre first became an obvious burden for *Orange*'s cultural capital, similar to *The Good Wife*, in the Emmy Awards nomination procedure, initially revolving around its hour-long episode length.

In response to the accelerated blending of comedy and drama in prestige hour-long American television, the Television Academy announced several changes to its Emmy nomination rules in 2015. One of the most controversial of these concerned the categories in which a series could be nominated, from that year on determined not by content but by length: Only series shorter than 30 minutes could compete in comedy categories, whereas longer programs were considered drama (Birnbaum 2015b). To offset the new rule's rigidity, programs could petition for reconsideration of their category; their eligibility was decided by a panel of industry members. All the series that used the opportunity to apply for category changes, including *Orange*, were hour-long series switching from drama to comedy; and only *Orange* was denied this and had to compete as a drama in 2015 (Birnbaum 2015a). The media commentary on this new rule and its controversial effect on programs' chances at winning soon honed in on *Orange*'s problem, specifically on the industry's efforts to shoehorn it into one generic category, upsetting its cultural position as quality television (Viruet 2015). *Orange*'s reputation in media discourses as sidelined in the industry's annual evaluations of its value hierarchies echoed *The Good Wife*'s notoriety as ever the underdog on the awards circuit.

Although *Orange*'s position does not revolve around straddling aesthetic-narrative practices associated with different institutional backgrounds but rather around generic categorizations, the root cause for its neglected status is similarly its appeal to cultural value by upsetting gendered expressive traditions. Netflix executive Ted Sarandos's comment on the Emmy ruling highlights this status; he called *Orange* "a truly pioneering series and an iconoclast which has always defied genre or easy categorization" (Birnbaum 2015a). If *Orange* is a "pioneering" and "iconoclastic" series, this reputation has everything to do with its novel concentration on marginalized female subjectivities, rectifying a blind spot for television. Into this reputation of marginality and iconoclasm feeds *Orange*'s institutional background, questioning whether it is television at all—the streaming era's reorganization of gendered value hierarchies and audience targets further influenced the series' understanding as hovering on the fringes of those established categories of quality that had dominated industry and media discourses in the previous decade.

In the following sections I provide detailed analyses of each series' configurations of their quality status in connection with genre and their alignments with female-centered and discursively feminist storytelling.

NO "CHEAP MELODRAMA": *THE GOOD WIFE* AND GENDERED GENRE DISTINCTIONS

As noted, critics and academics alike discuss *The Good Wife*'s cultural value in terms of a tension between institutional background and aesthetic-narrative achievement (Lowry 2015; T. C. Miller 2016, 5). Nussbaum (2014) also underlines this in her *New Yorker* review. She likens the series to *The Wire* for its similar invisibility on the awards circuit; but at the same time she distinguishes it from prestigious cable output by outlining a dualism between contemporary notions of quality and the nostalgia for network television that this show emanates for her (Nussbaum 2014). Her argument is worth quoting at length.

> The show didn't even get nominated for best drama at this year's Emmys (although the snub might be a point of pride: *The Wire* was never nominated for best drama at all). As sharp and as deep and as witty as *The Good Wife* is, it lacks all the Golden Age credentials. The series' showrunners, Robert and Michelle King, a married couple, don't have a pugnacious-auteur reputation or Hollywood glamour. They're collaborative workhorses, producing twenty-two hour-long episodes a year, more than twice as many as their peers on HBO, FX, or AMC. . . . Their series débuts every September, on schedule—no year-and-a-half-long hiatuses for them to brood about artistic aims. (Nussbaum 2014)

Nussbaum celebrates *The Good Wife* both because of and despite its institutional origins: for sticking to the formula of network prime-time drama without the arty navel-gazing of cable shows; for adhering to the constraints of commercial breaks, product integration, and censorship; and for the sharpness that in her description emerges mainly as a result of these constraints, because it keeps the—in this context suspicious—creative freedom of television producers in check. Nussbaum also laments that the show's liminality entails a gendered aspect, demonstrated by an anecdote where a male TV executive dismisses it as "being 'for women'" (Nussbaum 2014). Her praise thus exposes and expresses frustration with a gendered double standard in the industry where the network-cable dualism also involves a gendered differentiation of quality (see also T. C. Miller 2016; Nygaard and Lagerwey 2016). Yet in her analysis of the series' subtlety emerges another, this time only implied, duality: gendered *genre* hierarchies. Nussbaum describes the season 5 plot twist of major character Will Gardner's (Josh Charles) death (so far, he had been a vertex of the show's central love triangle) through the aesthetic difference between highbrow drama's subtlety and female-targeted melodrama's excess: "Instead of playing as cheap melodrama his death reinvented the series. . . . It also, daringly, broke *The Good Wife*'s primal link to a feminine TV narrative formula: the love triangle—the secret sauce for many female fans" (Nussbaum 2014).

For Nussbaum, then, it is the negotiated allure of and distancing from a tradition of feminine-coded network melodrama where *The Good Wife*'s cultural cachet becomes pivotal. In this echoes the common wisdom about the genderedness and rigid boundaries of the network-cable dichotomy, only this time it revolves around the question of different television forms. When Nussbaum defines the series' quality, she emphasizes what it is not—a feminine and "cheap melodrama" or "an empowerment procedural for the ladies"—and invokes by this the type of television that, according to industry wisdom, sells best to female audiences. Indeed, generic ambiguity is a prominent narrative-aesthetic device for the series' premise and promotion, starting with the title, which sarcastically invokes an archetypal female figure of American popular media to unhinge the associations that this epithet invites. The generic associations of melodrama and soap opera become reference points to be upset; in this we can see a play of distancing-while-invoking or absent presence, a method similar to that of network TV's female-centered comedy of distinction.

The pilot episode's much-discussed first scene (Leonard 2014b, 944; T. C. Miller 2016, 7) works out precisely this duality of gendered generic conventions in mise-en-scène, dialogue, and performance. The press conference in which Illinois State's Attorney Peter Florrick (Chris Noth) announces his resignation after his sex scandal is initially filmed focusing on him and the attending reporters; the slow-building tension promises a political drama revolving around *his* ordeal. The revelation that we are instead going to follow his wife's perspective comes as the scene's narrative surprise, with the camera discovering her quiet presence next to the orating husband. As both Leonard and Miller note, her face is first shown through a diegetic TV camera, indicating that the novel focus on the scorned wife will entail a scrutiny of the mediatized nature of political sex scandals (Leonard 2014b, 944; T. C. Miller 2016, 7). The dramatic-soapy slap that Alicia subsequently places on Peter's face backstage completes the scene not only to "transition . . . [her] into the star of the show" (Leonard 2014b, 944) but also to confirm the gendered complexity of generic TV traditions displayed here. The novel aspect of focusing on the marginalized female figure is complemented by Alicia's similarly novel and much-praised dogged silence and restraint (which, for Leonard, contributes to the series' feminist credentials), in the scene governing the power dynamics between husband and wife. If the cold open serves as Alicia's complex portrayal, it is unusual precisely because it lacks any dialogue from her. It relies on wordless performance, visual narration, and a characterization technique conveyed through character action (Alicia attempting to remove lint from Peter's suit and the slap that in this context is less melodramatic trope and more characterization method)—to the soundtrack of the male protagonist's speechifying. These stylistic choices demonstrate how the series emulates cable television's so-called cinematic filming methods, and they tap into the discursive dualism of average TV fare's feminine verbosity and image-driven highbrow drama. The aesthetic novelty is a consequence of the gendered novelty of characterization that associates powerful silence—and accompanying dominance of visual, putatively cinematic aesthetic—with the female protagonist, whereas verbosity, a traditionally feminine or feminizing trait of disdained TV genres, dominates our first impression of the male protagonist. Initially, this reversed setup describes the pompous politician–meek housewife scenario, but the premise (her centralization and the dynamic between her constraint and the unfolding narrative) makes full use of the medium's and the form's gendered associations to achieve the quality effect. The cold open's stylistic choices set up the terms on which the series positions itself as subtle and sophisticated television rising above average network offering and thus mobilize those features that in Nussbaum's assessment help to differentiate it from the suspicious stain of "cheap melodrama" and other feminine television.

Critics also routinely evaluate the program's storytelling, characterization methods, and aesthetics in comparison with contemporaneous series seen as its peers in terms of institutional origin, theme, genre, and gendered representation and cultural value. It is mainly the hit ABC shows produced by celebrated producer Shonda Rhimes's production company, Shondaland, such as *Scandal* (2012–2018) and *How to Get Away with Murder*, that become reference points for what *The Good Wife* is not. Although both Rhimes series debuted a few years after *The Good Wife*, discussions of their differences further illustrate how *The Good Wife* navigates gender and its associated television traditions. For critics the cultural importance of the Shondaland dramas revolves around the interconnected dynamics of race and gender in political and legal drama; and these representational methods contribute to the series' understanding as exceptional, accounting for the occasional quality label. Yet *Scandal, How to Get Away with Murder*, and other Shondaland series are *otherwise* considered fitting into female-targeted TV melodrama and soap culture (Leonard 2016, 8) with their fast-paced plotting, emphasis on romance and sex, narrative twists relying on scheming galore, and heightened emotionality and verbosity. Contrasted with this type of television, *The Good Wife* becomes for critics a laudable network TV anomaly. For a somewhat reversed demonstration, consider Noel Kirkpatrick's (2015) review of the season 7 episode "Cooked," which laments *The Good Wife*'s increasing reliance on intrigue as a gradual shift from cable-like narration toward Shondaland shows' "fast-burning and twisty" plotting.

If *The Good Wife* gains quality credentials in its negotiated difference from programs that thematically resemble it but are too reliant on established TV formulas, this difference involves a complex relationship to network television's feminine-coded reliance on verbosity and displayed affect. Again, the measured silence characterizing Alicia comes to bear on the program's aesthetics and its reputation as sophisticated TV complimenting viewer intellect rather than emotional response, in contrast with Shondaland shows' critical and academic evaluation. Investigating the dynamic between fan practices and Shonda Rhimes's authorship, TV scholar Anna Everett (2015) celebrates the latter by highlighting a defining emotionality and its effect on audience engagement in physical terms. Everett's description of the typical Rhimes drama as "ultrafast-paced, frenetic, and head-spinning storylines, as well as mind-blowing and off-the-chain plot points that mesmerize audiences every week" (36) speaks to a connection between these shows' mobilization of narrative and emotional excess and Linda Williams's (1991) "body" genres, whose centralized physicality and sensation are mimicked in audience reaction.

Theorizing melodrama as one of the "body" genres that Carol Clover (1987) identified in horror and pornography, Williams (1991) finds that all "low" genres fall under the expressive mode of melodrama, "encompass[ing] a broad range of films marked by 'lapses' in realism, by 'excesses' of spectacle and displays of primal, even infantile emotions, and by narratives that seem circular and repetitive" (3). Although this description already proffers a connection to the narrative practices of feminine-coded television forms, especially those of the Shondaland stable, it is the link between low cultural value and an overinvolved spectatorship that further confirms the similar context in which Shondaland series are positioned. If "the success of these genres is . . . measured by the degree to which the audience sensation mimics what is seen on the screen" (4), then their cultural value stands in reverse connection to this success because of the "apparent lack of proper esthetic distance, a sense of over-involvement in sensation and emotion" (5). Everett's description of the intense fan culture phenomenon surrounding Shondaland shows stresses viewer involvement in similar terms, locating its cultural importance in the democratizing, racially and socially inclusive interaction of fan communities and discursive author.

> Clearly, it was not only Rhimes herself who was yearning for the kind of brazenly postmodern, culturally reflexive, and visually tantalizing expressions of America's singularly pluralist societal composition, historically erased from mainstream television, that Shondaland consistently delivers to its gobsmacked or astounded viewers without apology. Like fans of horror and slasher films, who enjoy being scared in the dark, Rhimes' fans relish the hypersuspended disbelief that motivates their real-time tweets of delighted shock and awe. (Everett 2015, 36)

The mention of horror fandom similarly caught up in physical overinvolvement speaks to Williams's theorization of "body" genres, which Williams also interpreted as placed low in genre hierarchies for centralizing female bodies caught up in intense displays of physical action and reaction. But when Everett insists that Rhimes's oeuvre fits the bill of quality television, underlying her discussion of authorship, fandom, and media reception relations lurks an unease with aligning the programs with low and feminine-coded TV genres. She cites *Scandal*'s 2014 win of the Peabody Award as a triumph that finally "helped to quell somewhat unfair dismissals of *Scandal* as mere soap opera" (Everett 2015, 40). Everett struggles to save Shondaland programs for the quality brand according to the terms advocated by industry and reception discourses—here for gendered and raced political progressiveness, cult fandom, and discursive authorship—but the "mere soap opera" remark betrays her unquestioning acceptance of TV genres' gendered value hierarchies.

Nonetheless, associations with melodrama and feminine entertainment do underlie *Scandal*'s journalistic assessments. Nussbaum (2012b) frames this in a context she calls the show's "post-racial fantasy" and a connected lack of cultural prestige. That is, at a time when television's race politics and diversity are central talking points, these discourses tend to focalize other, more prestigious series, because *Scandal* is "the type of show the TV digerati don't care about: it's network, it's formulaic, and it fits squarely in the feminine junk drawer, with *Grey's Anatomy*, chick lit, and women's magazines, where few consumers go looking for artistry or deep meaning" (Nussbaum 2012b). Whether Nussbaum fairly assesses *Scandal*'s neglect in journalistic discussions of race politics is beside my point, but her argument demonstrates the cultural position of Shondaland programming as low-quality feminine television. Crucially, Nussbaum cites *The Good Wife* as a counterexample that tackles race in a more complex manner, again tapping into the terms on which this program signals its distinctive status on network television and distances itself from the codes of feminine entertainment.

The discursive contrast between these female-centered network dramas, then, involves a gendered body-mind dualism in relation to preferred modes of audience engagement and related genre conventions. *The Good Wife*'s cerebral sophistication means a negotiated distance from melodrama's displayed embodied affect. Despite thematic and genre similarities, the series is regarded as profoundly different from its network neighbors, celebrated for a cool intellectuality found lacking in the others. This discursive difference mostly hones in on Shondaland shows, with their proximity to Williams's "body" genres in terms of a feminine display of sensation and emotion, inviting audiences to mimic this. *The Good Wife*'s courting of viewer intellect is epitomized by the intellectualism and powerful reticence of its female protagonists—Alicia and most of the female attorneys, politicians, and clients appearing on the show. Further, the series often brings this characteristic into play to contrast it with the trope of female garrulousness and emotionality *as masquerade*. In a repeated gimmick the program uses memorable guest stars to play opposing counsel whose courtroom tactics involve performances, carefully emphasized as such, of stereotypical femininity, such as Nancy Crozier (Mamie Gummer) performing the ingénue or Patti Nyholm (Martha Plimpton) playing the overwhelmed mother (T. C. Miller 2016, 13). Portrayals of restrained female behavior and their oppositional relationship to these masquerades of femininity—enacted in Alicia's recurring eye-roll reaction shots in court scenes—further contribute to the series' prestige reputation and are contrasted with expected generic conventions per Nussbaum (2014).

Expectations of feminine self-presentation provide fertile ground for extended commentary on the series, thus demonstrating its high investment in these for establishing prestige credentials. The procedural story line of the season 2 episode "VIP Treatment" is an example of this, and it is also useful for further nuancing the series' self-distancing from melodrama conventions and mobilizing the feminism theme, both as individualized narrative and as political discourse (T. C. Miller 2016). The episode revolves mainly around a case of the week: High-profile masseuse Lara White (Natalie Knepp) walks into the law office accusing a (fictional) celebrity philanthropist of sexually assaulting her during a massage session just a few hours before, and she requests legal representation from Alicia. The episode recounts the events of a few hours in a series of backroom debates, revolving around whether Alicia's bosses Diane Lockhart (Christine Baranski) and Will will take up the suit.

Given the topic, this plot predictably focuses on issues associated with popular media treatments of sexual violence: women's agency, challenged credibility, sexuality as political issue, the power relations of those involved, and so forth. Here, these concerns emerge because the accused man (never shown in person and thus remaining a symbol, "the most beloved Democrat in America") is also a Nobel Peace Prize winner famous for his advocacy of women's rights in Africa. The plot foregrounds popular feminism not only as individualized narrative but also as politics, especially because it concentrates narrative tension on Diane's status as a powerful liberal feminist public figure. It revolves around her moral conundrum between believing the potential client and ruining a feminist organization's work by exposing its celebrity figurehead as a rapist.

The exposition already demonstrates how the series mobilizes political feminism as a narrative device to generate its smart status. I deal with the question of feminist politics and cultural value in chapter 6, but the detail I want to highlight here concerns Lara's portrayal and the series' relationship to melodrama's expressive modes that she signals. If the series strives to shake off the taint of "cheap melodrama" by presenting its plot as primarily a political issue, then this becomes overdetermined through Lara's portrayal as an excessively calm and eloquent woman. This is presented as an oddity from the moment she appears, given the circumstances, and intensifies the theme of credibility and character authenticity circulated in media treatments of real-life sexual assault scandals that the episode thematizes. Further, this makes Diane's dilemma especially poignant, creating the narratively productive irony where "the" feminist is the skeptical one about a woman's credibility who accuses a powerful man of sexual violence. The exchange between Diane and Lara in which this struggle culminates speaks not only to this narrative conundrum and moral, political dilemma but also to the series' own stakes in generating a tension between genre expectations and women's portrayals.

> **Diane:** Miss White, don't take this the wrong way but given that this happened five hours ago, you seem remarkably calm.
>
> **Lara:** I'm not sure how I'm supposed to take that the right way.
>
> **Diane:** Take it as the first of a long line of hard questions.
>
> **Lara:** Would it make a difference if I was crying?
>
> **Diane:** You were sexually assaulted. Wouldn't that make sense?
>
> **Lara:** When I was kicked out of college, I cried for an hour, then I stopped, and I never cried again. That's who I am. But if it helps, I wish this had happened to somebody who cried a lot.

Delivered with bone-dry sarcasm, the last line taps not only into expectations of female behavior in the context but, in terms of genre conventions, the associations of "women's issues" melodrama and its characterization and plot tropes. Lara's derisive description "somebody who cried a lot" evokes melodrama's excess as "body" genre in Williams's terms and signals the distancing that the program performs; it also adds a personalized clarification of the character's unmelodramatic behavior by means of a summary backstory. The need for this explanation signals the continued discursive importance of the personal-political dualism that crystallizes here both as an issue of television storytelling and as a historic feminist slogan. The plot negotiates between television's established method of individualizing and privatizing issues and efforts to politicize them. Generically, this surfaces in a negotiation between the excess of "women's issues" melodrama and the putative sophistication of contemporary quality drama. Lara has an intimate melodrama backstory that has evolved into intellectual drama. That this discursive evolution revolves around the program's refusal to use tropes of a disdained femininity is underlined by the immediate cut to Alicia's face after the last line. To boot, Lara is interviewed by Diane and others; Alicia has no lines throughout the scene and rarely has any reaction shots. The final cut to her medium close-up signals that, although Alicia is there only as silent observer, her presence is vital to the scene's effect. The exchange between Diane and Lara is presented in reverse-angle single shots, yet Lara's last utterance is completed not by Diane's reaction shot but by Alicia's, articulating a special resonance between them (Figure 8). Her emphasized stare at the client on which the scene ends confirms the similarity between the procedural plot's heroine and the program's star. This partly refers to the obvious parallel of the two women's involvements in high-profile sex scandals; but in the context of the preceding exchange it also highlights Alicia's by now customary depiction as similarly refusing to conform to expectations of feminine-coded behavior, replaced with excessive silence. As discussed, the program is at pains to link these expectations of femininity and genre traditions; thus a refusal to abide by the rules of one speaks to the struggle to shake off associations of the other.

The series, then, counters the excess of melodrama's displayed affect with an equally excessive refusal of emotive performance. However, this signifier of the melodramatic remains prominent through scarce outbursts of emotional and physical performance (what Anna Everett calls the "WTF moments" characterizing Shondaland series [2015, 38]). *The Good Wife*'s storytelling uses strategically placed and memorably grand displays of character breakdown that gain their significance from their scarcity and the sometimes season-long build-up to them. Positioned at distinct and accentuated points of the serialized narrative, they dominantly involve physical expressions of grandstanding and anger. The pilot's slap is an example; others include Will storming into Alicia's office, after finding out she had been plotting to abandon the firm, and knocking items on her desk to the floor in the season 5 episode "Hitting the Fan." The title indicates the binary of slow-burning tension and outbursts of crisis, signaling their plot device employment as self-reflexive smartness. Similarly, the same season's game changer episode in which Will is killed in the courtroom is titled "Dramatics,

Figure 8. Lara White (Natalie Knepp) as Alicia Florrick's (Julianna Margulies) symbolic double in *The Good Wife*.

Your Honor"—the metatextual admittance of relying on melodramatic twists highlights the series' constant negotiations of expressive modes.

Another instance of enacted excessive emotionality occurs in the season 7 episode "Iowa," in which campaign manager Eli Gold (Alan Cumming) admits to Alicia that years ago he erased a voicemail from her phone in which Will professed his love. This is an example of serial memory: Viewer attention is rewarded by recalling an unresolved conflict from six seasons ago. Mobilizing a textual feature of masculine-coded quality narration in a romance melodrama story line (the love triangle plot is feminine address for Nussbaum), the sequence following the confession juggles the requirements of both forms. Struggling to express the adequate affective response this moment invites, it keeps at arm's length the associations of melodramatic performance and mise-en-scène. Eli's confession is followed by Alicia's signature measured silence and composed "Get out," which then turns into a physical expression of anger: knocking over a chair, shoving away a table. The subsequent sequence balances the moment's heightened emotional stakes by mobilizing comedy and drama, in this mixed mode offsetting tropes of putatively sophisticated drama and melodrama aesthetics through dialogue-free performance. Alicia, struggling to hold back an outburst, slowly takes a stack of dishes out of the kitchen cabinet and sorts them into two piles by checking the inscriptions on the bottom. She then picks up the pile of cheaper china and flings them one by one at Eli, chasing him out of the apartment.

The emphasized calculatedness of physically enacted female anger transforms a (melo)dramatic trope into sophisticated slapstick in Margulies and Cumming's comic double act, and tellingly this mixture is present only when the female protagonist performs anger toward someone else. Once Eli is gone and Alicia loses her diegetic audience, the tone turns purely serious but continues to work out the tension between the character's composure and physical enactments of emotional upheaval. The next sequence in which Alicia returns to an open suitcase and continues packing and then flips it around before collapsing on the bed screaming complies with melodrama tropes and is arguably an anticipated payoff for a seven-year long audience hook (Figure 9).

These examples of expressions of anger mobilize character interactions, suggesting a correlation between quality aesthetics and the diegetic *performance* of melodramatic anger. This parallels Leonard's (2014b) interpretation of the series' treatment of mediated sexual behavior: For her, the program expresses skepticism in relation to notions of "sexual truth" in public dissections of sex scandals through its main character's exaggerated opaqueness (the "ethic of quiet refusal") and through its emphasis on *performance* (inauthenticity) of "sexual explanations" in public (953–56). If this stance informs both the putative feminism and high cultural status of the series, the scene in which Alicia enacts (as opposed to performs) an emotional breakdown is a break with this trend, because it provides us with an exclusive insight into

Figure 9. Alicia Florrick (Julianna Margulies) enacting "over-the-top" melodrama in *The Good Wife*.

her emotional turmoil—at a cost of aesthetic superiority, operating in full-on melodramatic mode. The episode's critical reception bemoans precisely this dualism, seeing the bedroom breakdown's over-the-top feminine melodrama as uncharacteristically direct, at odds with the usual subtlety of the series' aesthetics. The *Vulture* critic's dismissal of the episode's handling of performance is representative, finding Margulies's signature "subtle acting" irreconcilable with this "over-the-top reaction," effecting what "just feels like melodrama" ("*The Good Wife* Recap," 2016).

The analysis of the minutiae of this sequence gives an indication of the issues with which the series struggles, juggling cultural value, genre, and female subjectivity. It also exemplifies how it problematizes gendered affect in its link to television forms and narrative traditions. The program also navigates this by segmenting its serialized and procedural storytelling between the protagonist couple, into which feeds the discursive straddling of the line between cable television's high-concept storytelling (politician husband) and network TV's standard episodic narration (lawyer wife) with their respective cultural positions. Yet as these two aspects constantly bleed into each other, so does the series aspire to complicate the associated genderedness of these narrative forms. Alicia's centrality to the legal procedural aspect with its case-of-the-week formula, though fitting into traditions of female-centered television dramas and their tropes of femininity, becomes upset through character portrayal. The prestige drama aspect and empowerment-procedural-for-the-ladies aspect merge in the initial function that Alicia performs in the law firm: a draw for high-profile clients with her connections and reputation as a politician's wife. Her position connects these narrative strands. But this function extends pragmatism because, as established early on, her professional skills are enhanced by her exceptional empathy toward clients that the firm exploits—the procedural plot emphasizes the heroine's emotional availability counterintuitively manifested in restrained behavior (empathetic silences, curt but sensitive utterances). This emotional availability blends with her portrayal as a politician's wife refusing melodramatic excess, using silence "as a strategy of power rather than compliance" (Leonard 2014b, 955). This way, the series builds a mixture of gendered storytelling practices that meet in the titular figure's portrayal, determining the program's genre associations and position in the quality brand.

The heroine's portrayal revolving around silence and its relationship to power and affect determines the series' reputation as sophisticated television, embedded in genre hybridity. Another aspect of this sophistication is the cynicism with which the serialized narrative treats legal and political institutions, interpreted by critics as an island of grown-up entertainment in a sea of infantilizing popular culture. When *Slate* critic Willa Paskin (2014) calls the series "television for adults" for its "unprecedented depth and cynicism" in addressing corruption and political power, she draws on terms frequently used by critics to justify quality television's artistic value. But though Paskin, similar to Nussbaum, heralds the ways that the series exploits the constraints of network television, she unusually discusses these features as more mature, that is, more intelligent, than cable drama's modes of address. And although the series "understands power as both a more subtle and insidious force than series like *The Sopranos* or *Breaking Bad* do," its prestige is tainted by its procedural form (Paskin 2014). Paskin inscribes onto the values of programming context the dualism of infantilizing popular culture and mature art, meaning complexity and intelligence. But here it is cable television, not network drama, that falls short of a mature address of issues of morality and power.

Paskin's writing displays the common belief that quality TV overwrites historic understandings of television's cultural status as immature and feminine entertainment, an argument worth revisiting here in detail. To support her point about *The Good Wife* as "television for adults," Paskin cites *New York Times* film critic A. O. Scott's (2014) controversial article "The Death of

Adulthood in American Culture," a lengthy elegy over the demise of paternalistic, patriarchal maturity's legitimacy in contemporary popular culture. Uniting convergence media culture under the umbrella of an increasingly dominant juvenile aesthetic, Scott juxtaposes this aesthetic with the new culture's progressive gender politics, finding these processes (immaturity and gendered progressiveness) intertwined. Described as a "frontier," these processes culminate for him in television's cultural shift whereby prestige male-centered dramas codify the fall of patriarchy and virtually every other TV phenomenon participates in digging its grave. Because Scott lends great importance to popular feminism's simultaneous triumph—not least through the ubiquity of female-centered TV comedy and dramedy—his argument is another example of processes described earlier, whereby postrecessionary Western culture narrativizes itself as a crisis of patriarchy and consolidation of female success. With its link between immature culture and triumphant feminism, Scott expresses the associated genderedness of the grown-up/immature divide that continues to underlie cultural criticism, as feminist scholarship previously demonstrated (see chapter 1).[3]

Scott's article incited a wide array of commentaries that repeatedly pointed out its elitism and masculinism (Kalick 2014; Bustillos 2014; Sternbergh 2014). In this light, Paskin's reference to the article as underscoring her reading of *The Good Wife* as a member of the endangered species of "grown-up entertainment" is especially contradictory. Scott leaves no doubt about the connection between popular feminism's emergence, the crisis of adulthood associated with patriarchal authority, and television's recent generic legacies. He pits the "gloomy-man, angry-man, antihero dramas" against the half-hour comedy and dramedy series in which feminist discourses flourish. When he argues that these generic formulas accommodate "female rebellion," he also articulates this as resistance to prestige drama's "serious" and "mature" modes of expression. Consequently, Paskin placing *The Good Wife* into this nexus means that she has to abandon the

---

3 Tellingly, British film magazine *Sight and Sound* referenced Scott's piece in its 2014 end-of-year poll of best U.K. film releases to support leading film critics' lament of the "eclipse of what we think of as adult themes" and a growing "attachment to childhood" in Hollywood cinema, concluding that "mature" art has relocated to prestige TV drama manifested in the trio of *Mad Men, Breaking Bad*, and *The Sopranos* (Romney 2015). Here, television is the last bastion of cinema's best values, outperforming not just its own medium but cinema itself.

chain of associations on which Scott's writing is founded: If the program is one of the remaining few examples of mature TV while showcasing *female* subjectivity and dramatizing its relationship to social power, then this is at odds with the idea that the feminist attack on traditional patriarchal authority espouses juvenile modes of expression. Her gesture thus ensures that the program is understood as masculine-coded entertainment whose treatment of social power's seductive appeal is even subtler than that of male-led cable dramas.

The Good Wife once again becomes an anomaly in television culture. It politicizes female subjectivity and treats feminism as part of the political plot but complicates the generic associations and performance traditions that this seemingly invites by mobilizing the quality text's aesthetics. For Paskin, this aesthetic and political subtlety lands it in that disappearing cohort of adult *and* patriarchal, masculine-coded entertainment that Scott eulogizes. Evidently, the feature contributing to the series' importance for its supporters, namely, a feminine-coded address married with the distancing from melodrama's generic conventions, makes it uncategorizable for cultural gatekeepers' sense making of gendered TV trends.

THE "ICONOCLASTIC" AMBIGUITY OF GENRE IN *ORANGE IS THE NEW BLACK*

While *The Good Wife*'s awkward position in quality television discourses stems from the intertwined contexts of institutional background and gendered genre practices, for *Orange* the notion of uncategorizability is not simply a consequence of these contexts but an integral feature of the show's inception and publicity. Its flagship status for Netflix's foray into original programming bears down on every aspect of the show's economy, effecting its cultural status in the streaming media landscape as inseparable from Netflix's brand-building strategies. When Netflix executive Ted Sarandos calls *Orange* pioneering and iconoclastic to defend its aesthetics, this description also applies to the company's own self-positioning as a reformer of convergence-era television.

Touted innovative aesthetics, distribution models, and viewer engagement notwithstanding, these strategies still tie Netflix to existing television culture, as TV scholars demonstrate (e.g., Smith 2015; Jenner 2018). These analyses interrogate the company's efforts to position itself as innovative in its original programming's production and distribution, such as the promotion of autonomous viewing practices, as opposed to television's linear scheduling, and its effects on storytelling methods. The discourses problematized, especially those lauding Netflix as (r)evolutionary for its production, distribution, and consumption models that distinguish it from the cable and network context, are not new. They evoke the rhetoric mobilized in the late 1990s and early 2000s to celebrate premium cable TV's, and specifically HBO's, business model and branding strategies for its original programming. Tellingly, Netflix positions HBO as its main competitor in terms of both economic prowess and generational and aesthetic innovation (Spangler 2014; Jenner 2016, 261). The rhetorical contradiction of not-TV-ness is also familiar from this era, scrutinized in ongoing academic debates about the television industry's efforts to redefine quality. Smith (2015) demonstrates that, despite Netflix's and TV journalists' insistence that Netflix "invent[s] a new art form" that is "not quite TV and not quite film" (VanDerWerff 2015a), the narrative strategies of Netflix's programming adhere to television's storytelling conventions while accommodating a changed consumption context. Similar to HBO, whose status as a forerunner of quality programming presupposed the surrounding force field of discursively average television, Netflix's position as cable and network television's progressive other assumes their presence as complementing competitors.

Although similarities between HBO and Netflix's branding strategies and reception have been analyzed in academic literature (Jenner 2016, 2018), less has been written about the commonalities in the ways their first flagship series were segmented into respective gendered interests. Just as HBO established its reputation with two programs (*The Sopranos* and *Sex and the City*) that transgressively represented contemporaneous cultural identities in two different sets of gendered genre contexts, so did Netflix develop its iconoclast status with the double release of *Orange Is the New Black* and *House of Cards* (2013–2018). Accordingly, these two series' cultural significance was located in the interconnected areas of gendered address, aesthetic novelty, and genre hybridity. However, whereas HBO's reinvention of the quality brand involved the term's masculinization, Netflix prominently targeted young female viewers, which complicated its appeals to quality. Both programs were marketed as trendsetting and exceptional, but it was *Orange* that Netflix eventually heralded as the series that secured its position in the high-end programming market, even though *House of Cards* premiered before *Orange* by a few months. This is clear from the ways that Netflix established a hierarchal relationship among its programs through buzz marketing. The strategy was boosted by the company's secrecy about its viewership statistics, whereas competitors' ratings data were publicly available (Matrix 2014, 125). Lacking these numbers, the public had to rely on Netflix's communication, which frequently asserted in nebulous language *Orange*'s primacy in the ratings and its popularity among millennials (Kafka 2013; Spangler 2014; Hanson 2014). According to this narrative, young audiences contributed to the show's reputation as a surprise "word-of-mouth hit" (Harvey 2014), thanks to the series' popularity on social media, reportedly outperforming the *House of Cards* follower base on Twitter and Facebook (Wallenstein 2014).

Complemented by the enthusiastic critical reception, *Orange*'s novelty feature, namely, the focus on diverse femininities in an hour-long episode format and in a tone deemed unusual for female-centered narration, contributed to Netflix's hyped status as exceptional in the saturated quality television market. While *House of Cards* fit into the quality paradigm with its antihero male protagonist, goal-oriented narrative, milieu of national politics, polished aesthetics, promotional reliance on Kevin Spacey's name recognition as top-billed star, and the evocation of literary qualities ("Shakespearean" was a moniker mobilized by both the program and critical reception), *Orange* did not display these familiar signifiers of aesthetic superiority. Netflix promoted the program as subversive precisely through this contrast. It highlighted the unprecedented focus on multiple female subjectivities using a rhetoric of social realism and political critique associated with the prison setting and the show's dramatization of race, class, and sexual identity politics, without relying on the name recognition of cast members. Feminine address, representational politics, and social awareness were the signifiers that singled out the series in prestige television (Jenner 2018, 173–74).

Consider a promotional article commissioned by Netflix in 2014 on the *New York Times* website. The essay was timed to coincide with the series' season 2 launch and mimicked the format of investigative journalism that addresses institutional issues of women's incarceration in the United States (Deziel, n.d.). For a piece of native advertising, the most conspicuous thing about the article is its obfuscation about the show it sells: *Orange* and Netflix are mentioned only once in the lengthy piece, name-dropped once with ostensibly no promotional intent. This and a small banner on top of the page are the only hints that this article is a sponsored advertisement. The writing style applies techniques that are characteristic of investigative reporting to put forward its argument about women's incarceration, combining human interest stories with analyses of policies and statistics. Considered by marketing experts as the debut of a new type of multimedia campaign strategy (Moses 2014), this advertisement places the series in the context of a politically and socially argumentative journalistic tradition associated with a prestige newspaper and highlights the aspect of the series that mobilizes social awareness rhetoric to increase viewer interest.[4]

Promoting *Orange* as female-centered, politically subversive entertainment complements other aspects of Netflix's branding policies, most characteristically its popularization of online binge-watching culture, termed the Netflix effect by Sidneyeve Matrix (2014). Her examination of Netflix's promotion of binge viewing embeds this in young consumers' (or "screenagers") uses of digital media platforms. Matrix challenges media discourses that position binge watching as problematic youth consumership because of its associations with physical and mental passivity ("couch potato culture") and exposure to inappropriate (mature) content. Contesting the historically familiar moral panic through audience research, Matrix demonstrates a "participatory cultural citizenship" among millennial audiences who use social media (134).

Binge-watching culture and its promotion by Netflix have become a key focus of what we can call Netflix scholarship (e.g., McDonald and Smith-Rowsey 2016; Jenner 2018; Broe 2019), including the term's changing gendered associations. Because *binge* etymologically originates in describing excessive drink and food consumption, it "suggests some form of shameful indulgence, and a lack of control" (Ramsay 2013), whether describing drunkenness, eating disorders, or compulsive shopping. Couched in discourses about excess consumption, *binge* evokes twentieth-century thinkers' critique of late modern capitalism, which for feminist scholars (Petro 1986; Joyrich 1996; Brunsdon 1997) betrayed a gendered understanding of consumerism (feminine passivity, uncontrollability, indulgence, short attention span). Without engaging with gendered implications of the initial cultural distrust of binge watching, Debra Ramsay (2013) evokes these earlier

---

4 Promotional methods highlighting *Orange*'s social and political relevance started to become dominant only around the launch of season 2, that is, *after* audience and critical buzz hailed *Orange* as a novel text of women's representation. For more on how *Orange*'s promotional strategies capitalize on issues that the series problematizes, see DeCarvalho and Cox (2016).

discussions about gender and hierarchal cultural values applied to disparate media, highlighting that the intensive consumption of literature or classical music is never called bingeing, because these art forms have higher cultural currency than television.

Jenner (2016) argues that binge-watching culture derives from DVD box-set culture, which is associated more with cult television and a "valorization . . . of . . . texts as symbolically bounded and isolatable 'objects' of value" (Hills, quoted in Jenner 2016, 265). Here the operative term of consumption is "marathon viewing," a more respectful description of watching multiple episodes of a series, as Ramsay notes. To return to Matrix's analysis of surveys among teen audiences, the binaries she pinpoints fit into these oppositional hierarchies of media consumption practices. She exemplifies notions of a "mediated culture of instant gratification" (the online availability of a program's entire seasons) and "guilty pleasure" viewing with a quote from a teenage girl who admits to "eat[ing] that sappy teen drama up like it's my Grandma's spaghetti" (Matrix 2014, 130), which Matrix counters with "active" fan practices such as criticism and interpretation (133). The derision toward *binge* that Matrix describes is reminiscent of the terms mobilized by A. O. Scott's (2014) apocalyptic vision of grown-up culture's demise: Because Scott's influential think piece directly links generation with gender politics, it is safe to assume that Scott would have shared the worried rhetoric around binge watching as a feature of the increasing dominance of an "immature," feminized mediasphere.

When Netflix incorporated binge watching into its brand identity as the preferred mode of audience engagement, it simultaneously strove to upset the existing implications of a lazy consumption culture. The role it assigned to *Orange* as purveyor of this effort and its address to young female audiences speak to the company's recognition of the binge phenomenon's underlying genderedness. *Orange*'s quality moniker was generated around the text's socially aware epistemology, which in turn engendered viewer engagement practices that were aimed at challenging notions of a feminized, passive, infantilized viewer culture. These dynamics coalesce around binge watching, the cultural meanings of which Netflix keeps under tight control: The company markets its products as "instant gratification" and escapism while also tactically upsetting this by simultaneously promoting *Orange*'s political realness.

As Netflix maneuvered its entrance into the quality television business by means of controversial distribution and consumption practices and *Orange*'s gendered subversions, difficulties of categorization emerged in the program's other attributes as well. As noted, this surfaced poignantly in the nomination process for the Emmy Awards. *Orange*'s form as a mixture of drama and comedy with hour-long episodes, evidently clashing with expectations of a female-centered address, confused the industry's categorization models that undergird evaluation. Yet another aspect of *Orange*'s putative iconoclasm involving a gendered assessment of its merits was Netflix itself marginalizing the series on its online interface as female-targeted entertainment. Sarah Arnold (2016) calls this Netflix "ghettoizing" both the strong-female-lead-type subgenre and the targeted audience demographic (56–57). Arnold challenges Netflix's supposed liberation of the viewer from scheduled broadcasting traditions—itself accused of imposing ideals of taste and cultural value—by showing how its personalized recommendation system imposes gendered and raced viewer identities that are determined by an algorithmic analysis that creates genre subcategories based on the user's viewing history. Arnold demonstrates this by noting that the recommendation system suggests programs categorized under the header "strong female lead" once the viewer has finished watching *Orange*, whereas "similar tags do not exist for whiteness . . . or maleness" (57). This undermines appeals to scientific objectivity in the algorithmic method's personalization system, highlighting that Netflix's gender- and race-coded address stems from the social audience's demographic categorizations. Netflix's production of a "ghettoized" female audience as one homogeneous taste group betrays its unease in positioning *Orange* as the figurehead of the company's novel programming and business model, which originated in the choice of packaging these as feminized configurations of cultural value.

Even though *Orange* is considered one of Netflix's signature series, it nevertheless carries the moniker "female-centered" in a way that, though capitalized on for its iconoclasm, also encapsulates anxieties about how and to whom it is marketed. This is evident in the series' media reception, which celebrates *Orange* for its representational politics and for catapulting Netflix into the quality TV market; it is "a bull's-eye with the sort of premium-cable space the distributor is eager to carve out with its original efforts" (Lowry 2013). In their praise, media discourses frequently discuss the assumed problem of *Orange*'s female-centered address, evidenced in articles aimed to convince male audiences to watch the series. For instance, both Dockterman (2014) and Outlaw (2013) argue for the series' accessibility to male audiences by highlighting features that help situate it in discourses about prestige drama, either by comparing it to HBO's prison drama *Oz* (1997–2003;

Dockterman 2014) or by the reassurance "This is no *Sex in* [sic] *the City* fashion show" (Outlaw 2013). These examples demonstrate yet again the discursive connection between aesthetic evaluation practices and a gendered address in the quality discourse.

Again, the specific feminization strategy in the quality category—women in central roles and dramatizations of gender politics—is a site of tensions, inscribed onto questions of established generic, aesthetic, and narrative conventions. Similar to the other programs I examine, much of *Orange's* notoriety as something other than its peers is predicated on its textual-discursive upsetting of these conventions, which follow from the politicized centrality of women and their allocated televisual spaces. As seen in the cases of *30 Rock* (women's sitcom, comedian comedy, satire), *Parks and Recreation* (women's sitcom, comedian comedy, mockumentary), and *The Good Wife* (melodrama, political drama, legal drama), this female presence disturbs the masculine-coded format's genre signifiers, and this disturbance becomes a problematized focus both of the text and its paratexts. For *Orange*, contestations over the show's cultural position and its decoding revolve around the dubiousness of situating its female-centered themes in a dramedy format that has hour-long episodes instead of the tried-and-tested half-hour length of female-targeted quality programming.

As discussed in chapter 1, the form I call postfeminist dramedy developed by the end of the 1990s as a female-targeted televisual template of mediating changing gender scripts. Popularized by its urtext *Sex and the City*, this is also the format in which the tonal mixture of blue comedy and melodrama allows for transgressively thematizing changing sexual mores. Although Showtime's replication of the format did not necessarily involve themes of risqué sexuality à la *Sex and the City*, shows such as *Nurse Jackie*, *Weeds*, *The Big C*, and HBO's *Enlightened* and *Girls* still use the template to explore female subjectivities whose portrayal clashes with assumed norms of white middle-class femininity. For *Girls*, the most culturally resonant of these series, the generational and tonal updating of the *Sex and the City* formula similarly offers a politically committed focus on female subjectivity (for a comparison between the two series, see Winch [2013]). In addition, the program's and media critics' focus on central star Lena Dunham's body as both anatomically transgressive and sexual agent also drives home the point that female transgression is the issue at stake here. Individualized idiosyncratic femininity is thus the common operative description that determines these programs' generic-aesthetic properties as half-hour dramedies. Although genre hybridity is an expected trait for expressing such transgressions in quality television, the half-hour format's predominance speaks to an assumed closeness of these themes to the comic mode. The half-hour length is historically associated with the sitcom, a legacy that may have been upset with the dawn of convergence-era television and its generic hybrids, but the ubiquity of the female-centered half-hour dramedy reveals a tight link between gendered address and a long-standing format paradigm.

The discussed controversies around the 2015 Emmy nomination process indicate as much, with the Television Academy codifying the connection between episode length and genre, paradoxically in an effort to address the increased hybridity of television genres. The task of the new category system was to eliminate the issue of genre precisely for its contemporary elusiveness, using episode length instead as a presumably more objective classificatory method. Thus, when media debates translated the decision back into genre terms, this illuminated the continued hold of the tight link between genre and episode length, betraying taste hierarchies. The decision tied fixed generic descriptors to series such as *Orange* whose pioneering status revolved around their mixed tone and hour-long episode length (Viruet 2015). That cultural hierarchies between drama and comedy governed tensions around the new nomination process surfaced in critical agreement that the drama category was more competitive than the comedy category, which Viruet (2015) also mentions in discussing *Orange*. When the Television Academy panel ruled that only *Orange* had to compete in the hour-long (i.e., drama) category out of those series that petitioned for the half-hour (i.e., comedy) category, not only did this telegraph industry confusion over the program's generic standing—the Screen Actors Guild Awards and the Golden Globe Awards both continued to nominate *Orange* as a comedy—it also diminished its chances for winning the Emmy, the most coveted award in the industry. In the drama category *Orange* counted as an outlier that was too light to compete with dark prestige dramas, among them *House of Cards*.[5]

---

5 One of the reasons that Netflix preferred *Orange*'s classification as a comedy was to avoid awards competition with *House of Cards*, its other prominent nominated series (Viruet 2015). This again shows a strategic split linked to gendered generic address and marketability that governed the company's choice of its pair of signature series.

The promotion of *Orange* also favors the comedy description, evidenced in a tongue-in-cheek tweet on *Orange*'s official Twitter account reacting to the ruling. The post reads, "Drama Category? We got this . . ." and includes an embedded video showing a season 1 scene in which fan favorite character Suzanne "Crazy Eyes" Warren (Uzo Aduba) comically recites a monologue from *Coriolanus*.[6] The choice of scene is characteristic of the series' self-promotion as generically subversive, here through tweaking the meaning of *Shakespearean*, a term frequently applied to male-centered prestige dramas (including *House of Cards*). The tweet plays with the series' slippery position as a mixture of drama and comedy interpreted as transgressive. The choice of character is also significant: Suzanne is a popular Black female character who functions as a tragicomic jester figure, quoting tragedy Shakespeare in a comic scene; further, Aduba is, as frequently highlighted in media commentary, only the second actor after Ed Asner to have won Emmy awards for the same role in both the comedy and drama categories (Donnelly 2015).[7]

Relative lack of industry awards and discourses about them were pivotal sites on which *Orange*'s treatment of gender, genre, and cultural value were publicly negotiated and considered problematic to reconcile with existing paradigms. If *Orange*'s attraction as quality TV lies in its politicized examination of the U.S. prison industrial system and women's incarceration by focusing on individualized stories of diverse womanhood, this topic sits uncomfortably in the hour-long comedy/drama format per industry judgment. Emmy nomination controversies suggest that *Orange*'s episodes either need to be a half-hour long to secure a familiar generic position or need to lose the comic tone (tied to nonnormative womanhood) to be considered drama.

Issues of tone connected to a gendered focus are also the subject of Emily Nussbaum's (2015) analysis and advocacy of the series, and given Nussbaum's prominence in American TV criticism, it is worth examining in depth how she articulates this. Nussbaum's article is especially relevant for

---

6 https://twitter.com/OITNB/status/578981803748237313.

7 The difference between Aduba's and Asner's wins, overlooked by the commentators, is that Asner's wins for the role of Lou Grant in two different generic categories were due to the fact that he was nominated for two, generically different programs, *The Mary Tyler Moore Show* and *Lou Grant*. In chapter 1 I examined this character's prominence in MTM's two prestigious series and how it exemplifies the quality discourse's historic development in terms of genre and gender. In contrast, Aduba won for the same series in 2014 and 2015.

my argument because it compares *Orange*'s cultural work with acclaimed prestige drama *Show Me a Hero* (2015), an HBO miniseries produced by celebrated TV auteur David Simon. In many aspects that are similar to Simon's earlier series *The Wire* and *Treme* (2010–2013), the miniseries exemplifies the ideal of a complex TV drama, providing a point of reference for unpacking issues of tone, gender, and cultural value for Nussbaum.

Recounting the story of a housing desegregation scandal in the city of Yonkers, New York, in the late 1980s, *Show Me a Hero* is the quintessential authorly text, conceived in Simon's politically argumentative approach to discuss race and/as social class in America, expressed in documentarist aesthetics. Nussbaum (2015) argues that the "social issue" interest of Simon's work, "with plots torn not from the headlines but from the op-ed page,"[8] might form a key part of Simon's auteur status, but this approach is not that exceptional in television: It is prevalent in less respected forms such as "comedies, shows aimed at women and teens," of which she calls *Orange* "the most striking example." Nussbaum's argument recalls historic notions of television's political and social responsibility to reflect reality, steeped in the medium's assumed immediacy. But postmillennial trends shift cultural value onto aesthetic-narrative complexity, whereas television's traditional pursuit of political realism is refocused onto less revered programming that foregrounds diversity rhetoric and/or female presence, exemplified in *How to Get Away with Murder*'s Annalise Keating. The basis on which Nussbaum compares *Show Me a Hero* and *Orange* is a shared appeal to political advocacy, or a "mission to educate and to illuminate." The difference in their critical evaluation and categorization lies in their gendered governance of generic-aesthetic address: *Show Me a Hero* displays signifiers of quality drama, that is, "realism, male protagonists, big-name Hollywood directors," whereas *Orange* has a "tonally perverse" genre hybridity that leaves the TV Academy puzzled (Nussbaum 2015).

Nussbaum (2015) describes the two series' different aesthetics in the "realistic drama" versus "vaudevillian comedy/drama" dualism, but there is an even more demonstrative difference between their expressive modes tied to gendered traditions that goes unmentioned. As part of their efforts to narrativize political advocacy, both series use raced and classed femininities inscribed with political meanings. Nussbaum (2015) notes that the inmates of Litchfield "are demographic cousins of the women on *Show Me a Hero*,"

---

8   Shades of Netflix's native advertisement in the *New York Times*.

the difference being that *Orange*'s portrayals are "blown up, not life-size" representations. But *Show Me a Hero*'s reputation is not tied to centralizing previously neglected *femininities*; instead, it is the series' treatment of race and class as sites of social tensions that critics herald in its subject matter. Yet its storytelling allocates fixed gendered and generic codes to narrative strands to make its socially conscious argument, an aspect that remains unexamined in critical reception. The plotting structure repeats methods that Simon used in earlier series by employing parallel story lines about characters representing different social strata, producing a tableau of a community observed in its complexity. The central story of Yonkers mayor Nick Wasicsko (Oscar Isaacs), who is battling local government to get new low-income housing built in white middle-class neighborhoods, is contrasted with microstories of Black and Latina *women* living in the projects, functioning as illustrations of the lived realities of racially segregated communities that politicians argue about in the abstract. The multiple-focus feature of *The Wire* and *Treme* is here separated along gendered lines: Wasicsko's privileged white masculinity pitted against multiple victimized and raced femininities.

Show Me a Hero thus works out race and class issues by means of a gendering that informs aesthetic modes allocated to these multiple story lines: Wasicsko's story uses codes of tragedy, whereas the women's stories operate in the melodramatic mode. Simon's earlier work frequently uses melodrama, but as Linda Williams's (2014) analysis of *The Wire* demonstrates, both that series and its producer's comments struggle to shake off associations with the genre. Williams's reconsidered concept of melodrama helps her ameliorate this tension, as she posits that melodrama at its core is not about feminized excess but about powerless individuals' struggles against fate.[9] But Williams also proposes that some story lines of *The Wire* do exhibit features of classic tragedy, particularly in Stringer Bell (Idris Elba) and Frank Sobotka's (Chris Bauer) stories as "important members of their community who try to make change but when fate overcomes them, they accept it," while recognizing the system's oppressive nature (103). For Williams the crucial difference between melodrama and tragedy lies in the protagonists' differing relation to justice, fate, recognition, and victimhood: *The Wire* is ultimately an "institutional melodrama" in its rage against an unjust social system, presenting stories of

---

9   Jason Mittell (2015, 233–60) incorporates this definition into his concept of "complex" serial television to prove the paradigm's political progressiveness and to fend off accusations of its "masculinism." See chapter 6.

socially vulnerable individuals who are defenseless against and even unaware of a "predetermined fate" (104). These are in contrast to Bell and Sobotka's *tragic* stories, yet these stories are embedded in "a larger melodrama that seeks justice and that is governed by the outrage that so little justice exists for the poor and the black" (104).

A similar generic struggle characterizes the multiple story lines of *Show Me a Hero*, clearly delineated between Wasicsko's central narrative and the victimized Black and Latina women's parallel, cumulative microstories. The title openly communicates the discursive intent to interpret *his* story as tragedy. Coming from the F. Scott Fitzgerald quote "Show me a hero and I'll write you a tragedy," the text makes this literary reference explicit through a character's utterance. The generic struggle is telegraphed by the text itself, complementing Simon's own struggles to associate his oeuvre with this genre to signal its political-aesthetic superiority. And Wasicsko's story *can* be interpreted by means of Williams's concept, making him a prototypical tragic hero in his attempts to change fate (hubris), in his "tragic knowledge," that is, his recognition of the full picture's significance (Williams 2014, 104), and in his acceptance of his struggles' failure through suicide. The series negotiates a portrayal of the tragic hero's exceptionalism and institutional melodrama's concerns. Unlike *The Wire*, however, it inflates the tragic hero's narrative importance: Nussbaum (2015) finds that the women's stories suffer from a "peripheral quality." This negotiation between tragedy and institutional melodrama displays clear gendered oppositions, a feature not this prominent in Simon's earlier work—Williams (2014) remarks that *The Wire* exhibits a "hard dominant masculinity" and misogyny (161), arguing that this institutional melodrama inscribes its political argument exclusively onto stories of men. When *Show Me a Hero* uses raced female suffering to articulate its meanings, it does so by simultaneously inflating the male hero's individual tragedy in a more pronounced way than *The Wire*.

To return to Nussbaum's (2015) piece, her comparison not only highlights oppositional tonal and gendered strategies tied to the two "educational" quality texts but also points to a specific generic function of racially minoritized womanhood. In the contrast between these two texts, *Orange*'s iconoclasm emerges from its outrageously comic tone and sexual explicitness, making it inappropriate for classification as authentic message drama: "With its scenes of shower sex, [the series] has got the side eye from those who prefer their prison politics straight, so to speak" (Nussbaum 2015). Yet recall McHugh's (2015) analysis of *Orange*'s title sequence highlighting a documentary realism that may well be regarded as an aesthetic signifier of a straight(forward) politics. "Realism" becomes a key word in paratextual promotion as well, witnessed in series creator Jenji Kohan's statements about *Orange*'s mixed tone: "Dramas that are only dramatic are a lie, because life isn't just a drama and if you're reflecting reality, part of it should be humorous. When you have just a dry hour, I don't think it's reality" (Fienberg 2013). For an hour-long series, realism as an aesthetic mode to exhibit social awareness becomes especially fraught with definitional tensions when it comes to centralized raced femininities. In *Show Me a Hero* prestige drama's educational ambition places racially minoritized women in sidelined melodrama contexts as narrative support to the male hero's tragedy, cumulatively producing the social realism intent. In *Orange*, reversing the narrative focus results in a discursive realism that embraces grotesque and sexually explicit comedy. On the one hand, this helps to promote the series in an existing female-centered generic paradigm—the half-hour dramedy with which Kohan herself is associated through her work on *Weeds*. On the other hand, this strategy clashes with traditions of allocating high cultural value in quality drama discourses, as *Show Me a Hero*'s generic-aesthetic negotiations demonstrate. These tensions ultimately stem from the uncertain location of socially and racially marginalized femininities in quality television's generic traditions: If their centralized presence signifies political progressiveness—that is, a serious message as benchmark of cultural worth—it is also entrapped in the struggles over how their specific realism can be channeled and at what cost to cultural value.

6

FEMALE-CENTERED PRESTIGE DRAMA AND (POST)FEMINISM

"STRONG FEMALE CHARACTER" TO THE RESCUE

In chapter 3 I argued that the foregrounded gender politics in *30 Rock*'s and *Parks and Recreation*'s "comedy of distinction" produced an acute nervousness in media discourses about these series' interpretation, which surfaced in their competitive comparisons. Simultaneously, critical debates inscribed the gender politics of Tina Fey's and Amy Poehler's respective comedies onto their discursively feminist star personas. The journalistic questions of who and which series is the better feminist originated from the comedy genre's specifics; comedian comedy's transparency between discursive author and performed alter ego invites this condensation of attributed meanings onto the comedian. The twenty-first-century popularity of feminist-identified female *comedians* in American television demonstrates that the comedy form is well suited to configuring its cultural significance as political meaning. This owes to its status as a relatively low genre, the entangled relationship between authorship and performance, and the assumed tension between its aesthetic aim (funniness) and feminism's serious political aim. In short, the two comedies' status as quality television hinges on their modes of engagement with feminist politics, concentrated onto their central performers' celebrity personas.

If these comedies' cultural significance involves the ambiguous critical interpretation of their textually emphasized gender politics, then this is in contrast to the interpretation of hour-long female-centered dramas in critical debates. Rather than centering on notions of an adequate feminism, critical and industry discourses reveal more confusion about the appropriate forms and programming contexts of *The Good Wife* and *Orange Is the*

New Black. This is not to say that gender politics do not feature in their evaluations; but the way these two series upset the perceived norms of quality television surfaces primarily in critical and institutional unease about their aesthetic-generic positioning. I also do not imply that genre is not a contested issue for *30 Rock* and *Parks*, because the two comedies undoubtedly struggled to situate themselves in gendered comedy traditions. But they are still firmly positioned as quality comedies in critical evaluations; the two dramas, however, though critically acclaimed, occupy more contested generic spaces. As shown, *The Good Wife* straddles the hierarchal expressive modes of network and cable television and also struggles to shed the taint of melodrama and the "ladies' empowerment procedural" label (Nussbaum 2014). *Orange* upsets both the half-hour dramedy formula and the sincere tone of so-called message drama, resulting in award season controversies. All four case studies are objects of critical and institutional contestations that originated in their foregrounded gender politics, but for the hour-long series this primarily revolves around how to place them in genre categories and programming contexts.

The programs' treatment of the relationship between postfeminism and feminism derives from genre traditions too, namely, from the postfeminist dramedy's influence on the four series (and other female-centered programming) as their immediate ideological precursor. A. O. Scott's discussed rhetorical link between feminism and immature culture's twenty-first-century triumph emphasizes *Sex and the City*'s significance for American culture's gender politics: Scott (2014) calls the program "in retrospect the most influential television series of the early 21st century," responsible for the ubiquity of female-centered half-hour dramedies and comedies. But Scott avoids mentioning female-centered prestige *drama*. Comedies appear to be traceable back to the millennial half-hour dramedy and gain cultural significance on this basis; but this lineage is less easy to establish for hour-long series. The critical and institutional unease with the discussed series' generic categorization partly originates in their contested relationship to this formula. The choice to narrativize female subjectivity using putatively sophisticated and masculine-coded drama rather than half-hour dramedy formats creates this unease and relative marginality. Moreover, the two comedies both use opportunities to reference historic predecessors (female-led sitcoms) to establish generic validation, which is a less viable avenue for female-centered prestige drama because of the form's scarcity in American TV history. For the comedies, genre provides a reliable framework, and it is rather the specific insertion of gender politics into it that incites critical debates; female-led drama has no such framework to fall back on, evidenced in the discussed ambiguities of genre categorization.

While form is a contested issue for *The Good Wife* and *Orange* in critical discourses, there is more consensus about their significance as politically novel programming, an agreement that derives from their categorization predicated on the strong or complex female lead trope. The phenomenon variously called feminist or female-centered quality programming, in which female protagonists' narrative centrality signifies feminism, lends programs the aura of political novelty and thus quality. It is this category into which *The Good Wife* and *Orange* fit unequivocally and through which their cultural value is most recognized (O'Keeffe 2014; Blay 2015). Because of the category's defining aspect—the centrality of a type of fictional figure—issues of genre and expressive modes are not a priority for this discourse, apart from celebrating the breadth of genres and subgenres in which the female lead is present (O'Keeffe 2014; Blay 2015).

The complex female lead, then, is indeed a complex figure inasmuch as several ideological and aesthetic presuppositions converge in her cultural status. As a symbol of a triumphant feminism and diversity on television, she accounts for a representational realism that lends programs novelty value. This figure provides proof for critics that the white masculinist paradigm of quality television has been overcome; if Annalise Keating is a female Walter White, then this makes *How to Get Away with Murder* a *Breaking Bad* for (Black) women (O'Keeffe 2014). The strong female character's signifying power outranks issues of generic and aesthetic positioning and becomes the main carrier of prestige. In a presumed evolutionary trajectory, she is charged with a responsibility to represent various previously marginalized identity formations. This ascription of political progressiveness thus follows a trajectory that in feminist scholarship's terms is described as struggling to overcome postfeminist representational traditions to embrace intersectional feminism. Amanda Lotz (2007, 2014) applies this logic to some extent. Her optimism about television's increasing engagement with feminist representational ideals feeds into her work on prestige cable television's development and corresponds to media critics' reliance on the strong female character as proof of this progression narrative. Symptomatically, O'Keeffe's (2014) article about the "TV renaissance for strong women" includes quotes from Lotz to lend academic authority to its argument, but O'Keeffe evades issues of generic-aesthetic practices and their value hierarchies in his rhetoric about political innovation.

The understanding of the strong female character as purveyor of feminism is also prominent in scholarship that primarily engages with quality television as an *aesthetic* object, an approach dominant in Jason Mittell's influential book *Complex TV* (2015a). Given the broad academic influence of Mittell's concept, its implications for the issue of feminism and postfeminism in quality TV, and the fact that his work provides insight into scholars' ideological divide about the quality TV category and its relationship to gender politics, in the following discussion I engage with the concept at some length.

Mittell looks at the specifics of the "narrative complexity" phenomenon, a term coined for his earlier article on the subject (2006). As such, this examination concentrates on the aesthetics, or as he calls it, *poetics*, of storytelling in convergence-era television, building on literary theory and film studies models. He contrasts this approach with the analytic focus on the *politics* of television by describing a transition in television scholarship since the 1990s away from a primary interest in issues of representation, political economy, and identity (i.e., politics). This development has led to what Lury (2016) calls the "aesthetic turn" (120): scholarly preference for examining how television texts express aesthetic innovations, or poetics (Mittell 2015a, 3–4).

Mittell (2015a, 206–32) advocates against an excessive scholarly focus on quality TV's problematic nature; for him, this is an unproductive dead end because it shuts down possibilities of evaluation based on aesthetic achievements. Instead, he proposes the description "complex TV," which for him does not imply evaluative hierarchy but an apolitical designation of a narrative trend. His argument thus attempts to mediate across the aesthetic-political divide in television scholarship (see Zborowski 2016). Nonetheless, Mittell agrees with Sudeep Dasgupta (2012), who advocates for shunning Bourdieusian critical concepts about quality TV and quality audiences. Dasgupta finds it a patronizing, elitist position from academics such as Newman and Levine, Jane Feuer, or Michael Kackman to assume a direct correlation between "the people" (social audiences) in need of ideological defense and the TV texts they presumably consume. The debate forms along the lines of poetics versus politics in television scholarship, similar to the discipline's earlier periods, and Mittell's intervention intends to shun this framework of "quality" versus "antilegitimation" discourses by "return[ing] to questions of aesthetics and value to open up the possibilities of evaluative criticism of popular arts" (Mittell 2015a, 215).[1]

---

1   For more on the debate, see Nannicelli (2016), Logan (2016), and Piper (2016).

It is significant that Mittell's endeavor to offer a pure aesthetic evaluation of television texts devoid of ideological complications relies on political (i.e., gendered) interpretation in one particular area: genre and expressive mode. The "Serial Melodrama" chapter (Mittell 2015a, 233–60), on genre hybridity, explores the predominant use of melodrama in complex narratives. Mittell engages with melodrama's cultural standing as excessively feminine, stating that he used to refute the view that melodrama had any influence on complex serial drama with the latter's "intellectual seriousness, measured production style, and claims to authenticity and realism" (244). It was Linda Williams's (2014) argument that changed this position. The "engaging emotional response to *feel* the difference between competing moral sides as manifested through forward-moving storytelling" (Mittell 2015a, 244; italics in original) originates for Mittell in Williams's argument that melodrama's defining feature is not in gendered excess but in the construction of moral oppositions. It is thus through Williams's analytical framework that this intellectual and affective appreciation of complex texts gains academic validation, such that having a "good cry" over *The Wire*'s pathos is a nongendered reaction and also disproves claims that the program is deeply masculinist (248).

Although Mittell embraces melodrama's ubiquity in prestige drama through Williams's analysis, he also sets out to disprove the widespread agreement in TV theory that complex drama's formal aspects derive from soap opera. He supports this with a detailed investigation of the different historic production models and textual characteristics of American day-time soaps and prime-time dramas, concluding that in lieu of any formal or production background link between the two, there is no evidence that "contemporary serials 'masculinize' the soap opera form" (Mittell 2015a, 248). Rather, it is the melodramatic mode that informs television storytell-ing, and "the pervasive spread of serial melodrama has added an effeminate layer to traditionally masculinist genres such as crime dramas, espionage thrillers, and science fiction" (248). Mittell sees in this gendered genre mix-ing a politically progressive potential that breaks down gendered barriers of televisual traditions and viewing experiences (see Fiske 2011), such that melodrama, an "effeminate" mode, pervades television, effecting that tradi-tionally masculinist genres can accommodate female protagonists.

Mittell's example for this new accommodation is *The Good Wife*, whose narrative operation he sees as "complicating its gendered appeals" by mixing serialized and procedural narration through Alicia, "merging the familial, professional, romantic, and political, often within a single story thread, and exploring how these threads connect with the emotional and rational choices of its female protagonist" (Mittell 2015a, 258). Mittell celebrates the series for a feminist progressivism that derives from its aesthetic-generic choices; as such, the complex female character carries an *ideological* import here, the meaning of which is firmly located in gender politics. This is clear from the figure's centrality to the issue of genre mixing in complex TV's development, whose importance Mittell links to a feminist appeal. As such, complex TV's putatively nonideological, purely aesthetic examination relies on a biologically essentialist interpretation of gender to apply a narrative of genre progression and democratization.

> Male viewers weep at the sentimental melodrama of *Friday Night Lights* or *Lost*, female fans celebrate female power and analytic intelligence featured on *Alias* or *Veronica Mars*, and all viewers feel the affective interconnections of *The Good Wife's* personal and professional realms—such viewing experiences problematize strict gender dichotomies, offering sites of fluidity and empathy, however imperfect and partial, that seem consistent with feminist critiques of gender norms. (Mittell 2015a, 259–60)

Mittell's advocacy for redirecting academic focus on pure poetics becomes sidetracked around the theorization of genre hybridity, for which he relies on an appeal to progressive gender politics; in addition, he applies a selection of feminist theories tailored to boost his argument. This sabotages the claim of nonideological engagement, because the investigation's rhetoric glosses over an ideological (gender) bias masked as a focus on aesthetics. He mobilizes the complex female character as an ideological term to support complex television's meaning as an aesthetic term, laying bare complexity's (like quality's) own ideologically founded nature.

In the following discussion I briefly develop two intertwined areas, missing from Mittell's account, that are vital to an approach considering gender politics in television genre theory: the historic presence of feminism on television and cultural signifying processes that affect questions of genre. First, feminism's historic presence in television, a crucial area in feminist scholarship for discussing notions of progression and co-option, needs to be accounted for. As discussed, the postfeminism versus feminism issue had had a structuring importance for the field even before postmillennial quality television emerged. Declaring that all of complex TV's genre mixing is progressively feminist, as Mittell does, and invoking a fitting selection of feminist theories to do so misappropriates this scholarship's academic significance. The effort to demonstrate an aesthetic evolution putatively devoid of ideological implications relies on invoking political debates (about gender) to chart this evolution. The deployment of this methodology exclusively in the discussion of genre correlates to industry and critical contestations about the discussed series' genre categorizations and illuminates again that for serialized drama, aesthetic evaluations of genre are especially fraught with ideological implications around gender.

The other issue I raise relates to the cultural signifying processes that affect the contextual positioning of complex TV. Locating complex TV's narrative features outside the soap opera tradition dismisses this tradition's discursive dominance, and the view that "soapy" does not accurately describe a prime-time TV text avoids considerations not only of popular and industry uses of the term but also the fact that complex TV's aesthetics often explicitly rely on soap opera traditions. Indeed, *The Sopranos* has been analyzed for its textual and intertextual reflection on soap opera (Donatelli and Alward 2002); and journalistic think pieces about serialized drama's links to the form's narrative traditions and affect (e.g., Lyons 2015a) are products of a culturally ingrained chain of signification. Dismissing these phenomena undermines Mittell's own earlier analysis (2004) of genre as a cultural category produced in discursive formations operating in industry, audience, critical, and other cultural practices. This avoidance also leads to the deployment of Williams's concept of melodrama in Mittell's work in a way that ignores *her* earlier work's significance. Although Williams's more recent concept does demonstrate the melodramatic mode's ubiquity, it does not dismiss its cultural connotations as a bad object because of its centrality in female-targeted, female-centered entertainment but engages with this link's ideological implications.

The selective application of Williams's concept in Mittell's argument may serve to reconcile the melodramatic mode with complex TV by simultaneously removing connotations of suspicious femininities (such that crying over a male-centered drama becomes both the true appreciation of its complexity *and* proof of the text's feminist progressivism—these are acceptable femininities, then), recalling earlier academic contestations over the gendered meanings of television genres. Lynn Joyrich's (1996) scrutiny of cultural critics' engagement in the late 1980s and early 1990s with postmodernity and melodrama as television's prime expressive modes comes to mind (see chapter 1). Here I want to highlight Joyrich's critique of TV scholars, such as John Fiske, who claimed that male-oriented prestige TV dramas heralded progressive gender norms. That discussion is all the more relevant because Fiske's framing of historic television genres as polar opposites along gendered lines underpins Mittell's reasoning, to argue that complex TV's formal features progressively overwrite this setup (Mittell 2015a, 251). Joyrich (1996) is skeptical of Fiske's celebration of *Miami Vice*'s (1984–1990) "anarchic" self-liberation from "traditional meanings of gender by opening up the program to the postmodern pleasures of spectacle and style" (92), which for Fiske is "the ultimate political act" (cited in Joyrich 1996, 93). Her criticism highlights that Fiske's aesthetic analysis overlooks the social and ideological context in which the TV text is situated, concluding that

> the problem with this view [the purity of a nonideological plea-sure in style] lies not only in its reductive notion of ideology as a force which can simply be evaded or separated from pleasure and the formation of identity, but also in its misreading of the marketplace. . . . The same may be true of television's own repeated male displays: far from marking the end of gender and power divisions, TV's masquerades—a response to the discursive constructions that put television and its viewing subjects in their (feminized) place—contribute to these very disparities; indeed, the primary thing often masked in such male masquerades is the desire to be rid of femininity itself. (Joyrich 1996, 94–95)

Although Joyrich's criticism of both the TV texts and leading TV theorists' lopsided application of gender theory could be an eerily fitting rebuttal to Mittell's argument, my aim is not to reproduce it and refute Mittell's reading of complex television as progressively feminist. After all, my own reading of *The Good Wife* argues that the female character's centralization is fundamental to mixing television forms in ways that upset these forms' gendered meanings. Instead, my aim is to show that their emergence and contestations around cultural value continue to rely on gendered hierarchies, which are inseparable from the cultural purchase of the postfeminism-feminism debate. The reliance on a progressive feminism framework that we have seen in Mittell's argument about recombined television forms' aesthetic novelty points to this inseparability. But the putatively poetics-only approach renders TV texts' explicit negotiation of genre hierarchies' genderedness invisible, such as *The Good Wife*'s struggles with melodrama and its connotations of a suspicious feminine excess and the program's ambiguous standing in industry and critical discourses. Mittell's definition of melodrama works to limit the question of ideological and cultural context to an argument about gendered progression linked to aesthetic innovation.

Indeed, these considerations are not broadsides aimed at Mittell but a demonstration of a position and methodology that are representative of broader trends in television scholarship, historically divided along the lines of the poetics-politics approach; but the feminist quality television phenomenon has thrown this trajectory into even sharper relief. Fiske's analysis of postmodern TV genres strove to prove aesthetic innovation linked to progressive gender politics in an era when television was still viewed as aesthetically dubious. Joyrich's rebuttal to Fiske and other critics readjusted the focus, stressing that examining TV texts' political-ideological work is not an elective supplement to charting aesthetic developments but is intrinsic to understanding them. The problematic nature of this academic divide is even more pronounced in postmillennial prestige television, precisely because, as will be shown through the analyses, a significant segment of serial dramas are products of the aforementioned discursive struggles between postfeminism and popular feminism. Although this popular cultural contestation's visibility is undoubted in feminist scholarship, its notable absence from academic studies of quality or complex television suggests feminist literature's invisibility in the wider field. The cultural position of *The Good Wife* and *Orange Is the New Black* as exceptional in and for their programming contexts is embedded in promotionally and textually foregrounded gender politics, moving them to the center of feminist scholarship's analytical attention. Outside this field, the two series are considered mainly if the ideological context, like prestige drama's contested genderedness, requires it. This helps sustain the gendered split of the poetics-politics divide present in television culture and reproduced in scholarship.

Both *The Good Wife* and *Orange* represent the ways in which prestige drama centralizes contested gender politics, projected onto issues of genre categorization. This is evident in industry and media focus on the two programs' aesthetic volatility and contradictoriness and in accounts such as Mittell's, which frames the question of genre blending in a progressive gender politics using an isolated case study, an approach not dominant elsewhere in his book about narrative complexity. Such discussions rely on the strong or complex female lead for her fixed ideological importance that governs this programming's cultural novelty and complex genre treatment. Yet feminist theory shows that if this figure expresses complex female identity, then her ideological importance is not simply a putatively feminist influence on genre complexity but signals historic mediatized negotiations of the presence of feminist politics in popular culture. More specifically, she reflects the postfeminist cultural paradigm's changing context, problematized by means of the postrecessionary resurgence of a popular feminism and its contestations. Similar to the examined comedies, *30 Rock* and *Parks and Recreation*, which centralize these contestations in the relatively respected forms of satire and mockumentary, thus elevating this dialogue's discursive prestige, the examined hour-long series narrativize this politics in the high-end serial's framework. However, lending prestige to gender politics works more ambiguously here, coming to bear on negotiations of genre signifiers and testifying to the serialized drama form's especially fragile dependence on gendered (masculinist) ideals of cultural value.

"THE EDUCATION OF ALICIA FLORRICK": INSTITUTIONAL (POST)FEMINISM IN *THE GOOD WIFE*

The use of the complex or strong female lead in *The Good Wife* overlaps in her signification with the "independent woman" figure, a symbol in American culture of the achievements of the women's liberation movement and denoting an era's changing gender politics. A somewhat outmoded expression, the independent woman is still prevalent for narrativizing female identity in popular culture, especially television. This came to the fore in the four-part PBS documentary *America in Primetime* (2011), which focused on the evolution of different character types in American TV. The documentary's first episode, titled "Independent Woman," references *The Good Wife* extensively; as such, it provides useful insight into how American television's reflection on its own character type's evolution makes sense of the show's gender politics.

The episode charts the historic development of the independent woman figure from the postwar period across a variety of scripted programs and institutional contexts, making clear the industry's investment in signaling its influence on shifting ideas about gender politics in the United States. The narrative describes a progressive representational history that culminates in *The Good Wife*, supported by a curious structuring method: The otherwise historically linear narration opens with a detailed discussion of *The Good Wife* before moving on to its timeline's origin point, the postwar period's portrayal of the white middle-class housewife. After this, the documentary offers a whistle-stop tour of programming that corresponds to the narrative of growing female independence and character complexity, consistently linking this to contemporaneous American sociopolitical realities. For instance, footage of women's liberation movement rallies underlines *The Mary Tyler Moore Show*'s cultural importance. Magazine and newspaper clippings are used to illustrate gender discourses; the headlines in focus often highlight the word *feminist* in contexts of debate. *Roseanne* is discussed in relation to class difference and the realities of motherhood. *Sex and the City*'s appeal to women's sexual liberation is framed as a response to broadcast television's strict content regulations and its operation as a "business," as opposed to premium cable's putative freedom from these constraints.

Into this presentation of the independent woman's televisual history is blended the contemporary term *complex female character*. Whereas the independent woman evokes links with a historic and referential feminist politics, the complex female character focuses on individualized identity politics in fictional storytelling. In this context, singling out *The Good Wife* as the culmination of the independent woman's diachronic evolution—bookending the documentary's narrative, both outside linear history and as an endpoint to it—produces a slipperiness of the series' attributed meaning. That is, in interviews the creators and stars assert the program's political realism in referring to real-life political sex scandals[2] and invoke postfeminism's choice debates for the character's inception. At the same time, co-creators Robert and Michelle King frame this in a primary interest in ethical dilemmas of the sociopolitical world: Here, the celebration of female independence and the work-life balance discourse merge with the examination of the workplace as politicized space, complicating the independent woman trope. Michelle King says, "Alicia really is consistently trying to do the right thing, and it's just difficult because so much is being thrown at her." The documentary illustrates King's words with a scene from *The Good Wife* where Eli Gold tries to involve Alicia in a scheme to get rid of her workplace rival, Cary Agos (Matt Czuchry).

---

2 For more on this, see Leonard (2014b, 2016, 2018).

Viewers of the series can easily associate this with its general focus on political machinations within and outside Alicia's story line, providing both its viewing pleasures and critical approval. The producers interpret the independent woman figure in a way that foregrounds ethical and political dilemmas that complicate the meaning of progressive identity politics.

Here, the broader cultural work of *The Good Wife*, lauded for its critical take on institutional politics and law, comes into play. This aligns the series with the typical model of prestige television that reflects a public skepticism of these institutions, in series such as *House of Cards*, *Veep*, or producer David Simon's work. Because of the high cultural currency of this skepticism of institutions, associated with intellectual sophistication, *The Good Wife*'s focus on political scheming links it with this programming type. Yet the independent woman's centrality complicates both her meaning and the configuration of this political skepticism. That is, if this figure is associated with women's economic and psychological empowerment, then centering the narrative on her involves skepticism about the meaning of *this* character. As noted, the narrative often brings into play liberal feminism as a political force of organizational lobbying: In presenting political variables and influences, the series characterizes traditions of liberal feminism as one of the factors that put the independent woman heroine in a nexus of social power relations (T. C. Miller 2016). This emphasis on complicated social and political forces affecting the character creates the series' slippery meanings. The complexity of these forces provides its high cultural value, at the expense of the independent woman's ideological fixity as a sign of feminist progression: *The Good Wife*'s celebrated concentration on institutions and politics diverts the individualized identity politics toward an interest in the web of political power relations in spaces of American governance, law, and business. Yet the independent woman figure has crucial bearing on this interest for her centrality in popular culture's contestations of feminism and postfeminism.

The middle-class white woman is a preferred figure onto which popular culture tends to project ideas of shifting gender roles, from the postwar housewife to the postfeminist career woman. Feminist scholarship has shown how postfeminism imagines women's gain of (some) social power through *this* figure's successes, an image that by the 1990s had become ingrained in American cultural consciousness. This narrative of economic success and upward mobility contributed to the abandonment of feminist politics in the 1990s by a generation of young women. Lynn Spigel (1995) attributes this partly to television's role in promoting the idea of that present's "enlightened" gender scripts. In a survey project, Spigel interviewed American female college students about their notions of "women's progress" to see how television's canonized images inform these. She found that the medium's own perpetuated centrality to shaping popular memory through nostalgia shows contributed to students' unease with discussing feminism as a still relevant political factor. For these students, "television reruns and nostalgia shows might well have served the purpose of legitimation because they provide us with pictures of women whose lives were markedly less free than our own. . . . Faith in progress seemed to close off the need for a feminist movement in the present" (Spigel 1995, 27–28). Spigel's study shows how television's representational politics affected (some) young American women's interpretations of their own present's gender scripts in the 1990s. In retrospect, this is a symptomatic iteration of postfeminism's cultural work.

To the extent that what Spigel shows represents some of that period's dominant discourses affecting a generation of young educated women (dissociation from feminism, belief in gender progress), it is indicative that three of my case studies centralize fictional women who can be seen as part of this generation, now in their late thirties and early forties. Liz Lemon, Leslie Knope, and Alicia Florrick, the central characters of three network series about white women at the workplace, fall into an age bracket that affiliates them with Spigel's examined demographic group. With the caveat that this argument blends the real with the fictional, the three protagonists can be imagined as representative portrayals of early 1990s postfeminist womanhood, now fifteen to twenty years older, drifting out of the age group that female-targeted consumer culture prioritizes.

Positioning these three characters in workplace narratives that speak to political (including feminist) and institutional matrices affecting their social identity has crucial consequences. First, it reconfirms television's fascination with the shifting meanings of the affluent white career woman figure who possesses some social power gained at the height of postfeminism's cultural dominance, continuing to interrogate her identity as gendered and sexual subject.[3] Second, the three network series'

---

3   The industry backgrounds of the four series studied here are indicative of their preferred affiliations with specific fictional womanhoods and target audiences. The three network series focalize the mature career woman at the workplace; in contrast, the online streaming service invests in a story that initially focuses

foregrounding of social, cultural, and political forces as variably oppressive and confounding betrays a tendency to question the diachronic progress narrative of identity and institutional politics promoted in the West. This is evident in the treatment of late 1990s liberal feminism; critiqued by feminists as a realized political force, the programs also openly take institutional gender politics to task. In this regard, *30 Rock* and *The Good Wife* are ideological cousins for their overt skepticism about the realities of a visible, popular feminism.

The institutionalized liberal feminism in question is reminiscent of what McRobbie (2009) critiqued in her influential analysis of "gender mainstreaming," that is, the incorporation of *some* feminist concerns into governmental and institutional policymaking in the late 1990s under the banner of the elusive "human rights" discourse (152). McRobbie argues that this development removed the movement's radical aspects, especially those aspects that could be problematically absorbed into late capitalist institutions, such as postcolonial feminism or the critique of dualistic gender difference. I showed in chapter 3 how *30 Rock* enacts its skepticism about this mainstreamed version of feminism both in presenting Liz Lemon as a parody of the uninformed postfeminist/feminist possessing some social power and in commenting on the ways that political ideals play out in corporate capitalism and the television industry. Further, the four examined series thematize the problematic relationship of "gender mainstreaming" to race discourses, with the network programs narrativizing this as a matter of labor relations in the workplace, such as *30 Rock's* and *Parks'* mockery of race relations repeatedly brought into connection with gender politics.

The Good Wife regularly channels its criticism of realized feminist politics through Diane's character; as shown, the series often contrasts her political ideals and their institutional presence through backroom discussions

---

on a young postfeminist-coded woman and then gradually mitigates her role as subversive gesture, conceiving a putative future of progressive television storytelling that aligns itself with the future of television distribution and consuming practices. Network television can be contextualized in this generational conflict as negotiating its outdated reputation, struggling to survive in the postnetwork era and then in the streaming economy: It continues to invest in a figure to whose mediatization it has largely contributed, but it problematizes her cultural meanings in a way that confirms broadcast television's cultural relevance by mobilizing institutional and character skepticism.

and deals. On the one hand, the program promotes a discursive affiliation with second-wave feminist politics through Diane, as analyzed in detail by T. C. Miller (2016, 10–11). Ideological convictions and their complications dominate her story lines even when they depict her private life, as seen in her marriage to a conservative Republican. Further, the series deploys a range of female guest stars to portray lawyers and influential political figures whose politics determine their narrative significance, such as Maddie Hayward (Maura Tierney), a feminist Democratic businesswoman, and in one much-promoted instance, Gloria Steinem, in a cameo in Alicia's daydream to persuade her to run for state's attorney ("Dear God"). On the other hand, the institutional presence of liberal feminism is imbued with the same skepticism that characterizes the program, which, like *30 Rock*, extends to a criticism of its race politics. Consider the story line that focuses on Diane and Cary's condescending postrace attitudes as corporate bosses to Black employees in season 7 ("Lies") or the multi-episode portrayal in season 3 of systemic racism in the state's attorney's office, both plots using Black female lawyers to voice this criticism.

If these instances feed into *The Good Wife*'s cynicism about the state of affairs in American politics (a stance characteristic for a strand of prestige drama), then centralizing a female figure recognizable for her entrenched meanings in American gender relations throws into relief the question of her utility. How can the character function in this double bind that mobilizes both a gendered success story in the independent woman figure and also political skepticism, including the history of feminism? The central figure's specific paratextual and textual positioning is informative here. The previously quoted statement from co-producer Michelle King indicates that the character's function is not just that of the scorned political wife's fish-out-of-water story but an intensification of the dynamic between protagonist and environment. As narrative center, Alicia is a blank page on which different forces try to leave their ideological mark. Her signature sphinx-like reticence works, then, not only as gendered genre statement (see chapter 5) but also as the preferred presentation of a figure whose significance as a plot device lies in her lack of ideological affiliations.

The producers' comments are further reinforced by their other remarks interpreting the character's function; they frequently describe the show as "The Education of Alicia Florrick." This unofficial subtitle has featured at pivotal points of the program's production history, most resonantly in a series of Twitter posts after CBS announced the program's cancellation in its seventh season.[4] This communication is especially telling because it also reemphasizes earlier authorly statements about the narrative's closed nature, envisaged at its conception as a seven-season-long exploration of Alicia's education.

> Telling the story of the Education of Alicia Florrick is the creative dream of a lifetime. It was always our plan to tell it over 7 seasons. We wanted the story to have a beginning, middle, and an end—that's the only way actions can have real consequences—and it's the reason we had episode titles count up from one word to four, then back down again. . . . We're excited to celebrate the final 9 eps and bring the story to its natural conclusion. Here's a spoiler: the last episode will be called "End." (Producers' comments on Twitter)[5]

Quality drama's valorization of grand narrative, seriality, linear and goal-oriented storytelling, and implied authorly presence feed into the producers' communication, mitigating those aspects of storytelling that align it with so-called traditional television, such as procedurals' repetitive yet open-ended plotting. The grand narrative here denotes the character study of the independent woman, who, owing to her blank page status as privileged ex-housewife, functions less as a complex character and more as a catalyst for her social world's ideological and ethical complexities. Prestige cable drama's fascination with character complexity and concentrated psychological study of exceptional antiheroes is thus reorganized in the balance between social world and central character, a development that follows from network television's aesthetic-narrative constraints. In Mittell's analysis of cable drama's antihero, the complex aesthetic is matched with the focus on a protagonist "whose behavior and beliefs provoke ambiguous, conflicted or negative moral allegiance" (Mittell 2015b, 75). Alicia is not an antihero in this sense, yet the issue of moral corruption through social power is at stake in *The Good Wife*, providing the program's primary cultural distinction. Cable drama's focus on exceptional and morally "hideous men" (75) is countered here with Alicia's exceptional initial morality. In performance this translates into the character's signature silence that, as Leonard (2014b, 955) theorizes,

---

4   https://twitter.com/GoodWifeWriters/status/696499514316869632.
5   https://twitter.com/GoodWifeWriters/status/696499514316869632.

also speaks to a refusal to play along with media culture's scrutiny of public figures' sex lives.

The series' focus on Alicia Florrick's moral compass and relative morality, then, describes a trajectory in which these shift in a process of education through Alicia's encounters with social and political forces, similar to the Bildungsroman tradition in literature. The Kings' preferred description of the series, appealing to artistic status, confirms as much, considering that Bildungsroman's literal translation is "novel of education" or "formation," Anglicized as the coming-of-age story. In its original German versions the protagonist of the Bildungsroman is both central to the story and also negotiates a mere functionality; even though the protagonist's moral and emotional maturation is at stake, the narrative is often more interested in presenting the social environment they move through. As such, a tension dominates in the form between the hero's personal psychology and the social world's depiction, such that in its modern versions, the problematic reconciliation between the two surfaces in parody or satire and a "perversion" of the hero's portrayal (Slaughter 2011). *The Good Wife*'s cultural work and its producers' appeal to artistic significance recalls the satirical or parodic Bildungsroman's interpretation in literary theory: Both the notion of education and the denotation "good wife" as a reference to a trivial female role have a satirical tinge.

The Good Wife producers' ambition to present their show's cultural distinction, then, appeals to an established narrative tradition, drawing on its literary origins. The network drama competes with cable serials' discursive distinctiveness by projecting the antihero's complex (a)morality onto the social world, presenting it through a naïve protagonist's educational journey in the Bildungsroman tradition. As valorized modes of expression, cynicism and irony dominate these forms. In *The Good Wife* this is two-tiered, applying to both the described social world and the protagonist's cultural meaning as gendered subject. Both the title and the circulated subtitle signal an emphatically sarcastic interest in the "wife" as television culture's stock figure who represents the medium's historic femininity and an associated blandness and blankness of character. Alicia Florrick is extremely familiar from American culture (housewife, mother, career woman, Hillary Clinton allegory [Leonard 2014b]), and this familiarity includes millennial television's subversion of her meanings. That is, the program also builds on female-centered dramedy's portrayal of the "difficult mom" (Scott 2014). But the genre in which the figure is placed here upends this portrayal by way of the dialectic between her morality and the portrayed political culture's corruption—high-end legal-political drama rarely dramatizes domestic femininity at its narrative core.

Defamiliarizing the housewife figure is thus a fairly established trend for postmillennial television, but the political theme and generic environment reconfigure it as an ideological tug-of-war over her meaning and cultural utility. In the focus on "The Education of Alicia Florrick," opening up the narrative to the Bildungsroman formula (individual versus the social and political world) provides an avenue to negotiate the requirement of character complexity. The concentration on the figure and her cultural meaning's complexity differentiates the series from the two analyzed comedies' portrayal of the mature career woman: Both are embedded in the workplace comedy tradition, and as such they disperse narrative attention among the ensemble cast, of which the central comedian is one, albeit prioritized, member. The programs' titles also indicate this. Whereas the comedies designate workplaces, *The Good Wife* is explicit about its fascination with the central character's archetypal meaning. In contrast, consider Tina Fey's statement quoted in chapter 2 that rather than providing the career woman's singular viewpoint, *30 Rock* enacts its issue-based satire in the ensemble comedy, where each character stands for a particular ideological stance, of which Liz's middle-class white feminism is an emphasized yet equalized one. Contrastingly, *The Good Wife*'s intense interest in the central character requires that she is an outsider: She is portrayed as liminal to any ideological conviction, including feminism, and the series' commentary on politics and the protagonist's identity emerge from this liminality.

The confrontation between Alicia and the social world prominently inscribes her overdetermined meaning as a symbol of a historic femininity onto issues of liberal feminist politics, postfeminism, and, entangled in all this, the generational politics of feminism's waves (see T. C. Miller 2016, 10–15). That is, *The Good Wife* is engaged with Alicia's social status as a mature career woman and mother in her forties and with the awkward categorizability of this age and position in terms of both its affiliation with feminism and its location in cultural imagination. "Alicia's gender politics are in constant negotiation" as Miller posits (14), their meanings offered through her interactions with the numerous supporting female characters, who function primarily in their relative fixity contrasted with her shifting identity.

Diane is the clearest contrast figure, a childless second-wave feminist with explicit ideological convictions who possesses a great deal of social power.[6] In a *New York Times* article Michelle King expresses authorly interest in examining intergenerational relationships between women in a way that avoids portraying the older, and more powerful, career woman as a "bitch" (Hoffman 2011). This qualifier evokes the established narrative formula of inscribing a generational difference between women onto oppositional relationships to feminism and preferred routes to social power. In these narratives, prominent in postfeminist media, the older woman signals feminism's dangers to femininity and morality through her villainous or contradictory acquisition and use or abuse of power, as seen in the influential film *The Devil Wears Prada* (2006) (Rowe Karlyn 2011, 92–97; Winch 2013, 104–5). Glenn Close's early star text and career path also exemplify this postfeminist suspicion of female social power, in roles such as the Marquise de Merteuil in *Dangerous Liaisons*, *Fatal Attraction*'s (1987) pathologized single career woman, Cruella DeVil of *101 Dalmatians* (1996), and the duplicitous lawyer Patty Hewes in the television series *Damages* (2007–2012). This series was especially concerned with generational conflict and the symbolic avenues of morality that Patty's figure offered up to a young female attorney.

In the context of gendered generational conflict, *The Good Wife*'s Diane seems to fit the formula but also eschews it (as per King's statement) by not being portrayed as a villainous "bitch." Yet in the dynamic between Diane and Alicia, generational tension and distance still dominate. This is predicated on the question of feminist generations, given both Diane's portrayal as a feminist lobbyist and Alicia's extradiegetic understanding as a symbol of a postfeminist "retreatist" generation (Negra 2004). However, the millennial configuration of postfeminist generational conflict is mostly concentrated on young femininities and is often narrativized in teen-targeted genres (Rowe Karlyn 2011). Prestige drama's putatively grown-up aesthetic, and, in it, Alicia's portrayal as mother herself and mature woman, shifts this trope's meanings. The popular debate about the generational and biological rhetoric (mothers versus daughters) for feminism's history clearly informs the portrayal of Alicia and Diane's relationship but eludes dramatizing a "toxicity" of historic feminism in the way that a strand of mainstream cinema does (Bowler 2013, 191–92). This follows from the series' hyperfascination with

---

6 In addition, as T. C. Miller (2016) shows, *The Good Wife* translates its explorations of different types of feminism and femininity into a fascination with fashion as "surface area" (9), which for Diane means a preference for large power necklaces and "flamboyant" clothing (11).

its protagonist's complex cultural meanings, which emerge from the interplay between her symbolic simplicity (American television's housewife figure, the politician's scorned wife), her shifting position in the workplace environment, and the show's commentary on the good wife figure as existing through her mediatization in political discourses.

A story arc from the third season illuminates the dynamic of the "flexible feminist flow chart" (T. C. Miller 2016, 13), initiated by supporting character Caitlin D'Arcy's (Anna Camp) narrative and by the character relations that her appearance inspires. Caitlin is a newly hired junior associate with a short career at the firm, spanning between the episodes "Marthas and Caitlins" and "Long Way Home." Her figure is used, as customary for the series, to further refine the titular character's symbolic meaning. In "Marthas and Caitlins," Alicia is tasked with hiring a first-year associate, and the interview process presents a scenario where she has to choose between two women signaling two archetypal femininities ubiquitous in American popular culture: the homely, smart, and brown-haired Martha (Grace Rex) or the blonde, pretty, and seemingly superficial Caitlin, who is also equity partner David Lee's (Zach Grenier) niece. Alicia prefers Martha (she identifies with "Martha-ness"), but Lee and Will force her to hire Caitlin. Upon complaining to Will about the immorality of nepotism, he informs her that when she was hired at the firm, she was also a "Caitlin" competing against a more qualified "Martha"—meaning it was not her skills or qualifications that landed her the job but her friendship with Will, and Lee had approved her hire in exchange for Will's later vote for the niece. This inscribes onto the familiar dualistic imagery of women's sexual desirability the cutthroat intricacy of patriarchal office politics (the women are not hired for their desirability but for their connections with male bosses), both reinforcing the symbolism of female types in their iconographic allusions and also upsetting their meanings by throwing Alicia's identity into the mix, unsettling *her* position.

The twist exemplifies the series' much celebrated sophisticated cynicism, "wafting over you finely in a way that only *The Good Wife* can provide, that wonderfully bitter outlook on how to get ahead in life" (Sims 2011), dominating every further aspect that involves Caitlin's presence in the narrative. It also continues to relate to Alicia's signification both diegetically (the character's self-reflection) and in the extratextual shifting of how her already self-referential figure should be interpreted. In the next few episodes Alicia mentors Caitlin, whose initial image as a vapid blonde quickly disperses as the plot constantly confirms her professional skills and quick wit. Yet public performances of femininities continue to inform her story line and the two women's working relationship, culminating in the episode "After the Fall." The case of the week sees Alicia battling in court against Nancy Crozier, the attorney who notoriously enacts a naïve young femininity to manipulate judges' and juries' sympathies. As discussed, the series showcases masquerades of femininity and other performed personas in the courtroom (T. C. Miller 2016, 13), signaling its critique and Alicia's distance from them in her similarly showcased signature eye rolls.[7] But if we are to understand Alicia's professional performance of self as more authentic than that of her opponents, then this episode complicates this, inscribed onto other women's performances of femininity. Alicia is losing the case because the young male judge is enamored by blonde-haired Crozier's ingénue act, ignoring the older, deep-voiced, and brown-haired Alicia's arguments. In a new tactic she makes Caitlin argue in court, deploying her young, chirpy blondness against Crozier's. Caitlin quickly catches on and hyperperforms the role under Alicia's tutelage and silent approval, and a battle of two iterations of the same female stereotype ensues for the judge's sympathy. Diane is also present in court, and when Caitlin eventually wins the case, this earns her a promotion.

It is de rigueur by this point in the series to incorporate into the legal world's depiction the intricacies of institutionalized sexism and women lawyers' navigation of it by assuming a type of recognizable femininity, and this plot uses it to question the protagonist's distance from this strategy. The frequent assurance that this kind of posturing is beneath Alicia (through eye rolls, for instance), as an aspect of her morally sound character, is undermined when she uses Caitlin as her proxy, a tactic that still effects Alicia's sympathetic character portrayal as clever puppet master. She mobilizes a masquerade of femininity in another woman to professional ends with success and is not taken to task for it. Although the program avoids constructing a scenario where Alicia herself performs putatively inauthentic femininity, she still strategically deploys it in someone else, which allows her to continue with the disapproving eye rolls in later episodes. If the program's

---

7   The protagonist's signature eye roll is another common trait of Alicia and *30 Rock*'s Liz Lemon and is for both a self-referential punch line expressing the character's exasperation at and ideological distance from her environment. Both underline the respective series' lauded sarcasm and pessimism about the social world.

aim is to portray Alicia's "education" as a gendered initiation process into the ways in which politics and social power corrupt, it is also at pains here to limit this corruption to an extent that keeps her in a liminal position to everyone else's corruptness as a matter of semantic juggling.

Centralizing female lawyers' performance of feminine authenticity, the episode also continues to position them in a generational relationship. Alicia's mentorship and manipulation of Caitlin involves a generational aspect that puts the older woman in a role that invokes the Alicia-Diane dynamic. As T. C. Miller (2016) writes, "*TGW* doesn't offer much in the way of solidarity or sisterhood for its female characters" (12), a sentiment that dominates the three women's relationship. But the good wife's complicated meaning again effects an elusiveness of her ideological role, demonstrated in the next stages of Caitlin's story line. Because of Caitlin's quick promotion, Alicia starts to consider her a professional threat, complicating the already ambiguous mentor-protégé dynamic. Competitiveness surfaces in Alicia's growing paranoia about her job security in the recessionary workplace in relation to a younger female lawyer with talent, connections, and popularity. The program's signature paranoia and cynicism translate here into the protagonist's own, but they remain subjective and thus unreliable: The mise-en-scène and narrative highlight Alicia's suspiciousness about Caitlin's potential threat in a way that forebodes a misunderstanding, because her portrayal outside of her connection to Alicia remains neutral.

In Caitlin's final episode "Long Way Home," the underlying theme of competition becomes explicit. Following an incident that can be interpreted as Caitlin stealing Alicia's ideas and spotlight, Alicia confronts her using an oblique threat thinly disguised as mentor's advice. Alicia subsequently finds out from David Lee that Caitlin has given notice, thanks to Alicia's "mean girls act." If the plot has so far hinted in prestige drama's subtle fashion at the uncertainty of character morality (was Alicia right in her paranoia, or did she bully Caitlin into leaving?), then the resolution shifts these questions to the plane of gendered identity and generations of feminism articulated in the interactions among Diane, Alicia, and Caitlin. Guilt-ridden, Alicia tries to convince Caitlin to stay, upon which she reveals that the real reason for her leaving is not their conflict but her personal life: She is pregnant and getting married. As T. C. Miller (2016, 13) notes, the discussion among the three women recalls the postfeminist choice rhetoric: Against Diane's explanations about the company's generous maternity scheme, Caitlin declares that her life plan is "to be a mom." This utterance is positioned as the episode's comically shocking highlight. Alicia later apologizes to Caitlin, admitting that office politics "tend to make people paranoid," confirming that in this instance the series deployed its characteristic cynicism and paranoia to mislead the audience. This conflict was in fact about (post)feminist generational discourse about lifestyle and identity, with Caitlin declaring that "I *want* to choose. Maybe it's different for my generation but I don't have to prove anything. Or if I have to, I don't want to. I'm in love."

This conflict and utterance would not be out of place in an *Ally McBeal* episode, the legal series considered a quintessential signifier of 1990s postfeminist popular culture's relationship to feminism's historic influence on the workplace (Hermes 2006) and described by its feminist critics as shifting the concerns of feminist politics onto issues of individual choice. Caitlin's "choice" monologue could work as a summary of *Ally McBeal's* ending, which saw Ally giving up her legal career for full-time motherhood. In this context Alicia's character history recalls even more prominently a postfeminist past, picking up fifteen years later from where *Ally McBeal* left off. For Bonnie J. Dow (2002), *Ally McBeal*, and most American TV centrally concerned with gender politics, represents the movement as "lifestyle feminism": a narrative quest for the individualized heroine. But postfeminism especially turns feminist concerns into an issue of personal happiness, thus deflecting questions of institutional power and putting feminism on trial for complicating women's personal lives, particularly traditions of romance and marriage (Dow 2002).

Critical responses to the Caitlin twist were mixed, either dismissing it as dated or celebrating it for tackling the apparent real-life issue of young, educated women dropping out of the workforce to become housewives (Bosch 2012). Harnick (2012) lauded the swift elision of a story line of women's competition, noting that its suspense played with viewer recognition of this narrative tradition. The *AV Club* reviewer's analysis is perhaps most telling for bringing up the series' general tone in connection with this plot: The twist is both "refreshing"-ly innocent and idiosyncratic in the otherwise cynical and disillusioned world of *The Good Wife* and mockingly telegraphs an outdated conservative ideology with Caitlin going away to "liv[e] a life that belongs in a goddamn oil painting" (Sims 2012). Both *Ally McBeal* and *The Good Wife* thus betray American television's continued fascination with the singular female lawyer figure and her gendered meanings by means of lifestyle choices. But if *Ally McBeal* centralized the issue of postfeminist choice throughout its dramedy narrative, *The Good Wife* as recessionary political-legal drama parodies it as passé cultural phenomenon, a treatment that for its critics speaks to the series' ideological novelty.

The resolution of the Caitlin story line, then, stands out for its blatant callback to the millennial postfeminist retreatism trend. And again, following from the program's broader ideological and generic aspirations—painting a sociopolitical tableau of Chicago's legal world as the cynical education of a symbolic female figure—it is Alicia's diegetic position and identity that are at stake. Diane represents the second-wave feminist's familiar standpoint, commenting on Caitlin's decision that "I'm not sure the glass ceiling was broken for this," also comparing Caitlin's life choices to Alicia's: "She'll be back in fifteen years. Like you."[8] Alicia disagrees, and the two women's generational relationship remains ambiguous: Diane assumes that their shared social position as working women allows here for an ideological union, whereas Alicia distances herself from this. But if Caitlin represents a postfeminism that is similar to the 1990s postfeminism of Alicia's backstory, then this connection also has its limits because of the protagonist's present as a mature working mother with fiscal problems; the exchange between Diane and Alicia moves on to Alicia's requested pay raise and reminds viewers both of her relative financial hardship and the firm's recessionary struggles. Alicia's figure continues to stay liminal to diegetic ideologies and identities, a suitable central figure for the Bildungsroman narrative.

Sims's (2012) reference to the "refreshing" lack of cynical scheming that makes the twist so out of place further confirms the series' ambition to narrativize the immorality of law and politics, a concern allowing for the theme of gender politics and feminist generations to be discussed as collateral damage in institutional politics. The centralized symbolic female character allows the series to generate narrative tension around this political morality, and the refreshingness that the critic describes comes from the discrepancy between the Caitlin story line and this episode's other two plots, the case of the week and the serialized political narrative, both depicting the moral murkiness of their respective milieus.

The case revolves around a client, acquitted wife killer Colin Swee-ney (Dylan Baker), a recurring character notorious for his rotten sexual and social mores. Although critical reception dubbed Sweeney *The Good*

---

8   Caitlin returns sooner, namely, in the series' final season, as a divorced working mother, this way "eventually punished for [her postfeminism]," as T. C. Miller notes (2016, 13).

Wife's resident Hannibal Lecter for his sophisticated monstrosity, superior intellect, and intimate emotional connection to Alicia, the series is also at pains to demonstrate Alicia's personal distance from the sexuality he represents, depicted as perverted and predatory (which Lecter's portrayal lacks). At stake here is the ethical dilemma between fulfilling professional duties in institutions of the law and negotiating the hyperbolically opposed sexual and other mores between client and attorney. This dilemma is a favored theme in American cinema's narrativization of the legal world (Lucia 2005)—for instance, in *The Devil's Advocate* (1997) and *Primal Fear* (1996)—but television's episodic seriality and the centralized female protagonist both complicate ideological consequences. Because the series dramatizes issues of feminism as political factor and generational identity, this viewpoint feeds into its depiction of the legal world's, and the client's, rottenness. Sweeney's is a paternity case, an ex-colleague suing him for sexual harassment that had resulted in her pregnancy. The details of the case, characteristically for the series and its Sweeney plots, depict both parties as ethically and sexually depraved: Sweeney insists that the sexual encounter had been consensual and only oral, to which David Lee offers (correctly) that she might have used a turkey baster (implying that she spat his semen into a baster to later artificially inseminate herself). Lee's suggestion is followed by Diane's world-weary remark: "And so it devolves: from hopes, ideals, dreams, the glory of the law, to a turkey baster." Diane is often the voice of disillusionment with the realities of the legal world's morality, embedded in her portrayal as a left-leaning liberal feminist, a conviction that motivated her career trajectory. The series' suspicions about the world of law and politics surface through the contrast of Diane's established liberal feminist politics and this world's disappointing realities.

In addition, the same episode's serialized political plot concerns accusations by Black Assistant State's Attorney Geneva Pine (Renée Elise Goldsberry) of racist favoritism at the office and similarly verbalizes a discord between ethics and office politics. Pine dresses down her colleague Cary for having been unfairly promoted to deputy state's attorney over more experienced, and nonwhite, ASAs who had been fired for errors Cary himself had made. At the end of this scene, she voices her disgust over Cary's spinelessness for accepting the promotion in language similar to Diane's: "It's a bad economy for ideals." Both of these remarks construct an idealized past against which, in contrast, the present's realities of law and politics are found wanting, all embedded in feminist and race politics. Especially in

Diane's case, given her prominent status in the ensemble cast, her repeatedly expressed frustration with the law keeps the discursive women's empowerment narrative around the series ambiguous, into which feeds the sarcastic education context circulated by the producers.[9]

A great deal of the series' meanings emerge, then, from explorations of how legal systems are semantically manipulated: "Battles between the letter of the law and the spirit of the law come up again and again" (Yuan 2012). The program's ideological novelty is in combining this critical examination of American political and legal culture through the female lawyer's centralization, including the history of feminist politics she evokes. As mentioned, this conflict between individual and institutions is a favored popular cultural narrative, and its gendered implications became more foregrounded on second-wave feminism's cultural impact. Confronting patriarchal institutions of law making and law practicing through the female lawyer figure was a popular theme in the American cinema of the 1990s. Cynthia Lucia's book *Framing Female Lawyers* (2005) examines the cultural anxieties that these films express both about the idealized vision of the law and the increased inclusion of women lawyers in its institutions, expressed through Hollywood cinema's aesthetic tools. She finds that the "woman lawyer" film cycle negotiates contradictory ideological tendencies: first, that "the law is a stable, immutable force beyond the reach of transitory political and cultural influences" (3), and, second, that this is upended precisely by political and cultural factors (feminism), allowing women's appearance in its institutions. Feminism clashes here with traditions of law as patriarchal culture, onto which is inscribed psychoanalytic theory's symbolic meaning making (the Lacanian law as word of the father) (12). These two opposing tendencies produce the "uneasy acceptance of women in law," negotiated in these films by positing *her* as a symbolic problem to be resolved (3).

Women in legal film drama thus signal yet another putative crisis of patriarchy, here describing the symbolic equation of the law with male institutional power that the female lawyer figure upsets. However, instead of interrogating patriarchal power, these films "plac[e] the female lawyer

---

9   In addition, the producers explain the series' final scene, which mirrors the pilot's cold open—Diane slaps Alicia for a betrayal—as completing Alicia's education, defining this as a process in which "the victim becomes the victimizer" (Ausiello 2016). Alicia's moral corruption is complete once she openly betrays the (already ambiguous) feminist sisterhood (see Conclusion).

on trial, interrogating *her* role as woman and as lawyer" (Lucia 2005, 3). Lucia contrasts these films with those centralizing male lawyer protagonists and finds a structuring difference in the ways they dramatize the law versus justice discrepancy, a theme that the lawyer film typically interrogates. When cinema's male lawyers restore the balance between justice and law by putting the law to its proper use, they simultaneously resolve the crisis of patriarchy expressed in the initial imbalance (159). In contrast, the female lawyer struggles with a lack or ambiguity of professional and personal competence, signaling her inherent inability to acquire "the father's law" (159). Thus, rather than resolving the law-justice imbalance, she is its root cause as "a destabilizing presence who frequently is shown to subvert justice through her excess" (20).

Lucia considers the cinema context crucial for the ideological work of the 1990s "woman lawyer" film cycle. The female lawyer poses a problem for the law because hers is an *exceptional* presence, an anomaly that needs investigating. This meaning is fitting for cinema narration "which places individual agency above collective agency or action" (Lucia 2005, 21). Thus female presence's "singular/'symbolic'" (21) nature within the law is especially well suited for cinematic narratives, two systems that Lucia sees as similar in their patriarchal operation that negotiates popular feminist discourses: "'Success' for the female lawyer . . . [means a] 'right' to gain access to both these systems as lawyer and as protagonist" (21). The lack of a "female collective" in these films highlights her exceptional and exclusive status in male-dominated organizations (22). Cinematic narrative's discursive masculinism underlies this argument with its linear narrative, single focus, and closed ending, making it especially suitable for speaking to this theme. Lucia briefly notes that scripted television focusing on lawyers and law firms is less amenable to such ideologies because of its narrative traditions: The medium's use of ensemble casts and episodic story lines allows for a "far less intensive interrogation of the female lawyer" (238).

Lucia's concept is useful for unpacking television's use of the legal theme and the female lawyer's centralization in relation to a discursive feminism. A conspicuous issue is cinema's single-character focus versus television's ensemble cast, which Lucia theorizes as the key reason for television's less intense interrogation of its female protagonist. Yet for scripted television, narrativizing an evolutionary course of women's social roles has been a lucrative strategy for establishing the medium's cultural status through character-focused "independent woman" programming. Negotiating episodic ensemble storytelling with the single character focus is network TV's specificity, with its wide audience target favoring upscale women viewers and with its mixed serial and episodic structure allowing for thematizing sociopolitical concerns without resolution. Thus television's fascination with the independent woman speaks to narrative and ideological differences between the two media's treatment of the woman-and-law theme. If the woman lawyer is an anomaly in the dual patriarchal systems of cinema narration and legal institutions, then television seems a better home to accommodate the career-woman-as-political-symbol theme.

Nonetheless, as Lucia remarks, woman lawyers are usually members of an ensemble cast in procedural and serialized series. In this regard *Ally McBeal* and *The Good Wife* are somewhat exceptional for their centralization of a singular female lawyer and for linking their cultural status both to popular feminist and quality discourses. Both series investigate their central character's identity in the legal framework to an extent that allows for Lucia's concept to be mapped onto their cultural work. As discussed, *Ally McBeal* represents for Dow (2002) an extreme privatization of feminist politics; the title character is a career woman who "searches her soul *a lot*" (261; italics in original), and the show is more concerned with inspecting this than with legal issues, making it the quintessential postfeminist text. The episodic formula resolves the tension between legal world and central character by thematizing concerns of gender politics through legal cases that reflect the heroine's own soul searching about romance and changing gender scripts. This formula aligns the series with *Sex and the City*; the journalism framework allows for Carrie to muse over similar concerns. For Joke Hermes (2006), the two series signaled a new moment in television culture as "key agents in establishing the era of quality popular programming, or 'must see' television" (79), and as key texts of postfeminism mobilizing introspective discourses about gender roles. Lucia's notion that female lawyer films put women, and indirectly feminism, on trial in the law versus justice discourse is relevant for *Ally McBeal*'s postfeminism too: Interrogating the heroine's social position as a single career woman fueled the series' narrative, utilizing the putatively objective domain of the law as an instrument for scrutinizing women's lifestyle issues. *Sex and the City*'s use of journalism and *Ally McBeal*'s use of legal discourse serve similar ends, mobilizing professional labor contexts in service of investigating the intimate gendered self. The putative feminization of legal discourse, then, with its supposed disruption of the boundary between the feminine-coded private and the masculine-coded public domain (Cooper 2001), still keeps the dualism intact under the governance of postfeminism and its valorization of gendered self-surveillance.

If *Ally McBeal*'s lifestyle feminism privatizes the public and patriarchal domain of the law through the dramedy framework's focus on the female lawyer's emotional journey, then *The Good Wife*'s appeal to quality drama status involves the tactical probing of these dualisms. Mapped onto this is network drama's hybridization of episodic (legal) and serialized (political) narratives, centralizing a recognizable female character type as the catalyst of both types of narrative with the aim to upset their hierarchal connotations. For Leonard (2014b), the good wife figure gains her significance in the text's transparent admission that she is a media creation, signaling this both in the diegesis and in the intertextual link to American political and television culture. Diegetically, this emerges through the tension between her authentic self and its sexualized mediation in politics, a storytelling device that Leonard argues highlights the "fundamental unknowability of personal desire and sexual exchange" (946). This insistence reinforces the central figure's enigmatic character, suitably aligned with quality drama's emphasis on image rather than verbosity.

Extradiegetically, as discussed, the titular character operates as a multiply signposted critical reflection of the housewife figure, American television's icon of respectable womanhood. This overdetermined commentary on her media-created nature is familiar from *30 Rock*'s treatment of the urban career girl trope: To establish cultural status, both series critically reflect on mediatized femininities and their consequences for women's precarious command of public and professional spaces. If commentary on mediatized femininity undergirds both programs' prestige on network television in the respective legal-political drama and workplace comedy genres, then it explains another common feature: their problematizing of a sexual truth as ideological motivation. *The Good Wife*'s safeguarding of the unknowable sexual self recalls Fey's comments that as a female comedy author she refuses to enact sexual desirability or desire unless in the grotesque comic mode, a discursively far less realistic representation than drama. As shown in chapter 2, Fey articulated this insistence, which became an integral part of her star text, as self-distancing from *Sex and the City*'s introspective concentration on female sexuality. Safeguarding the privacy of protagonists' and/or performers' sexual selves informs both *30 Rock* and *The Good Wife* as politicized refusal of the postfeminist capitalization on female sexual agency and informs their status as quality texts. This also fits with network television's institutional constraints regarding sexually explicit content, a vital component in the cultural distinction between the kinds of quality that cable and network television are sanctioned to produce.

Key to the enactment of this politics of refusal is the placing of the action in public institutions of law and national politics, effecting that the rhetorical boundary between dichotomies such as private and public, private and political, feminine and masculine, emotion and intellect, and justice and law are shown to be products of cultural-political discourses similar to the scorned and retreatist wife's mediated image. If for Lucia the 1990s female lawyer film negotiates the contradiction of woman and law in a closed narrative trajectory that defends the ideal of an immutable and patriarchal justice system against the disruptive force of feminism, then broadcast narration's episodic structure is well suited to enact a reverse course: A key narrative hook of the series is its investigation of the legal system's endless mutability, fickleness, and instability. In its case-of-the-week plots, *The Good Wife* notoriously highlights fine curiosities and shortcomings of the American legal system, and narrative pleasure is derived from how its practitioners navigate its semantic traps and loopholes. This narrative interest is embedded in episodic TV's circular and endlessly recyclable storytelling formula, a tradition that also accounts for the medium's low reputation and gendered connotations. Linking this theme with the serialized political plot through the female protagonist associates political institutions with the same suspicious and endlessly recyclable fickleness. In addition, the recurring reference to a nostalgia for an idealized past of political and legal justice is, as shown, embedded in feminist and occasionally race discourses. This maps a divide between the present and the past, and an attendant dualism of gender politics, onto the law-justice divide—the glorious past of second-wave feminism versus the disappointment with its contemporary involvement in political and legal scheming.

The profound genderedness of law and politics is also exemplified in the gender-balanced makeup of the Lockhart & Gardner law firm with its symbolic consequences for the protagonist. Often called the "mom and dad" of the firm, Diane and Will represent network TV's historic portrayal of polarized American worldviews and identities—the other two network series I analyze also operate with lead figures in similar capacities. For *The Good Wife* this contrasts Diane's second-wave feminism and disillusioned legal idealism with Will's cocky and opportunistic masculinity, both portrayed sympathetically for their command of the law-justice dynamic, as they symbiotically navigate the firm through the economic crisis. But unlike the comedies' centralized pairing (with the female protagonist on one pole), Alicia is an outsider to this dynamic, yet she is instrumental to both sides' ideological and narrative relevance. Her connection to Will mobilizes the romance narrative, fueling its intimate melodrama component whose affective significance looms large for the program's critical estimation as women's entertainment. The professional and pragmatic connection between Diane and Alicia concerns feminist generational politics at the workplace. Will's drastic removal from the drama emphasizes this difference of relationships: His absence continues to inform the melodrama as intimate character portrayal but indicates that it is the Diane-Alicia dynamic that is crucial to the character's education: her final estimation as corrupted by social-political power. In her overdetermined symbolism—as commentary on mediatized femininity, postfeminist womanhood, a historic blandness of American womanhood in the housewife figure, the career woman, and so on—Alicia's character enacts an outsider function that allows her an intermediary position among narrative forms and modes, realms of the private and public, and ideological divisions of gender politics. She is a fitting symbolic figure for network television's response to industry-driven reconfigurations of masculine-coded quality drama.

NO "TV TITTIES" HERE: *ORANGE IS THE NEW BLACK* AND THE MARGINALIZED POSTFEMINIST ANTIHEROINE

The symbolic position of Piper Chapman, *Orange*'s central protagonist, is similar to Alicia's in mediating a shift in women's representational traditions. This politically driven function contributes to the program's novel generic hybridity and Netflix's brand identity. Most of the female-centered American series that became iconic for their unconventional portrayals of female protagonists operated in this vein (*The Mary Tyler Moore Show*, *Roseanne*, *Cagney and Lacey*, *Sex and the City*, *Ally McBeal*, etc.), registering a discursive past of women's representation with which the protagonist's contextually progressive identity dialogued, which informed the text's narrative-aesthetic strategies and cultural value. In *Orange*, however, the symbolic progression for which critics commend the series reverses this narrative tradition: It is the protagonist herself who denotes a discursive past of representational politics. Like Alicia Florrick, whose titular description evokes ironically a trope of women's portrayals, Chapman functions as a conduit between putatively outdated stereotype and subversive gender politics. This comes from the tense encounter between the protagonist and her new social environment, but whereas *The Good Wife* focuses attention on the protagonist's shifting identity ("the education of Alicia Florrick"), paratextual discourses about *Orange* insist that Chapman's narrative function is exactly that, a function: Her identity is important insofar as it contrasts with a realism of social context represented in the ensemble cast. Although the subtitle "the education of Piper Chapman" could describe *Orange* as well, the two programs use the protagonist differently as a signifier of a mediatized and outdated femininity. If *The Good Wife*'s premise of disrupting women's established portrayals is located in the protagonist herself, *Orange* finds narrative and political novelty in using Chapman's discursively stereotypical figure to disrupt historic portrayals of *other* and *othered* women and their stigmatized social worlds. The narrative strategy underlines this, using multithreaded and flashback storytelling to gradually mitigate Chapman's symbolic centrality.

As previously discussed, the term *realism* is used frequently by producers to highlight *Orange*'s cultural significance, exemplified in Jenji Kohan's reference to the role of genre hybridity in this. Her interpretation of the program's blend of comedy and drama invokes a realist intent, framing it as artistic necessity while mapping the opposite poles of comic and serious onto a presumed referential reality. In her statement "dramas that are only dramatic are a lie, because life isn't just a drama" (Fienberg 2013), Kohan challenges highbrow drama's connotation between realism and seriousness to demand cultural recognition for dramedy. The hierarchal status of comedy and drama is at stake here again, which for *Orange* involves physical comedy and sexual explicitness around marginalized female bodies. The defense also refers to the cultural confusion surrounding *Orange* for its generic "perversity" (Nussbaum 2015) or, in Netflix programming chief Ted Sarandos's wording, its "iconoclasm" that both hinders its institutional recognition and produces its popularity.

The slippery genre position and the discursive link to realism are thus intertwined with *Orange*'s gender politics, expressing an iconoclastic transition from established portrayals of women to a realism of a stigmatized social environment. Kohan's ubiquitous metaphor for Chapman as her "Trojan horse" is representative; Chapman serves as a point of identification for the upscale female demographics prioritized by the television industry and facilitates the discovery of a more diverse social world through her fish-out-of-water story.

In a lot of ways Piper was my Trojan Horse. You're not going to go into a network and sell a show on really fascinating tales of black women, and Latina women, and old women and criminals. But if you take this white girl, this sort of fish out of water, and you follow her in, you can then expand your world and tell all of those other stories. But it's a hard sell to just go in and try to sell those stories initially. The girl next door, the cool blonde, is a very easy access point, and it's relatable for a lot of audiences and a lot of networks looking for a certain demographic. It's useful. (Kohan 2013)

Onto the tension between the supposedly typical heroine and a multiplicity of diverse femininities can be mapped the tension between postfeminism and popular feminist discourses criticizing prerecessionary media's narrow focus on the lifestyle politics of privileged womanhood. Quality television's narrative requirement of a Big Idea—promising both overarching linear narration and the possibility of open-ended plots—is grounded here in such a use of feminism. *Orange* narrativizes a clash between a mediatized postfeminist (and consequently unreal-coded) femininity and a putative realism of femininities, which locates differences between real and unreal in embodied and demographic signifiers (class, ethnicity, nationality, sexuality, gender, age, body image). Promotional paratexts like Kohan's quote above emphasize this grand narrative of a political collision of femininities and also mobilize a clash between the singular author persona's political-aesthetic progressiveness and the television industry's conservatism.

As customary for the quality brand, authorship discourse is essential to *Orange*'s publicity, articulated as the author's ideological resistance to industry constraints and demonstrating the text's unique attributes as evidence of the creator's singular vision, which dissents from average, medium-specific fare. Creators of male-centered prestige dramas routinely express this in the art versus television dichotomy, at the same time praising the permissive attitudes of cable channels such as HBO that ensure their artistic freedom. Such communications court the host programmer for granting the author artistic license, thus strengthening the symbiotic link between the program's marketed singularity and the company's unique brand identity. For *Orange*, however, publicity discourses, such as the quote from Kohan, entail a narrative of ideological distance between institutional host and authorly intent, according to which Chapman's centralization was a necessity for

Netflix commissioning the series. This discourse presumes an audience whose feminist awareness and resistance to the cultural industries' capitalistic directives affect their consumption practices. The gender politics governing this resistance are reproduced in the program's narrative: Kohan's supposed resistance to industry standards corresponds to the postfeminism-feminism tension inscribed onto the Chapman versus prison-as-social-environment plot. Chapman stands for an industry-standard mandatory postfeminism, and the prison inmates speak to Kohan's subversive, authorly, and feminist narrativizing of diverse womanhoods and critique of the prison industrial complex, themes otherwise excluded from television's traditional narratives.

Representational resistance as realism becomes interpreted as unruly genre hybridity (hour-long comedy-drama) which opposes itself to the seriousness of highbrow drama, positioned as a conservative, outdated, and inauthentic norm. Simultaneously, this generic complexity is positioned as a feminine and feminist address that exists outside quality television's categories. But if realism links gender politics (postfeminism versus feminist resistance) with genre hybridity (serious drama versus dramedy), then its use is at odds with its discursive formation. Consider Nussbaum's (2015) article, discussed earlier, comparing the difference in tone between *Orange* and *Show Me a Hero* in their treatment of female characters. For Nussbaum, *Orange* "rejects realism," and she summons such descriptors as "tonal perversity," "vaudevillian," and "blown up, not life-size" characters to explain the series' generic indecipherability, contrasted with the David Simon–esque message drama's "educational" intent. "Surreal" is another word habitually used to describe the series; for instance, an initial concept for the title sequence was apparently meant to evoke "the surreal contrast" between Chapman's old and new lives ("*Orange Is the New Black* Opening Credits," 2013). Not only does this qualifier, which upsets the connotations of *real*, inscribe this onto a clash between privileged and demographically othered femininities, but it also implies body and sexuality politics. The existing title sequence depicts real bodies as surreal; for McHugh (2015) it denotes documentarist realism (featuring actual formerly incarcerated women), but the extreme close-ups of facial details and skins evoke a surreal closeness to the filmed subjects.

Orange's discursively progressive representations of female bodies are a contested notion in scholarship. As noted, McHugh (2015) celebrates it, briefly mentioning *The Good Wife* as a contrasting example of a reactionary postfeminism for using female attire as a signifier of social status, whereas *Orange*'s prison uniforms eliminate the possibility of consumerist indulgence. McHugh thus pits a postfeminist conservatism of female consumption against a progressive feminist politics of refusal (22). This verdict eludes examining different institutional, generic, and narrative contexts that influence the two series' cultural work; in addition, the production values of a series need not correlate with the *diegetic* look and class specifications of costuming and sets. But my point is that for McHugh the dichotomy is located in body politics, specifically in the costuming's symbolism as a site of negotiated femininity and feminism (see also T. C. Miller 2016).

McHugh's argument about the significance of women's attire can be extended to the contrast between the two shows' use of the female face as the bearer of gender politics. Alicia's or Kalinda's Kabuki-mask faces, always in full makeup, denote impenetrability and undecipherability, whereas *Orange*'s title sequence with its extreme close-ups promises a revelation of truths about its female subjects to the point of uncomfortable intimacy. These opposing meanings follow from the two series' different production contexts and the avenues they offer for invoking feminism as a source of cultural status. Leonard (2014b) considers it feminist that *The Good Wife* refuses to offer insight into the protagonist's sex life and that it critiques mediatized attempts to arrive at sexual truths around scrutinized female public figures. This notion of progressivism adheres to the visual and thematic constraints of network television. Because the program is in a double bind between its chosen theme (sex scandal in politics) and institutional regulation of sexually explicit imagery, it uses this contrast by turning the ban into a politics of refusal and explores the various power negotiations within the scenario. These negotiations are inscribed onto female characters' faces and costumes (as opposed to their corporeality), which extratextually include a struggle between the publicity value of the female star's eroticized image and the feminist power of refusal. Consider the promotional posters that depicted Margulies in suggestive poses and lingerie at odds with the series' tone and aesthetic (T. C. Miller 2016, 9) or the symbolism of Kalinda's attire, her leather jackets and stiletto boots linking the notion of commanding female silence to fetishized female glamour (the dominatrix iconography). Contrastingly, Netflix's institutional approval of sexually and otherwise explicit content propels a discursive feminism in *Orange* that finds a suitable site of tensions in corporeally rendered body politics, which the prison environment makes especially fraught with ideological meanings.

Inseparable from these discursive negotiations is the issue of race and class involved in constructions of a feminist resistance. *Orange* appeals to representational diversity by using a classed lack of glamorous femininity that follows from the prison setting, itself inviting interpretations of social inequity expressed on the Foucauldian surveilled body. The previously discussed *How to Get Away with Murder* and Annalise Keating's symbolic importance in critical discourses offer another comparison. Although that series is associated with feminine and middlebrow viewing pleasures, Keating functions as the *embodied* revelatory realism of Black femininity, securing the program's political significance. The famous transition scene (getting rid of makeup and wig) also inscribes tensions between race and class and between private and public: Whereas the series privileges classed public spaces (courtroom, classroom), this discursively revelatory scene is set in a private space, signaling secrecy and intrigue apposite to the generic tone. This generic tone also aligns the series with network television's narrative traditions. As such, the show's race and class politics are linked to the programming context's restrictions: The revelation around the raced and classed female image centers on masquerade of the face but not of the body. Contrastingly, critical reception of *Orange* lauds it for a brutal honesty foregrounding the corporeal in its critique of the prison industrial complex. The series exploits Netflix's permissiveness around explicit content by establishing its quality aesthetic in the focus on a social space where a revelation around marginalized female bodies is diegetically moot—yet is mobilized in the fish-out-of-privileged-water story. In the prison setting female bodies are constantly exposed and surveilled in a transitory space between the private and the public, whereas Keating's revelation happens in the darkness of her bedroom. The political realism of race, class, and gender is inscribed onto the visual renditions of bodies, which contributes to Netflix's institutional configurations of the program's quality features.

Danielle Hancock (2016) argues that the othered bodies of *Orange*'s inmates correspond to Mary Russo's (1995) concept of the female grotesque. This concept is central to feminist scholars' examinations of the liminal and excessive female body in popular culture, especially in its subversive potential for women's comedy (Rowe Karlyn 1995b; Arthurs 1999). Hancock draws attention to the contradictory mobilizations of the grotesque in the first season of *Orange*: By distancing Chapman's classical, clean, bourgeois body from those of the prison inmates, these become associated with a threatening abject physicality. Because Chapman functions, as reiterated by Kohan, as a middle-class audience's "host" body—that is, the viewer's "adopted identity"—the threat of intrusion that the surrounding grotesque bodies express is rendered a threat to *this* audience. The text's emphasis on the physically overbearing presence of the women around Chapman reconfirms the distance between postfeminist femininity and othered femininities, keeping *her* audiovisual portrayal aligned with codes of conventional femininity. The program's seriality allows for gradually mitigating the grotesque's threatening aspect: Although Chapman remains an "isolated body," the other inmates' grotesqueness becomes contextualized through the use of the explanatory flashback technique and their shifting narrative importance. Moving the others toward the narrative center effects a portrayal of institutional victimization, such that the grotesque turns from alienating character trait into a consequence of the "monstrous" prison environment, generating sympathy for its victims (Hancock 2016).

Hancock's argument is helpful for unpacking how the series uses the grotesque to inform its quality status and the postfeminism-feminism tension. If the difference of cultural and social status between protagonist and othered inmates is located in the body, the distance between them can also be measured in their shifting ideological-cultural difference. The opening sequence of the pilot ("I Wasn't Ready") revolves around Chapman's showering habits and is, as Hancock remarks, characteristically linked to the physical. The flashback montage of self-cleansing appears as a nostalgia-fueled fantasy contrasted with the dank prison shower's "harsh reality." Chapman's subsequent exchange in the prison shower with fellow inmate Tasha "Taystee" Jefferson (Danielle Brooks) is our first glimpse into her prison interactions. Strikingly, Taystee not only violates Chapman's personal space but makes comments on her body's cultural connotations: Catching a glimpse at Chapman's breasts, she exclaims, "You got them TV titties. They stand up on their own all perky and everything." The dialogue puts into corporeal terms Kohan's comments about Chapman as familiar media fantasy, rendered in the as-yet-alien point of view of a Black, loud, and large fellow inmate (Figure 10). If Chapman is the viewer's "adopted identity," then the dialogue stresses through the comment on her body that this is predicated on television culture's iconographic traditions.

The "TV titties" comment gains further significance through the image preceding the exchange. The scene opens on a seminaked nameless extra and her large sagging breasts. The issue of mediatized femininity versus reality becomes visualized in the difference of what kinds of breasts are eligible for what kinds of narration. If Chapman's "TV titties" are an anomaly in the prison environment, symbolizing her postfeminist femininity, then the unglamorous extra's chest as backdrop promises a putatively realist body politics through which the program communicates its difference from cable television's uses of female nudity. Considering that Netflix positions HBO as its main competitor and that HBO's legacy of courting controversy involves showing explicit sex and eroticized female nudity, *Orange*'s visual rendering of female bodies telegraphs a challenge to these institutional practices right in the opening scene. Although this beginning also mobilizes Taystee as a grotesque alien threat to stress the

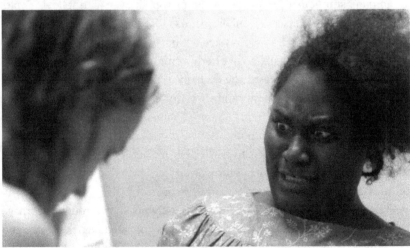

Figure 10. Tasha "Taystee" Jefferson (Danielle Brooks) comments on Piper Chapman's (Taylor Schilling) breasts in *Orange Is the New Black*'s opening scene.

embodied difference of Chapman's postfeminist femininity from the others, it also communicates that the female grotesque is in fact the "real" femininity, its othering being a consequence of its exclusion from quality TV traditions.

Chapman continues to mediate the tension between these femininities through body politics, aligned with the discursive positioning of Netflix in a transgressive contrast with cable TV culture and corresponding to the postfeminism-feminism dichotomy. Consider the season 3 story line in which Chapman sets up an illegal business operation selling fellow prisoners' worn underwear online. This plot contributes to Chapman's increasingly negative portrayal, where the former underdog turns into a gang boss: She manipulates inmates into giving her their underwear in exchange for flavor packets that make the horrible prison food more palatable, keeping the business profits for herself. She becomes a prison queenpin doling out sophisticated punishment, establishing a social hierarchy by the misuse of her class and educational privilege. Her transformation is paralleled with the prison privatization plot depicting how the corporation's inhumane labor practices exploit incarcerated women: It is her new prison job sewing women's underwear in a sweatshop that prompts Chapman's idea of the "dirty panties" business. As Hancock (2016) notes, the critique of the corporate prison's exploitation of women uses the female grotesque, whereas Chapman's portrayal as villain maintains her iconographic physical distance. If she was characterized in earlier seasons as different from the others with her clean femininity, linked with her hipster entrepreneurship (she used to sell artisanal soaps), then this portrayal involves her exploitation of other inmates' physicality in a business venture. With her white-collar business savvy, she recognizes the profitability of *other* female bodies, going from merchandising obscure toiletries to a middle-class market to her small-time capitalization on fellow inmates' leaking bodies. Aligning her portrayal with that of the corporate prison's exploitative practices reaffirms the dichotomy between postfeminist protagonist and a feminist-coded portrayal of the exploited others. The critique of the postfeminist woman links her meanings to corporate capitalism's modus operandi.

Chapman's quasi-villainy is thus expressed in her economic exploitation of othered women's bodies. Critical reception interpreted this shifting portrayal, combined with the increased narrative attention on other protagonists' plots and characterizations, as akin to male antihero figures. Alan Sepinwall (2015c) commented that "Pipes had been broken bad," and Orli Matlow (2015) saw the "villainous Piper" theme linked with the series' political commentary on how the prison industrial complex corrupts prisoners. This resulted in a portrayal reminiscent of—who else's—Walter White's (Bryan Cranston) character trajectory: "It may be panties instead of meth, but Piper's trajectory from where she started is growing just as stark as Vince Gilligan's famous 'Mr. Chips–to–Scarface' paradigm" (Matlow 2015).

Akin to *How to Get Away with Murder*, *Breaking Bad*'s antihero is the template against which critics measure Chapman's complexity, but for both series the female antihero's establishment is directly linked to an embodied femininity involving classed and raced identity politics. Further, critics' comparisons ignore a difference between the cultural position of Walter White's and Chapman's villainy. Chapman's growing unpopularity in fandom, noted by Matlow, is in stark contrast to the popularity and iconic status of Walter's Heisenberg alter ego, evident in the figure's prominence in merchandising (Murray 2014).

Chapman's inclusion into quality television's antihero paradigm is contingent on her inception as a quintessential postfeminist woman, a rendering that the narrative links to her physical depiction and, in season 3, to her antiheroic rise to social power in prison. Because of the character's hipster postfeminism, the nature of criticism inherent in *her* Mr. Chips–to–Scarface trajectory yields specifically gendered results that are different from *Breaking Bad*'s. Abuse of unethically gained social power is a central concern of both series, and the ideological chain of associations around morality offers a juxtaposition between the male-centered drama's discursive expression of a patriarchy in crisis and *Orange*'s expression of a postfeminism in crisis. But in this comparison, gendered differences in fan popularity, narrative centrality of character, and genre descriptors have key consequences for the two series' cultural positions.

Male-centered prestige dramas such as *Breaking Bad* possess high cultural status for recombining televisual forms while offering compelling examinations of troubled patriarchal male identities. As discussed, the core contradiction in this paradigm is that, although it denotes for cultural critics a crisis of traditional masculinities, it does so by mobilizing cultural forms that leave the fictional male figure's ideological-narrative centrality intact, raising him to or keeping him at the center of cultural attention. The cultural fascination with the psychological complexities of these masculinities, depicting identity crises, lays the foundation for a set of programs to be canonized as attaining the highest achievement in television storytelling. This continues to normalize male experience, however troubled, by means of dominant norms of aesthetic judgments.

Mittell (2015a) discusses the gendered difference between the stories of Walter and his wife, Skyler White (Anna Gunn), in *Breaking Bad* as linked to generic traditions. As a thought experiment, he recites the program's narrative arc from Skyler's point of view to argue that, although the promotional-textual treatment foregrounds crime drama's masculinity, the text gradually emphasizes *her* story of being the victim of emotional abuse at the same time as Walt's "patriarchal role and masculine prowess begin to crumble and erode" (Mittell 2015a, 257). Mittell adds that "of course, it is not Skyler's story" (256), and as a side note he acknowledges that her "presence serves as an irritant for some viewers" (257). This is a tamed-down allusion to the social media controversy about Skyler's apparently too foregrounded narrative presence. The controversy, which critical responses challenged for fan discourses' blatant misogyny (Poniewozik 2013), eventually devolved into an online bullying campaign against Anna Gunn. The escalating harassment led Gunn to write an opinion piece in the *New York Times*, calling out gendered online vitriol that conflates fictional characters with the actors portraying them (Gunn 2013). Setting aside Mittell's rhetorical mitigation of the incident and the gendered and misogynistic expectations for quality drama forms that it signals in fan cultures, his final remark about Skyler's story betrays similar assumptions about character gender and its suitable forms of storytelling: "By considering Skyler's perspective, *Breaking Bad* functions in part as a 'women's film' in reverse, told through the rationalizing perspective of the abusive spouse whom we only slowly grow to recognize as the villain" (Mittell 2015a, 257). As *supporting* character, Skyler participates in a masculine crime drama and is a minor player in a story concentrating on the troubled patriarch's complex identity; were *she* the central character, we would be in "women's melodrama" territory, centralizing domestic female victimhood. What Mittell overlooks is that this type of drama would exist in a different (feminine) programming context aimed at a different (feminine) demographic and would likely not be positioned in the quality paradigm—but at least not inserting such an alien narrative into a masculine crime drama would presumably help avoid fandom outrage.[10]

---

10 Gunn's op-ed also cites as a troubling trend the unpopularity of "unhappy suburban wife" characters in other male-centered prestige dramas, for example, Carmela Soprano (Edie Falco) of *The Sopranos* or Betty Draper (January Jones) of *Mad Men* (Gunn 2013). Mittell's argument about the "women's melodrama" positioning equally fits these characters, further signaling both quality TV's reliance on this gendered dynamic and the similarly gendered value judgments in fan reception.

I considered *Breaking Bad*'s gender dynamics and fan responses to them at length because of the invocations of the series in *Orange*'s critical analyses for making sense of Chapman's growing villainy. If her plot can be interpreted as postfeminism-in-crisis, akin to prestige drama's patriarchy-in-crisis narratives, then the textual interest in and fan responses to it betray a different attribution of cultural significance. *Orange*'s discursive feminism-as-quality involves mitigating the character's centrality to the narration, articulated as justified both textually (character flashbacks increase fellow inmates' narrative significance, and dialogue frequently calls out Chapman's class and racial privilege) and paratextually. Her villainy revolves around her social status, in obvious contrast to male-centered prestige drama's obsession with the troubled patriarch's psyche, whose putative crisis similarly signals a postrecessionary cultural interest in shifts in socioeconomic identity. Fan discourses dismissing Chapman further confirm the text's explicit suspicions about its protagonist, which counterintuitively aligns her cultural position with that of Skyler White. The postfeminist antiheroine's villainy does not echo the male antihero's in that *his* character trajectory is subject to sustained textual, critical, and fan fascination. Rather, she starts from a space of social privilege for which both the series and the fan discourses punish her by removing her *narrative* privilege, coinciding with the diegetic time when her character reaches antihero status (learning to navigate the prison space and asserting a higher status in its power structure). Lotz (2014) celebrates the male antihero quality drama for mobilizing feminism in reflecting on patriarchal men grappling with historically shifting gender norms. Chapman's postfeminist antihero is similarly conceived in a political shifting of identities and stands for a putative past of gender scripts linked to social privilege. But unlike in the male-centered prestige drama, this shift emphasizes the gesture of turning narrative attention away from her and toward those overshadowed by her social, cultural, and narrative centrality, a trajectory not demanded of patriarchal male antiheroes. *Orange* defines both its feminism and its quality status by this gesture. In this it fulfills more literally the promise of a discursive crisis for its examined system of privilege and cultural paradigm than does the male-centered drama.

CONCLUSION

In this book I have examined the emergence of a group of American TV programs characterized by their use of feminism as a historical reference and political force to establish their position in the postmillennial quality television paradigm. Associating American television with feminist politics through specific programming, audience targeting, and publicity strategies is a well-worn path for broadcasters to ascribe cultural value to their scripted output. But the cultural and technological sea change around quality TV discourses in and after the 1990s means that the postmillennial feminist quality TV phenomenon tends to be understood as a reaction to and consequence of both mainstream, masculine-coded prestige television and a postfeminist cultural paradigm. By the mid-2010s the phenomenon solidified to the extent that its narrative-generic and characterization patterns, production backgrounds, and institutional positioning were recognizable signifiers of a subcategory of television for various stakeholders, including journalists, audiences, and cultural critics.

THE COMPLEX FEMALE CHARACTER

Symptomatically, the so-called complex or unlikable female character is claimed to possess such cultural influence as to have developed her own subcategory of "antiheroine" television in transnational TV culture (Buonanno 2017). The American reception of BBC3's transatlantic hit comedy *Fleabag* (2016–2019) provides a representative example. TV critics Stassa Edwards (2016) and Emily Nussbaum (2016) praise the series as a novel entry in the "unlikable woman" or "bad girl" comedy genre, updating the trope with an "aggressive" tone (Edwards 2016). The journalists emphasize how the comedy articulates the eponymous character's (Phoebe

Waller-Bridge) moral ambiguity in terms of her conflicted relationship to feminism, quoting the heroine's confession, "I'm a greedy, perverted, selfish, apathetic, cynical, depraved, morally bankrupt woman who can't even call herself a feminist" ("Episode 1"). Completing the litany of antiheroic personality traits, the reference to feminism imagines the movement as another, albeit unattainably positive, identity marker. Bonnie Dow (2002) describes millennial postfeminist television as "lifestyle feminism" in that it provides "a narrative *quest* for central female characters" to work on the self (261; italics in original), but this is an already failed quest for Fleabag: Over before the narrative begins, its failure is fodder for comedy (Gill 2017).

For Jason Mittell (2015b) quality comedy's (male) antiheroes allow the audience to "root . . . against them . . . , watch . . . them fail for our amusement as well as laugh . . . at their boundary-pushing behavioral extremes" (75). In *Fleabag* these faults and extremes stem from the heroine's failed connection to a putatively ubiquitous feminism, as Nussbaum (2016) notes in describing a scene in which Fleabag and her sister visit a feminist seminar: "A dignified older woman . . . asks the audience, 'If you could lose five years of your life to have what society considers the perfect body, would you?' Everyone else stays still, but Fleabag and her sister shoot their hands straight to the ceiling." For Nussbaum the sequence expresses the two characters' "feminine masochism," but it also recalls *Orange*'s treatment of its central character, Piper Chapman. Both series establish the protagonist's classed postfeminist femininity as something to be scrutinized and critiqued as the basis of her unlikability or complexity, presented in a social space in which this femininity signals an inappropriate, exceptional position (the scene ends on Fleabag whispering into the awkward silence, "We are bad feminists"). Traces of *30 Rock*'s "Liz Lemonism" are noticeable here (recall Liz's "failed" or uninformed feminism), and *The Good Wife*'s treatment of Alicia's character arc also falls into the pattern. *The Good Wife*'s most resonant gimmick of serialization, namely, the narrative and visual mirroring of the pilot's cold open with the series finale's last scene, grounds its affective resonance in condemning the heroine's abandonment of female/feminist solidarity (Leonard 2018, 181). Diane's slap signals that Alicia's moral corruption in the world of politics and corporate labor is complete: She betrayed a character whom the series portrays as a robust symbol of (and a nostalgia for) the virtues of second-wave feminism. This betrayal, like the "failed feminisms" in the other examples, is predicated on a narrative that politicizes the private sphere: Alicia betrays Diane by destroying her marriage to boost her own political ambitions.

Although comedy and half-hour dramedy have been the preferred narrative forms for this character-specific subgenre (because of these genres' historic amicability to discursively authored female performance), prestige drama in the mid-2010s increasingly used the tension between character and historic feminism as serialized arcs, as seen in *The Good Wife*. Nostalgia television set in the 1960s and 1970s favors this route: Consider the references in *Masters of Sex* to second-wave feminism affecting the female protagonists' lives, or Amazon's *Good Girls Revolt*, a fictionalized account of the 1969–1970 class action lawsuit brought by female employers of *Newsweek* against the paper's gender discrimination practices. Cable channel Lifetime's first successful effort to fix its reputation as provider of female-targeted mediocre programming was *UnREAL* (2015–2018), an hour-long series killing several birds with one stone to secure industry prestige. Set backstage at a fictitious dating reality show called "Everlasting," *UnREAL* allows for the kind of self-referential, self-critical tone that has characterized many series—at least since *The Mary Tyler Moore Show*—appealing to quality audiences' teleliteracy and presumed smart suspiciousness of television. The dating contest show setup satirizes the kind of content associated with feminine viewing pleasures, the lifeblood of basic cable channels like Lifetime. Concentrating on the personal and professional drama among the (mainly female) producers, *UnREAL* also presents as key conflict these characters' corruption by the television industry, articulated as a betrayal of the feminist cause and progressive race politics. Rachel (Shiri Appleby), the midlevel producer of "Everlasting," is an expert at manipulating contestants ("producing" them in insider parlance) to shoehorn them into female-centered reality TV's reductive character types. She first appears in the pilot wearing a T-shirt with the slogan "This Is What a Feminist Looks Like" ("Pilot"); and she had read women's studies at college before joining the production. The conflict between the TV industry's sexist mediatization of womanhood and one of its midlevel female members' background as a has-been feminist provides a central drama of feminist politics. The series dramatizes Rachel's exploitation of the contestants' personal lives to produce "good TV" (another recurring phrase) *as* failed feminism. Reminiscent of *30 Rock*'s setup, this antiheroine personifies an ideological clash between political, academic feminism and "low" television culture, this way consolidating the program's cultural value.

FAILED FEMINISM, POSTFEMINISM, AND CULTURAL VALUE

The feminism that these antiheroines fail to achieve is implicitly presented as a morally right choice and social-political backdrop, in contrast to the feminism that Dow (2002) describes in relation to millennial postfeminist television. Dow's critique stresses that the *Ally McBeal*–type dramedy strategically conflates personal affect and social policy to blame feminism for personal ills: "If feminism was supposed to make women's lives better, this logic goes, why are they unhappy? . . . The central problem with this equation is that it confuses feminism with women's personal fulfilment. . . . Feminism has never promised women happiness—only justice" (263). Although still connected to "personal fulfilment," feminism does not cause the (predominantly white and affluent) antiheroine's ambiguous morality. Rather, *her* failure to live up to its expectations does. The areas in which the heroine fails demonstrate where these expectations lie: female solidarity, body acceptance, resistance to mediatized femininity, social consciousness, and awareness of racial, class, and other privileges. Postfeminism's choice rhetoric (between career and domesticity, singledom and marriage, motherhood and childlessness) has been critiqued by feminist scholars as false dualism, offering only the appearance of options by presenting socioeconomic and governmental policy issues as matters of domestic decision making. In contrast, these series' critique of their protagonists' failed feminisms offers a dualism (and choice) between "good" feminist behavior and "bad" complicity with patriarchal institutions, dissected in the heroines' intimate psychological portrayals. This configuration of a tense relationship between historic feminist politics and female protagonists and/as antiheroes continued to gain traction in prestige television toward the end of the 2010s—partly responding to the Trump presidency—and surfaced perhaps most directly in the FX miniseries *Mrs. America*. In retelling the story of the 1970s feminist movement's failure to pass the Equal Rights Amendment, the series presents as its central antiheroine, and is most interested in the psychology of, conservative lobbyist Phyllis Schlafly (Cate Blanchett), whose historic antifeminist influence is portrayed as a key agent in laying the foundations of the Trump era's far-right extremism.

As stressed throughout, the generic-aesthetic signifiers of feminist quality TV discursively emerge as a challenge to the quality TV paradigm's masculinism, evident in frequent competitive comparisons of complex female characters to iconic male roles, including narrational features.

Nussbaum (2016) compares Fleabag to "that tragicomic asshole Larry David." Maureen Ryan (2016a), of *Variety*, describes *UnREAL*'s set as "Westeros, but with more headsets and walkie-talkies," and the two female protagonists' friendship as "one of the most complicated and fascinating bonds on TV, now that Walter White and Jesse Pinkman of *Breaking Bad* are gone." Both *Masters of Sex* and *Good Girls Revolt* were claimed to capitalize on and function as the feminist correctives of *Mad Men*'s cultural influence (H. Miller 2013; Prudom 2016). These rhetorical contrastings of feminine- versus masculine-coded TV continue to express ambiguity about ascribing cultural value to the aesthetics of female-centered quality TV. They suggest that this programming exists primarily in relation to its mainstream male-centered counterpart and has evolved by departing from male-centered quality TV's gendered political signifiers. The rhetorical dualism allows for celebrating and canonizing female-centered series for their political significance while leaving the terms on which aesthetic evaluation in the quality TV era has developed unquestioned.

Simultaneously, TV institutions also promote several of the discussed series as responses to ideals of quality in gendered terms and frequently as tools to brand or rebrand the programmer. I demonstrated how Netflix used *Orange* in this capacity, but CBS's promotion of *The Good Wife* was equally borne out of tactically affiliating quality with feminism. As T. C. Miller (2016) shows, the channel reanimated its own promotional strategies from its 1970s female-led sitcom cycle, this time by contrasting cable TV's "rampant, old-timey" sexism (7) with broadcast TV's modern political progressiveness, to disprove CBS's outdated status. NBC used *30 Rock* and *Parks and Recreation* in similar capacities, as demonstrated in the detailed analyses. *UnREAL* was seen as being mandated with fixing Lifetime's bad reputation and as cleverly exploiting this reputation to produce quality drama (Lyons 2015b). Streaming services cultivate a form of half-hour dramedy that associates the companies with modern edginess both aesthetically and politically by narrativizing identity politics through American independent cinema's aesthetics (e.g., *Master of None* [2015–2017], *Easy* [2016–2019], *Transparent*, *One Mississippi* [2015–2017]).[1]

---

1   See Havas and Sulimma (2018).

BODY POLITICS AND CULTURAL VALUE

The use of feminist and identity politics in the analyzed series also illuminates a tight but conflicted relationship among quality TV's genre conventions, gender, and body politics. Notable in the programs' invocation of feminism as the basis of aesthetic exceptionality is the significance attributed to body politics, which affects their appeal to cultural value and its media reception. The generic exceptionalism of both *30 Rock* and *Parks* affects the female comedians' uses of physical comedy: Paratexts articulated *30 Rock*'s increasing use of the female grotesque and its simultaneous reliance on cartoonesque satire as responses to the postfeminist dramedy's oppressive dominance and to the pretty/funny dilemma faced by the female comedian. But critical reception considered Fey's feminist comic star text, popularized in magazine discourses as a negotiation between female glamour and humor, as being at odds with the grotesque femininity mobilized on *30 Rock*. This led to debates about the series' feminist and quality credentials in the backlash years of Fey's celebrity. *Parks*' more unanimous reputation as feminist quality TV stems from the series' tonal change after its first season, which involved downplaying Amy Poehler's physical comedy, situated in mockumentary's cringe aesthetic, and instead emphasizing her verbal and impersonation skills. Changes in gendered bodily performance affected the two comedies' genre signifiers and their associated cultural value.

Body politics are a similarly pivotal issue for the quality feminism of hour-long programs. As T. C. Miller (2016) shows, *The Good Wife* uses high fashion and the female ensemble's iconography to articulate the series' production values and relationship to feminism. And as discussed, the female face and masquerades of femininity serve symbolic functions for the program's sophisticated aesthetics and gender politics. In the context of streaming culture, *Orange*'s touted iconoclasm concerns its promoted realism around both the female body and genre conventions, where the female body is strategically contrasted with premium cable television's gratuitous female nudity and with postfeminist femininity. Similarly, the premise of *Masters of Sex* is grounded in a transgressive connection between sexual and feminist politics: Charting the revolution in the historic academic research of human sexuality, it links this research to the cultural influence of the women's liberation movement.

Thus female sexuality and body politics continue to be pivotal yet contested areas for feminist quality TV, given the body's centrality to visual arts and the historic debates surrounding representations of the female body. As shown, the programs' modes of expression and their representations of the female body and sexuality are interrelated: Dramatic series lend much significance to a discursively progressive realism of dealing with the (sexual) corporeal as claims to authenticity and exceptionality (*Orange*, *Masters of Sex*). This applies to *The Good Wife* too in reverse: Institutional regulations of network television restrict promoting such notions of realism around the female body, which the program exploits by emphasizing the *masquerade* of femininities among its female cast, complicating the dualism of artifice and reality.

For comedy this connection is less straightforward because of the perceived conflict between funniness and serious or realistic political intentions. The entrenched understanding of seriousness as the default human expression lies at the core of this contrast. Because comedy and funniness are seen as deviations from this norm and require clear signals to be decoded, the use of the female body and sexuality in comedy as sites of serious politics is bound to be controversial. This cultural ambiguity partly accounts for the emergence of half-hour dramedies about identity and sexual politics on cable and online platforms (*Girls*, *Transparent*, *One Mississippi*, *Master of None*, etc.). In industry awards shows these series fall into the comedy category without exception, following from their production backgrounds, especially in cases where they are developed from a comedian's stand-up persona (e.g., Aziz Ansari, Tig Notaro). Yet they deal in discursively progressive treatments of sexual and identity politics in ways that appear to require the dramatic tone's increased influence. *Fleabag* is perhaps a more demonstrative example of this, given its raunchy sexual comedy and its roots in Waller-Bridge's stand-up. The blue comedy of women's sexuality is played initially for laughs but creeps toward psychological drama, and the narrative twist in the first series' last episode dramatically reveals that Fleabag's funny promiscuity is rooted in unprocessed trauma. For critics the seriousness with which these dramedies treat sexual and identity politics accounts for much of their cultural value, expressed in tonal changes from the comic toward the dramatic.

THE AESTHETIC TURN AND FEMINIST SCHOLARSHIP

These considerations of these series' cultural work in the wider landscape of mid-2010s American television have a crucial bearing on television scholarship, to which I finally return. As stated, my argument aims to intervene in ongoing discussions in television studies about the aesthetic evaluation practices of TV texts: This "aesthetic turn" (Lury 2016) has been met with suspicion in the cultural and media studies community. Throughout this book I have combined the methodologies of feminist media studies, aesthetic analysis, critical reception studies, industry analysis, and celebrity studies to examine the feminist quality TV phenomenon, arguing for the necessity of considering the interconnection of these aspects in teasing out this programming's cultural significance. Mobilizing feminist media studies alongside aesthetic analysis was motivated only partly by an emancipatory gesture of, in Nygaard and Lagerwey (2016) words, "reclaim[ing] TV studies' feminist roots" (7). Although I share their concern that the debate sidelines the discipline, or rather treats it as an obligatory constituent of political approaches, I find the role of feminist analysis in the debate more complicated than this suggests.

I demonstrated in chapter 6 through the scrutiny of Jason Mittell's work how the championing of the aesthetic exceptionality of certain TV programs draws selectively on feminist analysis to argue their *political* exceptionality as an auxiliary feature. Applying tools of feminist media analysis in similarly selective ways crops up frequently in academic debates. Another characteristic example can be found in James Zborowski's (2016) intervention, which aims to reconcile the "TV aesthetics" approach and the "media and cultural studies" approach. Zborowski engages with the two camps' opposing arguments and quotes Jason Jacobs and Stephen Peacock (2013) to demonstrate the untenability of this divide. The quoted passage discusses a scene from *Mad Men* that has a specifically gendered theme (centralizing the 1960s housewife's subjectivity in a domestic dispute) in order to show that, although the scene offers itself for feminist analysis, this would be "critical hubris" (Zborowski 2016, 13), because this method would not allow for capturing the scene's "expressive *punctum*," or aesthetic significance (13). Zborowski critiques the false dualism, arguing that "to analyze a text for its representations of particular dimensions of sociocultural identity and to treat it as an aesthetic object are different activities, but not necessarily mutually exclusive ones" (12). He claims that our understanding of the "aesthetic achievements" of series such as *Mad Men* or *The Wire* can be enriched by enlisting history, sociology, and so on "as tools that might fine tune our ability to do justice to the[se] aesthetic achievements" (13).

Although Zborowski's point is laudable in its reconciliatory effort, it also lays bare a representative problem with customary approaches to the debate. For discussing this, I set aside for now another issue with his argument, namely, the implicit assumption that scholarly inquiry has a mission to "do justice" to aesthetic achievement. Similar to skepticism in feminist media studies about the scholarly usefulness of trying to prove a media text's feminist achievements (the feminist ur-article per Charlotte Brunsdon [2005]), it is unclear how aesthetic judgment furthers existing academic knowledge and methods.[2] But I want to highlight in Zborowski's account that the dialogue it joins invokes feminist analysis as an *example* to make its broader point about different academic approaches. This is a representative and tendentious method in the field, ensuring that feminist analysis does not necessarily become ignored (as Nygaard and Lagerwey warn) but is strategically displayed as a prominent mode of sociopolitical engagement, in the process mischaracterizing its usefulness. This utilitarian logic is similar in both Jacobs and Peacock's and Zborowski's positions, despite their disagreement about feminism's role in aesthetic analysis, and recalls Mittell's examined strategy that reduces feminist analysis to a toolkit to be cherry-picked from to prove (or to "do justice to") the text's political achievements. This reduction means that a whole set of scholarship becomes glossed over, likely those views that could derail the respective rhetoric of achievement.

Staying with *Mad Men* as our example, we can note that the series has been subjected to feminist scholarship's scrutiny as postfeminist nostalgia television. Mimi White (2011) suggests that the program's promotional materials place its fictional women in "historic/realist representation, despite their often stereotypical referents" (157). The appeal to historic realism produces a contradiction for the program's own relationship to its women characters, because it both positions them as types of mediatized womanhood within its mythologizing aesthetic and also associates them with discourses of social history. As a result, "the very artificial (sometimes parodic) representations of women are turned into the stuff of history" (157). Lynn Spigel (2013) also scrutinizes *Mad Men*'s gender politics, arguing that the program's nostalgia

---

2   This question gained traction in media studies in the mid-2010s; for instance, the journal *Screen* devoted its summer 2016 special issue to it.

rewrites the historic significance of second-wave feminism: Although the series clearly deals in representing the era's gender politics, it never refers to the women's liberation movement, an evasion made even more conspicuous by constant textual references to *other* social-political events and by creator-producer Matthew Weiner's statements that his prime inspirations for the series were Betty Friedan's *The Feminine Mystique* and Helen Gurley Brown's *Sex and the Single Girl* (272). This way, Spigel suggests, the show imagines a prefeminist past that has organically led to a postfeminist present, without ever depicting the political struggles of actual feminist movements in the middle (275).

White's and Spigel's accounts provide only two examples of incisive feminist criticism problematizing *Mad Men*'s cultural work, and their arguments around the slick aesthetics of nostalgia television in relation to gender politics are at odds with the language of political-aesthetic achievement used by Jacobs and Peacock and Zborowski. They also expose that "treat[ing a TV text] as an aesthetic object" and considering their social, political, and promotional context are not "different activities," as Zborowski (2016, 12) has it, and combining them (along with other approaches necessitated by the text's cultural position) should not serve to further foster already ongoing processes of canonization but to interrogate the cultural forces underlying them. To boot, a hypothetical investigation of the emergence of post– or anti–*Mad Men* nostalgia television such as *Good Girls Revolt* and *Masters of Sex* would need to prioritize Spigel and White's arguments over a mainly aesthetic analysis.

My aim in this book has not only been to challenge the TV aesthetics debate but also to expose its false dichotomies by demonstrating by means of the analysis of postmillennial feminist quality TV the necessity of synthetizing approaches. It could be argued that examining this particular group of texts and the cultural context in which they exist obviously calls for feminist analysis alongside aesthetic study or, in fact, could work without considering aesthetics and issues of cultural value. But if we are to understand these programs' significance in television culture and how as a group they signal shifting trends in the cultural position of gender politics in the American mediasphere, these approaches cannot be divorced from each other. This applies to the examinations of most aspects and trends of the medium but become essential in the digital "Peak TV" era. After all, from the medium's beginnings, television culture, and certainly quality television culture, has been conceived by the industry and public discourses as a specifically gendered set of practices. Aesthetics-focused television scholarship, in its evaluation of narrative and formal achievements, tends to mitigate or misinterpret the role of this genderedness and the relevance of feminist scholarship for its analysis. But equally, feminist scholarship often evades querying the role of form, aesthetics, and attendant cultural status in its ideological analysis of gender and television, instead passing judgments on the gendered progressivism or conservatism of TV texts. The conflation of analysis with appreciation of achievement is thus an unfortunate bridge in the contrived rift between political and aesthetic approaches to TV culture. Television studies needs to reconsider its relationship to these approaches; otherwise it risks undermining its usefulness for interrogating the forces that govern the shifting cultural presence of early-twenty-first-century television, eminently displayed in the feminist quality TV phenomenon.

BIBLIOGRAPHY

Adalian, Josef. 2016. "Super Bowl Shocker: *The Good Wife* Will End in May." *Vulture*, February 8. http://www.vulture.com/2016/02/super-bowl-shocker-the-good-wife -to-end-in-may.html.

Adams, Erik. 2012. "Showrunner Michael Schur on Building *Parks and Recreation's* Fourth Season (Part 3 of 5)." *The AV Club*, June 20. http://www.avclub.com/article/ showrunner-michael-schur-on-building-iparks-and-re-81531.

Adams, Sam. 2012. "Has Liz Lemon Become 'Dumbass Homer'?" *Slate*, February 10. https://slate.com/culture/2012/02/liz-lemon-and-homer-simpson -is-30-rock-getting-stupider.html.

Albrecht, Michael Mario. 2015. *Masculinity in Contemporary Quality Television.* Farnham, UK: Ashgate.

Arnold, Sarah. 2016. "Netflix and the Myth of Choice/Participation/Autonomy." In *The Netflix Effect: Technology and Entertainment in the 21st Century*, ed. Kevin McDonald and Daniel Smith-Rowsey, 49–62. New York: Bloomsbury Academic.

Arthurs, Jane. 1999. "Revolting Women: The Body in Comic Performance." In *Women's Bodies: Discipline and Transgression*, ed. Jane Arthurs and Jean Grimshaw, 137–64. London: Cassell.

———. 2007. "*Sex and the City* and Consumer Culture: Remediating Postfeminist Drama." In *Television: The Critical View*, 7th ed., ed. Horace Newcomb, 315–31. New York: Oxford University Press.

Arthurs, Jane, and Jean Grimshaw. 1999. "Introduction." In *Women's Bodies: Discipline and Transgression*, ed. Jane Arthurs and Jean Grimshaw, 1–16. London: Cassell.

Ausiello, Michael. 2016. "*The Good Wife* Creators Explain That Striking Final Scene: 'The Victim Becomes the Victimizer.'" *TV Line*, May 9. http://tvline.com/2016/ 05/08/the-good-wife-finale-slap-interview-robert-king-explains/.

Baldwin, Kristen. 2015. "Tina Fey: The EW Interview." *EW.com*, January 17. https:// ew.com/article/2012/09/28/tina-fey-ew-interview/.

Banet-Weiser, Sarah. 2018. *Empowered: Popular Feminism and Popular Misogyny.* Durham, NC: Duke University Press.

Bathrick, Serafina. 1984. "*The Mary Tyler Moore Show*: Women at Home and at Work." In *MTM: "Quality Television,"* ed. Jane Feuer, Paul Kerr, and Tise Vahimagi, 99–131. London: BFI.

Baysinger, Tim. 2015. "*Parks & Recreation*: 'Must-See' You Later." *Broadcasting & Cable*, February 23.

Berlant, Lauren Gail. 2011. *Cruel Optimism*. Durham, NC: Duke University Press.

Bianculli, David. 2000. *Teleliteracy: Taking Television Seriously*. Syracuse, NY: Syracuse University Press.

Bignell, Jonathan. 2013. *An Introduction to Television Studies*. London: Routledge.

Bigsby, C. W. E. 2013. *Viewing America: Twenty-First Century Television Drama*. New York: Cambridge University Press.

Birnbaum, Debra. 2015a. "*Orange Is the New Black* Emmy Petition Denied: Jailed in Drama Category." *Variety*, March 20. http://variety.com/2015/tv/news/orange-is-the-new-black-emmys-1201456619/.

———. 2015b. "TV Academy's Bruce Rosenblum on Emmy Rule Changes, Younger Voters, and Diversity." *Variety*, June 3. http://variety.com/2015/tv/spotlight/emmy-awards-rule-changes-diversity-1201508452/.

Bishop, Bart. 2015. "The Joker as Sexual Predator: Rape, Queer Readings, and Anticipatory Outrage for *Suicide Squad*." *Bleeding Cool: Comic Book, Movie, TV News*, May 14. http://www.bleedingcool.com/2015/05/14/the-joker-as-sexual-predator-rape-queer-readings-and-anticipatory-outrage-for-suicide-squad/.

Blay, Zeba. 2015. "How Feminist TV Became the New Normal." *Huffington Post*, June 18. http://www.huffingtonpost.com/2015/06/18/how-feminist-tv-became-the-new-normal_n_7567898.html.

Bosch, Torie. 2012. "*The Good Wife* Tackles Tricky Subject of Women Opting Out of Work." *Slate*, March 12. https://slate.com/human-interest/2012/03/the-good-wife-educated-women-dropping-out-of-workforce.html.

Bowler, Alexia. 2013. "Towards a New Sexual Conservatism in Postfeminist Romantic Comedy." In *Postfeminism and Contemporary Hollywood Cinema*, ed. Nadine Müller and Joel Gwynne, 185–203. New York: Palgrave Macmillan.

Boyle, Bridget. 2013. "Bits and Bumps: Gender, Comedy, and the Body." *Ejournalist* 13(1): 85–101.

———. 2015. "Take Me Seriously. Now Laugh at Me! How Gender Influences the Creation of Contemporary Physical Comedy." *Comedy Studies* 6(1): 78–90. doi:10.1080/2040610X.2015.1028167.

Broe, Dennis. 2019. *Birth of the Binge: Serial TV and the End of Leisure*. Detroit: Wayne State University Press.

Bronfen, Elisabeth. 1996. *Over Her Dead Body: Death, Femininity, and the Aesthetic*. Manchester, UK: Manchester University Press.

Brooks Olsen, Hanna. 2015. "A Leslie Knope in a World Full of Liz Lemons." *Medium*, January 22. https://medium.com/@mshannabrooks/a-leslie-knope-in-a-world-full-of-liz-lemons-61726b6c6493.

Brown, Laura. 2009. "Tina Fey Rocks." *Harper's Bazaar*, July 10. http://www.harpersbazaar.com/celebrity/news/tina-fey-interview-1109.

Brunsdon, Charlotte. 1990. "Problems with Quality." *Screen* 31(1): 67–90. doi:10.1093/screen/31.1.67.

———. 1997. *Screen Tastes: Soap Opera to Satellite Dishes*. London: Routledge.

———. 2005. "Feminism, Postfeminism, Martha, Martha, and Nigella." *Cinema Journal* 44(2): 110–16. doi:10.1353/cj.2005.0005.

Buonanno, Milly, ed. 2017. *Television Anti-Heroines: Women Behaving Badly in Crime and Prison Drama*. Bristol, UK: Intellect.

Bustillos, Maria. 2014. "The Birth of Adulthood in American Culture." *The Awl*, September 15. http://www.theawl.com/2014/09/the-birth-of-adulthood-in -american-culture.

Butler, Jeremy G. 2010. *Television Style*. New York: Routledge.

Cardwell, Sarah. 2007. "Is Quality Television Any Good? Generic Distinctions, Evaluations, and the Troubling Matter of Critical Judgment." In *Quality TV: Contemporary American Television and Beyond*, ed. Janet McCabe and Kim Akass, 19–34. London: I. B. Tauris.

Carter, Bill. 2011. "*30 Rock* to Continue Even If Alec Baldwin Leaves, NBC Says." *New York Times*, August 2. http://www.nytimes.com/2011/08/03/arts/television/30 -rock-to-continue-even-if-alec-baldwin-leaves-nbc-says.html.

Chaney, Jen. 2013. "The Liz Lemon Effect." *Slate*, January 30. http://www.slate.com/ articles/double_x/doublex/2013/01/_30_rock_finale_the_legacy_of_tina_fey _at_the_nbc_show_s_final_episode.html.

Clayton, Alex. 2007. *The Body in Hollywood Slapstick*. Jefferson, NC: McFarland.

Clover, Carol J. 1987. "Her Body, Himself: Gender in the Slasher Film." *Representations* 20: 187–228. doi:10.2307/2928507.

Cooper, Brenda. 2001. "Unapologetic Women, 'Comic Men,' and Feminine Spectatorship in David E. Kelley's *Ally McBeal*." *Critical Studies in Media Communication* 18(4): 416–35. doi:10.1080/07393180128092.

Creeber, Glen. 2004. *Serial Television: Big Drama on the Small Screen*. London: BFI.

Crenshaw, Kimberlé. 1989. "Demarginalizing the Intersection of Race and Sex: A Black Feminist Critique of Antidiscrimination Doctrine, Feminist Theory, and Antiracist Politics." *University of Chicago Legal Forum* 140: 139–67.

Crider, Michael. 2011. "*30 Rock* Season 6 to Be Its Last, Says Alec Baldwin." *Screen Rant*, April 6. http://screenrant.com/30-rock-season-6-ending-alec-baldwin -mcrid-109620/.

Cuen, Leigh. 2016. "*Game of Thrones* Season 6 Is the Most Feminist of All—and Here's Why." *Mic*, June 20. https://mic.com/articles/146562/game-of-thrones-season-6-is -the-most-feminist-of-all-and-here-s-why.

D'Acci, Julie. 1994. *Defining Women: Television and the Case of Cagney & Lacey*. Chapel Hill: University of North Carolina Press.

Dailey, Kate. 2010. "Leslie Knope, Liz Lemon, and the Feminist Lessons of NBC's *Parks and Recreation*." *Newsweek*, April 8. http://www.newsweek.com/leslie -knope-liz-lemon-and-feminist-lessons-nbcs-parks-and-recreation-222734.

Dale, Alan S. 2000. *Comedy Is a Man in Trouble: Slapstick in American Movies*. Minneapolis: University of Minnesota Press.

Dasgupta, Sudeep. 2012. "Policing the People: Television Studies and the Problem of 'Quality.'" *NECSUS European Journal of Media Studies* 1(1). http://

www.necsus-ejms.org/policing-the-people-television-studies-and-the-problem-of-quality-by-sudeep-dasgupta/.

DeCarvalho, Lauren J., and Nicole B. Cox. 2016. "Extended 'Visiting Hours': Deconstructing Identity in Netflix's Promotional Campaigns for *Orange Is the New Black*." *Television and New Media* 17(6): 504–19.

Deziel, Melanie. n.d. "Women Inmates: Why the Male Model Doesn't Work." *New York Times*. http://paidpost.nytimes.com/netflix/women-inmates-separate-but-not-equal.html (accessed January 22, 2016).

Dockterman, Eliana. 2014. "What Men Can Learn from *Orange Is the New Black*." *Time*, June 10. http://time.com/2848310/orange-is-the-new-black-men/.

Donatelli, Cindy, and Sharon Alward. 2002. "'I Dread You'? Married to the Mob in *The Godfather*, *GoodFellas*, and *The Sopranos*." In *This Thing of Ours: Investigating the Sopranos*, ed. David Lavery, 60–71. New York: Columbia University Press and Wallflower Press.

Donnelly, Matt. 2015. "Emmy Winner Uzo Aduba Is, in Fact, the New Ed Asner." *The Wrap*, September 20. http://www.thewrap.com/emmy-winner-uzo-aduba-is-in-fact-the-new-ed-asner/.

Douglas, Susan J. 2010. *The Rise of Enlightened Sexism: How Pop Culture Took Us from Girl Power to Girls Gone Wild*. New York: St. Martin's Griffin.

Dow, Bonnie J. 1996. *Prime-Time Feminism: Television, Media Culture, and the Women's Movement Since 1970*. Philadelphia: University of Pennsylvania Press.

———. 2002. "*Ally McBeal*, Lifestyle Feminism, and the Politics of Personal Happiness." *Communication Review* 5(4): 259–64. doi:10.1080/10714420214688.

Doyle, Sady. 2010. "13 Ways of Looking at Liz Lemon." *Tiger Beatdown*, March 24. http://tigerbeatdown.com/2010/03/24/13-ways-of-looking-at-liz-lemon/.

Duberman, Amanda. 2014. "Amy Poehler on Celebrity Feminism Conversation: It's an 'Attempt to Get Us to Talk Sh*t About Each Other.'" *Huffington Post*, October 28. http://www.huffingtonpost.com/2014/10/28/amy-poehler-feminism-celebrity_n_6064350.html.

Durham, Aisha. 2012. "'Check On It': Beyoncé, Southern Booty, and Black Femininities in Music Video." *Feminist Media Studies* 12(1): 35–49. doi:10.1080/14680777.2011.558346.

Edgerton, Gary R. 2009. "Introduction: A Brief History of HBO." In *The Essential HBO Reader*, ed. Gary R. Edgerton and Jeffrey P. Jones, 1–20. Lexington: University Press of Kentucky.

Edgerton, Gary R., and Jeffrey P. Jones, eds. 2009. *The Essential HBO Reader*. Lexington: University Press of Kentucky.

Edwards, Stassa. 2016. "Amazon's *Fleabag* Is a Complex Look at an 'Unlikable Woman.'" *The Muse*, September 26. http://themuse.jezebel.com/amazons-fleabag-is-a-complex-look-at-an-unlikable-woma-1787083404.

Escobedo Shepherd, Julianne. 2015. "The Women of Pawnee Ruled *Parks & Recreation* 'til the Very End." *The Muse*, February 25. http://themuse.jezebel.com/the-women-of-pawnee-ruled-parks-recreation-til-the-ve-1688037847.

Ess, Ramsey. 2013. "Looking Back at *30 Rock* with Tina Fey, Robert Carlock, and the Writers." *Splitsider*, March 1. https://www.vulture.com/2013/03/looking-back-at-30-rock-with-tina-fey-robert-carlock-and-the-writers.html.

Everett, Anna. 2015. "Scandalicious: *Scandal*, Social Media, and Shonda Rhimes' Auteurist Juggernaut." *Black Scholar* 45(1): 34–43. doi:10.1080/00064246.2014.997602.

Fallon, Kevin. 2010. "Showtime: Television for Women, for Everyone?" *The Atlantic*, August 16. http://www.theatlantic.com/entertainment/archive/2010/08/showtime-television-for-women-for-everyone/61535/.

Faludi, Susan. 1991. *Backlash: The Undeclared War Against American Women*. New York: Crown.

Feuer, Jane. 1984a. "MTM Enterprises: An Overview." In *MTM: "Quality Television,"* ed. Jane Feuer, Paul Kerr, and Tise Vahimagi, 1–31. London: BFI.

———. 1984b. "The MTM Style." In *MTM: "Quality Television,"* ed. Jane Feuer, Paul Kerr, and Tise Vahimagi, 32–60. London: BFI.

———. 2007. "HBO and the Concept of Quality TV." In *Quality TV: Contemporary American Television and Beyond*, ed. Janet McCabe and Kim Akass, 145–57. London: I. B. Tauris.

Feuer, Jane, Paul Kerr, and Tise Vahimagi, eds. 1984. *MTM: "Quality Television."* London: BFI.

Fey, Tina. 2011. *Bossypants*. New York: Little, Brown.

Fienberg, Daniel. 2013. "Interview: *Orange Is the New Black* Creator Jenji Kohan Talks Prison, Netflix, and Jodie Foster." *HitFix*, July 10. http://www.hitfix.com/the-fien-print/interview-orange-is-the-new-black-creator-jenji-kohan-talks-prison-netflix-and-jodie-foster.

Fiske, John. 2011. *Television Culture*, 2nd ed. London: Routledge.

Flint, Joe. 2013. "*The Good Wife* Will Have Multiple Partners in Syndication." *Los Angeles Times*, March 13. http://articles.latimes.com/2013/mar/13/entertainment/la-et-ct-good-wife-20130313.

Fox, Jesse David. 2015. "The History of Tina Fey and Amy Poehler's Best Friendship." *Vulture*, January 8. http://www.vulture.com/2013/01/history-of-tina-and-amys-best-friendship.html.

Friedlander, Whitney. 2014. "*Parks and Recreation*'s Hidden Political Commentary." *Variety*, March 19. http://variety.com/2014/tv/news/parks-and-recreations-hidden-political-commentary-1201139020/.

Frucci, Adam. 2011. "Entertainment Weekly Dubs *Parks and Rec* 'TV's Smartest Comedy.'" *Splitsider*, October 2. https://www.vulture.com/2011/02/entertainment-weekly-dubs-parks-and-rec-tvs-smartest-comedy.html.

Garber, Megan, David Sims, Lenika Cruz, and Sophie Gilbert. 2015. "Have We Reached 'Peak TV'?" *The Atlantic*, August 12. http://www.theatlantic.com/entertainment/archive/2015/08/have-we-reached-peak-tv/401009/.

Gilbert, Joanne R. 2004. *Performing Marginality: Humor, Gender, and Cultural Critique*. Detroit: Wayne State University Press.

Gill, Rosalind. 2007. "Postfeminist Media Culture: Elements of a Sensibility." *European Journal of Cultural Studies* 10(2): 147–66. doi:10.1177/1367549407075898.

——. 2016. "Post-Postfeminism? New Feminist Visibilities in Postfeminist Times." *Feminist Media Studies* 16(4): 610–30. doi:10.1080/14680777.2016.1193293.

Gjelsvik, Anne, and Rikke Schubart, eds. 2016. *Women of Ice and Fire: Gender, Game of Thrones, and Multiple Media Engagements.* New York: Bloomsbury Academic.

Goldberg, Lesley. 2016. "*Good Wife* Final Season Confirmed." *Hollywood Reporter,* February 7. http://www.hollywoodreporter.com/live-feed/good-wife-final-season -confirmed-862839.

Goodman, Tim. 2013. "Tim Goodman's 11 Best Network Dramas." *Hollywood Reporter,* December 23. http://www.hollywoodreporter.com/bastard-machine/best-network -dramas-2013-665636.

Griffin, Molly Marie. 2010. "How Tina Fey Ousted Carrie Bradshaw." *Salon,* May 20. http://www.salon.com/2010/05/20/tina_fey_recession_americas_carrie _bradshaw/.

Gunn, Anna. 2013. "I Have a Character Issue." *New York Times,* August 23. http://www .nytimes.com/2013/08/24/opinion/i-have-a-character-issue.html.

Hamad, Hannah, and Diane Negra. 2020. "The New Plutocratic (Post)Feminism." In *New Feminist Studies: Twenty-First Century Critical Interventions,* ed. Jennifer Cooke, 83–96. Cambridge, UK: Cambridge University Press.

Hamad, Hannah, and Anthea Taylor. 2015. "Introduction: Feminism and Contemporary Celebrity Culture." *Celebrity Studies* 6(1): 124–27. doi:10.1080/1939239 7.2015.1005382.

Hamamoto, Darrell Y. 1991. *Nervous Laughter: Television Situation Comedy and Liberal Democratic Ideology.* Westport, CT: Praeger.

Hancock, Danielle. 2016. "Give It a Week, You'll Be Pissing and Farting with the Rest of Us: Becoming Grotesque in *Orange Is the New Black.*" *CST Online,* March 17. http://cstonline.tv/oitnb.

Hanson, Evan. 2014. "What *Orange Is the New Black* Means to Netflix." *247wallst,* June 7. http://247wallst.com/media/2014/06/07/what-orange-is-the-new-black -means-to-netflix/.

Harnick, Chris. 2012. "*The Good Wife*: Alicia Florrick's Mentoring 101." *Huffington Post,* May 11. http://www.huffingtonpost.com/chris-harnick/the-good-wife -recap_b_1338134.html.

Harvey, Chris. 2014. "*Orange Is the New Black* Author: 'People Are Sexual Beings, Even If You Lock Them in a Cage.'" *The Telegraph,* June 5. http://www.telegraph .co.uk/culture/tvandradio/10877836/Orange-is-the-New-Black-author-People -are-sexual-beings-even-if-you-lock-them-in-a-cage.html.

Havas, Julia. 2017. "Tina Fey: 'Quality' Comedy and the Body of the Female Comedy Author." In *Hysterical! Women in American Comedy,* ed. Linda Mizejewski and Victoria Sturtevant, 347–78. Austin: University of Texas Press.

Havas, Julia, and Maria Sulimma. 2018. "Through the Gaps of My Fingers: Genre, Femininity, and Cringe Aesthetics in Dramedy Television." *Television and New Media* 21(1). doi:10.1177/1527476418777838.

Heffernan, Virginia. 2003. "Anchor Woman." *The New Yorker*, March 11. http://www
.newyorker.com/magazine/2003/11/03/anchor-woman.

Heisler, Steve. 2012. "'The Comeback Kid': *Parks and Recreation*." *The AV Club*, January 12. http://www.avclub.com/tvclub/parks-and-recreation-the-comeback-kid
-67479.

Hermes, Joke. 2006. "*Ally McBeal, Sex and the City*, and the Tragic Success of Feminism." In *Feminism in Popular Culture*, ed. Joanne Hollows and Rachel Moseley,
79–95. Oxford, UK: Berg.

Hight, Craig. 2010. *Television Mockumentary: Reflexivity, Satire, and a Call to Play*.
Manchester, UK: Manchester University Press.

Hinckley, David. 2014. "Emmy Awards 2014 Nominations: *The Good Wife*, Tatiana
Maslany, James Spader Among Biggest Snubs." *New York Daily News*, July 10.
http://www.nydailynews.com/entertainment/tv/good-wife-emmy-awards
-biggest-snubs-article-1.1861910.

Hoffman, Jan. 2011. "*The Good Wife* and Its Women." *New York Times*, April 29.
http://www.nytimes.com/2011/05/01/fashion/01CULTURAL.html.

Hollows, Joanne, and Rachel Moseley. 2006. "Popularity Contests: The Meanings of
Popular Feminism." In *Feminism in Popular Culture*, ed. Joanne Hollows and
Rachel Moseley, 1–22. Oxford, UK: Berg.

Holmes, Linda. 2012. "The Incredible Shrinking Liz Lemon: From Woman to Little Girl." *NPR.org*, February 9. http://www.npr.org/sections/monkeysee/2012/
02/09/146626983/the-incredible-shrinking-liz-lemon-from-woman-to-little
-girl.

Idato, Michael. 2014. "*The Good Wife* not Good Enough as Emmy Award Nominations Reveal Surprise Snubs." *Sydney Morning Herald*, July 11. http://www
.smh.com.au/entertainment/tv-and-radio/the-good-wife-not-good-enough-as
-emmy-award-nominations-reveal-surprise-snubs-20140711-zt3m9.html.

Imre, Anikó. 2009. "Gender and Quality Television: A Transcultural Feminist Project."
Feminist Media Studies 9(4): 391–407. doi:10.1080/14680770903232987.

———. 2016. *TV Socialism*. Durham, NC: Duke University Press.

Irving, Dan. 2008. "Normalized Transgressions: Legitimizing the Transsexual Body
as Productive." *Radical History Review* 2008(100): 38–59. doi:10.1215/0163654
5-2007-021.

Jacobs, Jason, and Stephen Peacock. 2013. "Introduction." In *Television Aesthetics
and Style*, ed. Jason Jacobs and Stephen Peacock, 1–20. New York: Bloomsbury
Academic.

Jenner, Mareike. 2016. "Is This TVIV? On Netflix, TVIII, and Binge-Watching." *New
Media and Society* 18(2): 257–73. doi:10.1177/1461444814541523.

———. 2018. *Netflix and the Re-Invention of Television*. Cham, Switzerland: Palgrave
Macmillan.

Jensen, Jeff. 2015. "*Parks and Recreation* Series Finale Review: Sorry, *Two and a Half
Men*, but This Is How You Make a 'Winning!' Finale." *EW.com*, February 26.
http://www.ew.com/article/2015/02/24/parks-and-recreation-series-finale
-review.

Johnson, Merri Lisa. 2007a. "Gangster Feminism: The Feminist Cultural Work of HBO's *The Sopranos.*" In *Third Wave Feminism and Television: Jane Puts It in a Box*, ed. Merri Lisa Johnson, 28–55. London: I. B. Tauris.

———. 2007b. "Introduction: Ladies Love Your Box—The Rhetoric of Pleasure and Danger in Feminist Television Studies." In *Third Wave Feminism and Television: Jane Puts It in a Box*, ed. Merri Lisa Johnson, 1–27. London: I. B. Tauris.

Jones, Bethany. 2014. "*Game of Thrones*, Sex, and HBO: Where Did TV's Sexual Pioneer Go Wrong?" *Jezebel*, May 6. http://jezebel.com/game-of-thrones-sex-and -hbo-where-did-tvs-sexual-pion-1586508636.

Joyrich, Lynne. 1988. "All That Television Allows: TV Melodrama, Postmodernism, and Consumer Culture." *Camera Obscura: Feminism, Culture, and Media Studies* 6(1[16]): 128–53. doi:10.1215/02705346-6-1_16–128.

———. 1996. *Re-Viewing Reception: Television, Gender, and Postmodern Culture.* Bloomington: Indiana University Press.

Kackman, Michael. 2008. "Quality Television, Melodrama, and Cultural Complexity." *Flow TV*, October 31. http://flowtv.org/2008/10/quality-television-melodrama-and -cultural-complexity%C2%A0michael-kackman%C2%A0%C2%A0university-of -texas-austin%C2%A0%C2%A0/#.

Kafka, Peter. 2013. "Netflix's No-Name Show Beating *House of Cards* and *Arrested Development.*" *AllThingsD*, July 23. http://allthingsd.com/20130723/netflixs-no -name-show-beating-house-of-cards-and-arrested-development/.

Kalick, Lila. 2014. "Please Step on My Grass: New Adulthood in American Culture." *Huffington Post*, September 16. http://www.huffingtonpost.com/lila-kalick/please -step-on-my-grass-n_b_5830978.html.

Karnick, Kristine Brunovska, and Henry Jenkins. 1995. "Introduction: Comedy and the Social World." In *Classical Hollywood Comedy*, ed. Kristine Brunovska Karnick and Henry Jenkins, 265–81. New York: Routledge.

Keller, Jessalynn. 2015. "Girl Power's Last Chance? Tavi Gevinson, Feminism, and Popular Media Culture." *Continuum* 29(2): 274–85. doi:10.1080/10304312.2015. 1022947.

Kerr, Paul. 1984. "The Making of (The) MTM (Show)." In *MTM: "Quality Television,"* ed. Jane Feuer, Paul Kerr, and Tise Vahimagi, 61–98. London: BFI.

Khamis, Susie. 2020. *Branding Diversity: New Advertising and Cultural Strategies.* Abingdon, UK: Routledge.

King, Geoff. 2002. *Film Comedy.* New York: Wallflower Press.

Kirkpatrick, Noel. 2015. "*The Good Wife* 'Cooked' Review: Intrigue Pile-Up." *TV.com*, October 19. http://www.tv.com/shows/the-good-wife/community/post/the-good -wife-season-7-episode-3-cooked-review-144520260733/. (URL inactive)

Kleeman, Saphie. 2014. "In One Perfect Sentence, Amy Poehler Schools a Guy in What It's Like to Be a Woman." *Mic*, August 27. http://mic.com/articles/97464/in-one -perfect-sentence-amy-poehler-schools-a-guy-in-what-it-s-like-to-be-a-woman.

Kohan, Jenji. 2013. "*Orange* Creator Jenji Kohan: 'Piper Was My Trojan Horse.'" *NPR. org*, August 13. http://www.npr.org/2013/08/13/211639989/orange-creator-jenji -kohan-piper-was-my-trojan-horse.

Lagerwey, Jorie, Julia Leyda, and Diane Negra. 2016. "Female-Centered TV in an Age of Precarity." *Genders* 1(1). http://www.colorado.edu/genders/2016/05/19/female-centered-tv-age-precarity.

Lauzen, Martha. 2014. "The Funny Business of Being Tina Fey: Constructing a (Feminist) Comedy Icon." *Feminist Media Studies* 14(1): 106–17. doi:10.1080/14680777.2012.740060.

Lawson, Richard. 2010. "Showtime Cornering the Market on 'Ladies with Problems' Shows." *Gawker*, March 24. http://gawker.com/5501286/showtime-cornering-the-market-on-ladies-with-problems-shows.

Lentz, Kirsten Marthe. 2000. "Quality Versus Relevance: Feminism, Race, and the Politics of the Sign in 1970s Television." *Camera Obscura: Feminism, Culture, and Media Studies* 15(1[43]): 45–93. doi:10.1215/02705346-15-1_43-45.

Leonard, Suzanne. 2014a. "Escaping the Recession? The New Vitality of the Woman Worker." In *Gendering the Recession: Media and Culture in an Age of Austerity*, ed. Diane Negra and Yvonne Tasker, 31–58. Durham, NC: Duke University Press.

———. 2014b. "Sexuality, Technology, and Sexual Scandal in 'The Good Wife.'" *Feminist Media Studies* 14(6): 944–58. doi:10.1080/14680777.2014.882372.

———. 2016. "'I May Need You, Peter, but You Sure as Hell Need Me Too': Political Marriages in *The Good Wife* and Beyond." *Television and New Media*, June. doi:10.1177/1527476416652484.

———. 2018. *Wife, Inc: The Business of Marriage in the Twenty-First Century*. New York: New York University Press.

Leverette, Marc. 2008. "'Cocksucker, Motherfucker, Tits.'" In *It's Not TV: Watching HBO in the Post-Television Era*, ed. Marc Leverette, Brian L. Ott, and Cara Louise Buckley, 123–51. New York: Routledge.

Leverette, Marc, Brian L. Ott, and Cara Louise Buckley. 2008a. "Introduction." In *It's Not TV: Watching HBO in the Post-Television Era*, ed. Marc Leverette, Brian L. Ott, and Cara Louise Buckley, 1–10. New York: Routledge.

———, eds. 2008b. *It's Not TV: Watching HBO in the Post-Television Era*. New York: Routledge.

Levy, Ariel. 2006. *Female Chauvinist Pigs: Women and the Rise of Raunch Culture*. New York: Free Press.

Logan, Elliott. 2016. "'Quality Television' as a Critical Obstacle: Explanation and Aesthetics in Television Studies." *Screen* 57(2): 144–62. doi:10.1093/screen/hjw020.

Lotz, Amanda D. 2001. "Postfeminist Television Criticism: Rehabilitating Critical Terms and Identifying Postfeminist Attributes." *Feminist Media Studies* 1(1): 105–21. doi:10.1080/14680770120042891.

———. 2006. *Redesigning Women: Television After the Network Era*. Urbana: University of Illinois Press.

———. 2007. "Theorising the Intermezzo: The Contributions of Postfeminism and Third Wave Feminism." In *Third Wave Feminism: A Critical Exploration*, ed. Stacy Gillis, Gillian Howie, and Rebecca Munford, 46–85. Basingstoke, UK: Palgrave Macmillan.

———. 2014. *Cable Guys: Television and Masculinities in the 21st Century*. New York: NYU Press.

Lovelock, Michael. 2016. "Call Me Caitlyn: Making and Making over the 'Authentic' Transgender Body in Anglo-American Popular Culture." *Journal of Gender Studies* 26(6): 675–87. doi:10.1080/09589236.2016.1155978.

Lowry, Brian. 2009. "Parks and Recreation." *Variety*, June 4. http://variety.com/2009/scene/markets-festivals/parks-and-recreation-1200507317/.

———. 2013. "Review: *Orange Is the New Black*." *Variety*, August 7. http://variety.com/2013/digital/reviews/orange-is-the-new-black-review-netflix-1200504709/.

———. 2015. "*The Good Wife* Reloads for Seventh Season with Eye on Politics, Redemption." *Variety*, October 2. http://variety.com/2015/tv/columns/the-good-wife-season-7-premiere-review-julianna-margulies-margo-martindale-jeffrey-dean-morgan-1201606771/.

Lucia, Cynthia. 2005. *Framing Female Lawyers: Women on Trial in Film*. Austin: University of Texas Press.

Lury, Karen. 2016. "Introduction: Situating Television Studies." *Screen* 57(2): 119–23. doi:10.1093/screen/hjw023.

Lyons, Margaret. 2015a. "How TV Fell Back in Love with Soaps." *Vulture*, October 29. http://www.vulture.com/2015/10/primetime-soap-operas-are-back.html.

———. 2015b. "Lifetime's *UnREAL* Is One of the Most Interesting Dramas in Recent Memory." *Vulture*, June 1. http://www.vulture.com/2015/05/lifetime-unreal-is-real-damn-good.html.

Marsh, Sarah. 2016. "*Game of Thrones* Fans Review Season Six: 'Misogyny Has Been Replaced by Breakneck Storytelling.'" *The Guardian*, June 28. https://www.theguardian.com/tv-and-radio/2016/jun/28/game-of-thrones-fans-review-season-six.

Martin, Brett. 2013. *Difficult Men: From* The Sopranos *and* The Wire *to* Mad Men *and* Breaking Bad. London: Faber & Faber.

Matlow, Orli. 2015. "Piper Is a Villain on *Orange Is the New Black* Season 3 and This Arc Has Been a Long Time in Coming." *Bustle*, June 16. http://www.bustle.com/articles/90677-piper-is-a-villain-on-orange-is-the-new-black-season-3-this-arc-has.

Matrix, Sidneyeve. 2014. "The Netflix Effect: Teens, Binge Watching, and On-Demand Digital Media Trends." *Jeunesse: Young People, Texts, Cultures* 6(1): 119–38. doi:10.1353/jeu.2014.0002.

McCabe, Janet, and Kim Akass, eds. 2004. *Reading Sex and the City*. London: I. B. Tauris.

———, eds. 2006. *Reading Desperate Housewives: Beyond the White Picket Fence*. London: I. B. Tauris.

———, eds. 2007a. *Quality TV: Contemporary American Television and Beyond*. London: I. B. Tauris.

———. 2007b. "Sex, Swearing, and Respectability: Courting Controversy, HBO's Original Programming, and Producing Quality TV." In *Quality TV: Contemporary*

American Television and Beyond, ed. Janet McCabe and Kim Akass, 62–76. London: I. B. Tauris.

———. 2009. "What Has HBO Ever Done for Women?" In *The Essential HBO Reader*, ed. Gary R. Edgerton and Jeffrey P. Jones, 303–14. Lexington: University Press of Kentucky.

McDonald, Kevin, and Daniel Smith-Rowsey, eds. 2016. *The Netflix Effect: Technology and Entertainment in the 21st Century*. New York: Bloomsbury Academic.

McHugh, Kathleen A. 2015. "Giving Credit to Paratexts and Parafeminism in 'Top of the Lake' and *Orange Is the New Black*." *Film Quarterly* 68(3): 17–25. doi:10.1525/fq.2015.68.3.17.

McRobbie, Angela. 2009. *The Aftermath of Feminism: Gender, Culture, and Social Change*. Los Angeles: SAGE.

———. 2011. "Beyond Post-Feminism." *Public Policy Research* 18(3): 179–84. doi:10.1111/j.1744–540X.2011.00661.x.

Meeuf, Russell. 2016. "Class, Corpulence, and Neoliberal Citizenship: Melissa McCarthy on *Saturday Night Live*." *Celebrity Studies* 7(2): 137–53. doi:10.1080/19392397.2015.1044758.

Middleton, Jason. 2014. *Documentary's Awkward Turn: Cringe Comedy and Media Spectatorship*. New York: Routledge.

Miller, Hilary. 2013. "Why *Masters of Sex* Is the New 'Mad Men.'" *Huffington Post*, December 7. http://www.huffingtonpost.com/2013/12/07/masters-of-sex-mad-men_n_4392519.html.

Miller, Taylor Cole. 2016. "The Fashion of Florrick and FLOTUS: On Feminism, Gender Politics, and 'Quality Television.'" *Television and New Media*, June. doi:10.1177/1527476416652486.

Mills, Brett. 2004. "Comedy Verite: Contemporary Sitcom Form." *Screen* 45(1): 63–78. doi:10.1093/screen/45.1.63.

———. 2005. *Television Sitcom*. London: BFI.

———. 2009. *The Sitcom*. Edinburgh: Edinburgh University Press.

———. 2013. "What Does It Mean to Call Television 'Cinematic'?" In *Television Aesthetics and Style*, ed. Jason Jacobs and Steven Peacock, 57–66. New York: Bloomsbury Academic.

Mittell, Jason. 2004. *Genre and Television: From Cop Shows to Cartoons in American Culture*. New York: Routledge.

———. 2006. "Narrative Complexity in Contemporary American Television." *The Velvet Light Trap* 58(1): 29–40. doi:10.1353/vlt.2006.0032.

———. 2015a. *Complex TV: The Poetics of Contemporary Television Storytelling*. New York: New York University Press.

———. 2015b. "Lengthy Interactions with Hideous Men: Walter White and the Serial Poetics of Television Antiheroes." In *Storytelling in the Media Convergence Age: Exploring Screen Narratives*, ed. Roberta E. Pearson and Anthony N. Smith, 74–92. Houndmills, UK: Palgrave Macmillan.

Mizejewski, Linda. 2014. *Pretty/Funny: Women Comedians and Body Politics*. Austin: University of Texas Press.

Morris, Wesley, and James Poniewozik. 2016. "Why 'Diverse TV' Matters: It's Better TV. Discuss." *New York Times*, February 10. http://www.nytimes.com/2016/02/14/arts/television/smaller-screens-truer-colors.html.

Morrison, Grant, and Dave McKean. 1989. *Arkham Asylum: A Serious House on Serious Earth*. New York: DC Comics.

Moses, Lucia. 2014. "New York Times Debuts the 'Snowfall' of Native Ads." *Digiday*, June 14. http://digiday.com/publishers/new-york-times-native-ad-thats-winning-skeptics/.

Murray, Jack. 2014. "*Breaking Bad* Merchandise Is Cheapening the Show's Legacy." *Vice*, September 12. http://www.vice.com/read/heisenberg-on-the-high-street-328.

Nannicelli, Ted. 2016. "In Defence of the Objectivity of Evaluative Television Criticism." *Screen* 57(2): 124–43. doi:10.1093/screen/hjw017.

Neale, Stephen, and Frank Krutnik. 1990. *Popular Film and Television Comedy*. London: Routledge.

Negra, Diane. 2004. "'Quality Postfeminism?' Sex and the Single Girl on HBO." *Genders*, no. 39. http://www.colorado.edu/gendersarchive1998-2013/2004/04/01/quality-postfeminism-sex-and-single-girl-hbo.

———. 2009. *What a Girl Wants? Fantasizing the Reclamation of Self in Postfeminism*. London: Routledge.

———. 2014. "Claiming Feminism: Commentary, Autobiography, and Advice Literature for Women in the Recession." *Journal of Gender Studies* 23(3): 275–86. doi:10.1080/09589236.2014.913977.

———. 2015. "'Orange Is the New Black' and the New Female-Centered Quality Television." Paper presented at the *Orange Is the New Black* and New Perspectives on the Women in Prison Genre Conference, Edinburgh, Napier University, June 5.

———. 2020. "Age Disproportion in the Post-Epitaph Chick Flick: Reading *The Proposal*." In *Cross Generational Relationships and Cinema*, ed. Joel Gwynne and Niall Richardson, 55–77. Cham, Switzerland: Palgrave Macmillan.

Negra, Diane, and Yvonne Tasker, eds. 2014a. *Gendering the Recession: Media and Culture in an Age of Austerity*. Durham, NC: Duke University Press.

———. 2014b. "Introduction: Gender and Recessionary Culture." In *Gendering the Recession: Media and Culture in an Age of Austerity*, ed. Yvonne Negra and Yvonne Tasker, 1–30. Durham, NC: Duke University Press.

Newman, Michael Z., and Elana Levine. 2012. *Legitimating Television: Media Convergence and Cultural Status*. Oxon, UK: Routledge.

Nussbaum, Emily. 2012a. "In Defense of Liz Lemon." *The New Yorker*, February 23. http://www.newyorker.com/culture/culture-desk/in-defense-of-liz-lemon.

———. 2012b. "Primary Colors." *The New Yorker*, May 21. http://www.newyorker.com/magazine/2012/05/21/primary-colors.

———. 2014. "Shedding Her Skin." *The New Yorker*, October 13. http://www.newyorker
.com/magazine/2014/10/13/shedding-skin

———. 2015. "Little Boxes." *The New Yorker*, August 31. http://www.newyorker.com/
magazine/2015/08/31/little-boxes.

———. 2016. "'Fleabag,' an Original Bad-Girl Comedy." *The New Yorker*, September 26.
http://www.newyorker.com/magazine/2016/09/26/fleabag-an-original-bad-girl
-comedy.

Nygaard, Taylor. 2013. "Girls Just Want to Be 'Quality': HBO, Lena Dunham, and
'Girls' Conflicting Brand Identity." *Feminist Media Studies* 13(2): 370–74. doi:
10.1080/14680777.2013.771891.

Nygaard, Taylor, and Jorie Lagerwey. 2016. "Broadcasting Quality: Re-Centering
Feminist Discourse with 'The Good Wife.'" *Television and New Media*, June.
doi:10.1177/1527476416652485.

O'Keeffe, Kevin. 2014. "TV's Renaissance for Strong Women Is Happening in a Surpris-
ing Place." *The Atlantic*, October 9. http://www.theatlantic.com/entertainment/
archive/2014/10/how-to-get-away-with-murder-and-the-rise-of-the-new
-network-tv-heroine/381021/.

"*Orange Is the New Black* Opening Credits Feature Real, Formerly Incarcerated
Women." 2013. *Huffington Post*, August 20. http://www.huffingtonpost.com/
2013/08/20/orange-is-the-new-black-opening-credits_n_3786127.html.

Ott, Brian L. 2008. "Introduction: The Not TV Text." In *It's Not TV: Watching HBO
in the Post-Television Era*, ed. Marc Leverette, Brian L. Ott, and Cara Louise
Buckley, 97–100. New York: Routledge.

Outlaw, Kofi. 2013. "5 'Girl Shows' That Guys Should Be Watching." *Screen Rant*, September 18. http://screenrant.com/tv-shows-girls-guys-male-female-demographics
-scandal-orphan-orange-new-black/.

Paskin, Willa. 2011. "'Parks and Recreation' and the Comedy of Super Niceness." *Vulture*, March 24. http://www.vulture.com/2011/03/parks_and_recreation_takes_all
.html.

———. 2014. "Television for Adults." *Slate*, September 18. http://www.slate.com/
articles/arts/television/2014/09/the_good_wife_season_6_starts_sunday_the
_cbs_show_is_better_than_ever.html.

Patterson, Eleanor. 2012. "Fracturing Tina Fey: A Critical Analysis of Postfeminist
Television Comedy Stardom." *Communication Review* 15(3): 232–51. doi:10
.1080/10714421.2012.701991.

Petro, Patrice. 1986. "Mass Culture and the Feminine: The 'Place' of Television in
Film Studies." *Cinema Journal* 25(3): 5–21. doi:10.2307/1225477.

Piper, Helen. 2016. "Broadcast Drama and the Problem of Television Aesthetics:
Home, Nation, Universe." *Screen* 57(2): 163–83. doi:10.1093/screen/hjw021.

Poehler, Amy. 2014. *Yes Please*. New York: Dey Street.

Poniewozik, James. 2013. "On Anna Gunn, the Skyler-Hating Sexists, and the Billion-
Megaphone Era." *Time*, August 26. http://entertainment.time.com/2013/08/26/
on-anna-gunn-the-skyler-hating-sexists-and-the-billion-megaphone-era/.

Prudom, Laura. 2016. "Amazon's 'Good Girls Revolt' Is Picking Up Where 'Mad Men' Leaves Off." *Variety*, August 7. http://variety.com/2016/tv/news/good-girls -revolt-fox-news-sexual-harassment-newsroom-mad-men-1201832412/.

"Questions for Tina Fey." 2007. *New York Times Blog*, September 22. http://questions .blogs.nytimes.com/2007/09/22/questions-for-tina-fey/.

Rabinovitz, Lauren. 1999. "Ms.-Representation: The Politics of Feminist Sitcoms." In *Television, History, and American Culture: Feminist Critical Essays*, ed. Mary Beth Haralovich, 144–67. Durham, NC: Duke University Press.

Ramsay, Debra. 2013. "Confessions of a Binge Watcher." *CST Online*, October 4. http://cstonline.tv/confessions-of-a-binge-watcher.

Raymond, Adam K. 2013. "12 Great Jump-Cut Montage Riffs on 'Parks and Recreation.'" *Vulture*, October 24. http://www.vulture.com/2013/10/12-great-parks -and-rec-jump-cut-montages.html.

Rodrigues, Sara. 2014. "'Yes Please' Is White Liberal Feminism in Full Force." *Popmatters*, December 9. http://www.popmatters.com/column/188928-yes-please -is-white-liberal-feminism-in-full-force/.

Rodriguez, Maddie. 2014. "3 Times Amy Poehler Said 'Yes Please' to Feminism in Her Memoir, and We're on Board, Naturally." *Bustle*, November 6. http://www .bustle.com/articles/47745-3-times-amy-poehler-said-yes-please-to-feminism -in-her-memoir-and-were-on-board.

Romney, Jonathan. 2015. "Getting Down with the Kids." *Sight and Sound*, January.

Rorke, Robert. 2014. "'Orange Is the New Black' Ignites a TV Revolution for Women." *New York Post*, June 5. http://nypost.com/2014/06/04/orange-is-the-new-black -ignites-a-tv-revolution-for-women/.

Rowe Karlyn, Kathleen. 1995a. "Comedy, Melodrama, and Gender." In *Classical Hollywood Comedy*, ed. Kristine Brunovska Karnick and Henry Jenkins, 39–59. New York: Routledge.

———. 1995b. *The Unruly Woman: Gender and the Genres of Laughter*. Austin: University of Texas Press.

———. 2011. *Unruly Girls, Unrepentant Mothers: Redefining Feminism on Screen*. Austin: University of Texas Press.

Russo, Mary J. 1995. *The Female Grotesque: Risk, Excess, and Modernity*. New York: Routledge.

Ryan, Maureen. 2014. "TV Writers Weigh In on Legacy of 'Hill Street Blues' as Classic Drama Hits DVD." *Huffington Post*, April 29. http://www.huffingtonpost .com/2014/04/29/hill-street-blues-dvd_n_5232710.html.

———. 2015. "What 'Parks and Recreation' Taught My Son About Feminism." *Huffington Post*, February 23. http://www.huffingtonpost.com/2015/02/23/parks-and -recreation-finale_n_6732338.html.

———. 2016a. "TV Review: 'UnReal' Season 2." *Variety*, June 2. http://variety.com/ 2016/tv/reviews/unreal-season-2-review-shiri-appleby-constance-zimmer -1201782340/.

——. 2016b. "Why TV Is Finally Embracing the Realities of Race." *Variety*, February 23. http://variety.com/2016/tv/features/television-race-diversity-ratings-1201712266/.

Sandberg, Sheryl. 2013. *Lean in: Women, Work, and the Will to Lead.* New York: Knopf.

Santo, Avi. 2008. "Para-Television and Discourses of Distinction: The Culture of Production at HBO." In *It's Not TV: Watching HBO in the Post-Television Era*, ed. Marc Leverette, Brian L. Ott, and Cara Louise Buckley, 19–45. New York: Routledge.

Savigny, Heather, and Helen Warner. 2015a. "Introduction: The Politics of Being a Woman." In *The Politics of Being a Woman: Feminism, Media, and 21st Century Popular Culture*, 1–24. Houndmills, UK: Palgrave Macmillan.

——, eds. 2015b. *The Politics of Being a Woman: Feminism, Media, and 21st Century Popular Culture.* Houndmills, UK: Palgrave Macmillan.

Sconce, Jeffrey. 2009. "The Girl from Pawnee." *Flow TV*, March 4. http://flowtv.org/2009/04/the-girl-from-pawnee-jeffrey-sconce-northwestern-university/.

Scott, A. O. 2014. "The Death of Adulthood in American Culture." *New York Times*, November 9. http://www.nytimes.com/2014/09/14/magazine/the-death-of-adulthood-in-american-culture.html.

Seidman, Steve. 1981. *Comedian Comedy: A Tradition in Hollywood Film.* Ann Arbor, MI: UMI Research Press.

Sepinwall, Alan. 2013. "Review: Netflix's 'Orange Is the New Black' Season 1." *HitFix*, August 13. http://www.hitfix.com/whats-alan-watching/review-netflixs-orange-is-the-new-black-concludes-a-triumphant-first-season.

——. 2014. "Review: 'Game of Thrones'—'Breaker of Chains.'" *HitFix*, April 20. http://www.hitfix.com/whats-alan-watching/review-game-of-thrones-breaker-of-chains-uncle-deadly.

——. 2015a. "How 'Parks and Recreation' Found All-Time Greatness in Simple Goodness." *HitFix*, February 23. http://www.hitfix.com/whats-alan-watching/how-parks-and-recreation-found-all-time-greatness-in-simple-goodness.

——. 2015b. "One Last 'Parks and Recreation' Q&A with Mike Schur." *HitFix*, March 4. http://www.hitfix.com/whats-alan-watching/one-last-parks-and-recreation-qa-with-mike-schur.

——. 2015c. "'Orange Is the New Black' Season 3 in Review." *HitFix*, July 21. http://www.hitfix.com/whats-alan-watching/orange-is-the-new-black-season-3-in-review.

Shales, Tom. 2005. "'Fat Actress': Jolly-Unsaturated." *Washington Post*, March 7. https://www.washingtonpost.com/wp-dyn/articles/A12720-2005Mar6.html?nav=rss_style/columns/shalestom.

Shapiro Sanders, Lisa. 2007. "'Feminists Love a Utopia': Collaboration, Conflict, and the Futures of Feminism." In *Third Wave Feminism: A Critical Exploration*, 2nd ed., ed. Stacy Gillis, Gillian Howie, and Rebecca Munford, 3–15. New York: Palgrave Macmillan.

Simon, Ron. 2009. "Sex and the City." In *The Essential HBO Reader*, ed. Gary R. Edgerton and Jeffrey P. Jones, 193–203. Lexington: University Press of Kentucky.

Sims, David. 2011. "'The Good Wife': 'Marthas and Caitlins.'" *AV Club*, October 23. http://www.avclub.com/tvclub/the-good-wife-marthas-and-caitlins-63748.

———. 2012. "'The Good Wife': 'Long Way Home.'" *AV Club*, March 11. http://www.avclub.com/tvclub/the-good-wife-long-way-home-70346.

Slaughter, Joseph R. 2011. "Bildungsroman/Künstlerroman." In *The Encyclopedia of the Novel*, ed. Peter Melville Logan, Olakunle George, Susan Hegeman, and Efraín Kristal, 1: 93–97. Malden, MA: Wiley-Blackwell.

Smith, Anthony. 2015. "Inside the Box: Exploring the Links Between Netflix Original Series and Television Industries." Paper presented at the Media Futures Research Center, Seminar Series 2015–2016, Bath Spa University, Bath, England, December 9.

Snierson, Dan. 2013. "Building 'Parks and Recreation.'" *Entertainment Weekly*, August 2. http://www.ew.com/article/2013/07/26/building-parks-and-recreation.

Spangler, Todd. 2014. "Netflix Originals 'House of Cards,' 'Orange Is the New Black' Watched by Fewer than Half of Subs, Study Finds." *Variety*, August 7. http://variety.com/2014/digital/news/netflix-originals-house-of-cards-orange-is-the-new-black-watched-by-fewer-than-half-of-subs-study-finds-1201277702/.

Spigel, Lynn. 1995. "From the Dark Ages to the Golden Age: Women's Memories and Television Reruns." *Screen* 36(1): 16–33. doi:10.1093/screen/36.1.16.

———. 2013. "Postfeminist Nostalgia for a Prefeminist Future." *Screen* 54(2): 270–78. doi:10.1093/screen/hjt017.

Sternbergh, Adam. 2014. "The Death of Adulthood and the Rise of Pleasure, or Why Seth Rogen Is More Serious than Woody Allen." *Vulture*, September 12. http://www.vulture.com/2014/09/death-of-adulthood-pop-culture-ao-scott-essay.html.

Stryker, Susan. 2008. "Transgender History, Homonormativity, and Disciplinarity." *Radical History Review* 2008(100): 145–57. doi:10.1215/01636545-2007-026.

Sulimma, Maria. 2021. *Gender and Seriality: Practices and Politics of Contemporary U.S. Television*. Edinburgh: Edinburgh University Press.

Tasker, Yvonne. 1998. *Working Girls: Gender and Sexuality in Popular Cinema*. London: Routledge.

———. 2009. "Comic Situations/Endless War: 'M*A*S*H' and War as Entertainment." In *War Isn't Hell, It's Entertainment: Essays on Visual Media and the Representation of Conflict*, ed. Rikke Schubart, Fabian Virchow, Debra White-Stanley, and Tania Thomas, 132–49. Jefferson, NC: McFarland.

———. 2011. "'Enchanted' (2007) by Postfeminism." In *Feminism at the Movies. Understanding Gender in Contemporary Popular Cinema*, ed. Hilary Radner and Rebecca Stringer, 67–79. Oxon, UK: Routledge.

Tasker, Yvonne, and Diane Negra, eds. 2007. *Interrogating Postfeminism: Gender and the Politics of Popular Culture*. Durham, NC: Duke University Press.

"*The Good Wife* Recap: Not Number One." 2016. *Vulture*, January 11. http://www.vulture.com/2016/01/good-wife-recap-season-7-episode-11.html.

Thompson, Ethan. 2007. "Comedy Verité? The Observational Documentary Meets the Televisual Sitcom." *The Velvet Light Trap* 60(1): 63–72. doi:10.1353/vlt.2007.0027.

Thompson, Robert J. 1997. *Television's Second Golden Age: From Hill Street Blues to ER*. Syracuse, NY: Syracuse University Press.

Thornham, Sue, and Tony Purvis. 2005. *Television Drama: Theories and Identities*. Basingstoke, UK: Palgrave Macmillan.

Traister, Rebecca. 2010. "The Tina Fey Backlash." *Salon*, April 14. http://www.salon.com/2010/04/14/tina_fey_backlash/.

Trantham, Holly. 2015. "10 Times Leslie Knope Was a Total Feminist Badass." *Bust*, February 24. https://bust.com/tv/13775-10-times-leslie-knope-was-a-total-feminist-badass.html.

Travers, Ben. 2014. "'The Good Wife' Debate: Should Emmy Voters Consider the Number of Episodes in a Season Along with Its Quality?" *IndieWire*, April 25. http://www.indiewire.com/article/television/the-good-wife-debate-do-emmy-voters-need-to-consider-the-number-of-episodes-along-with-the-quality.

VanDerWerff, Todd. 2015a. "Netflix Is Accidentally Inventing a New Art Form—Not Quite TV and Not Quite Film." *Vox*, July 30. http://www.vox.com/2015/7/29/9061833/netflix-binge-new-artform.

———. 2015b. "Starz's Hugely Successful 'Power' Proves Cable Should Be Targeting Diverse Audiences." *Vox*, June 13. http://www.vox.com/2015/6/13/8775375/power-season-2-starz-interview.

Vermeulen, Timotheus, and James Whitfield. 2013. "Arrested Developments: Towards an Aesthetic of the Contemporary U.S. Sitcom." In *Television Aesthetics and Style*, ed. Jason Jacobs and Steven Peacock, 103–11. New York: Bloomsbury Academic.

Viruet, Pilot. 2015. "How the Rise of the Hourlong Comedy Is Forcing the TV Academy to Change the Emmys' Rules." *Flavorwire*, March 18. http://flavorwire.com/510087/how-the-rise-of-the-hourlong-comedy-is-forcing-the-tv-academy-to-change-the-emmys-rules.

Wallenstein, Andrew. 2014. "'Orange Is the New Black' Trending Stronger than 'House of Cards.'" *Variety*, June 5. http://variety.com/2014/digital/news/orange-is-the-new-black-trending-stronger-than-house-of-cards-1201214225/.

Weidhase, Nathalie. 2015. "'Beyoncé Feminism' and the Contestation of the Black Feminist Body." *Celebrity Studies* 6(1): 128–31. doi:10.1080/19392397.2015.1005389.

West, Steve. 2009. "TV Recap: '30 Rock'—'The Natural Order.'" *CinemaBlend*, April 30. https://www.cinemablend.com/television/TV-Recap-30-Rock-Natural-Order-17229.html.

Wheatley, Helen. 2016. *Spectacular Television: Exploring Televisual Pleasure*. London: I. B. Tauris.

White, Mimi. 2011. "Mad Women." In *"Mad Men": Dream Come True TV*, ed. Gary R. Edgerton, 147–58. London: I. B. Tauris.

White, Rosie. 2018. *Television Comedy and Femininity: Queering Gender*. London: I. B. Tauris.

Wicking, Christopher. 1984. "'Lou Grant.'" In *MTM: "Quality Television,"* ed. Jane Feuer, Paul Kerr, and Tise Vahimagi, 166–82. London: BFI.

Wilkes, Karen. 2015. "Colluding with Neo-Liberalism: Post-Feminist Subjectivities, Whiteness, and Expressions of Entitlement." *Feminist Review* 110(1): 18–33. doi:10.1057/fr.2015.19.

Williams, Linda. 1991. "Film Bodies: Gender, Genre, and Excess." *Film Quarterly* 44(4): 2–13. doi:10.1525/fq.1991.44.4.04a00020.

———. 2014. *On the Wire*. Durham, NC: Duke University Press.

Winch, Alison. 2013. *Girlfriends and Postfeminist Sisterhood*. Houndmills, UK: Palgrave Macmillan.

Yabroff, Jennie. 2014. "Amy Poehler Preaches 'Lean Out.'" *The Daily Beast*, October 29. http://www.thedailybeast.com/articles/2014/10/29/amy-poehler-preaches-lean-out.html.

Yuan, Jada. 2012. "'The Good Wife' Recap: The Law Is a Strange, Sex-Addled Thing." *Vulture*, March 12. http://www.vulture.com/2012/03/good-wife-recap-season-3-episode-17.html.

Zborowski, James. 2016. "Television Aesthetics, Media, and Cultural Studies and the Contested Realm of the Social." *Critical Studies in Television: The International Journal of Television Studies* 11(1): 7–22. doi:10.1177/1749602015619632.

LIST OF TELEVISION PROGRAMS AND FILMS

TELEVISION SERIES AND PROGRAMS

24. 2001–2010. Fox.
30 Rock. 2006–2013. NBC.
Absolutely Fabulous. 1992–2012. BBC2, BBC1.
All in the Family. 1971–1979. CBS.
Ally McBeal. 1997–2002. Fox.
America in Primetime. 2011. PBS.
Arrested Development. 2003–. Fox, Netflix.
The Betty White Show. 1977–1978. CBS.
The Big C. 2010–2013. Showtime.
Boardwalk Empire. 2010–2014. HBO.
Breaking Bad. 2008–2013. AMC.
Broad City. 2014–2019. Comedy Central.
Buffalo Bill. 1983–1984. NBC.
Buffy the Vampire Slayer. 1997–2003. WB.
Cagney & Lacey. 1981–1988. CBS.
Cashmere Mafia. 2008. ABC.
The Comeback. 2005–2014. HBO.
Community. 2009–2015. NBC.
Crazy Ex-Girlfriend (2015–2019). The CW.
Curb Your Enthusiasm. 2000–. HBO.
Cybill. 1995–1998. CBS.
Damages. 2007–2012. FX.
Deadwood. 2004–2006. HBO.
Designing Women. 1986–1993. CBS.
Desperate Housewives. 2004–2012. ABC.
The Division. 2001–2004. Lifetime.
Easy. 2016–. Netflix.
Ellen. 1994–1998. ABC.
Enlightened. 2011–2013. HBO.

Entourage. 2004–2011. HBO.

The Fall. 2013–2016. BBC.

Fat Actress. 2005. Showtime.

Fleabag. 2016–2019. BBC 3, Amazon.

Friends. 1994–2004. NBC.

Game of Thrones. 2011–2019. HBO.

Girls. 2012–2017. HBO.

Good Girls Revolt. 2015. Amazon.

The Good Wife. 2009–2016. CBS.

Grey's Anatomy. 2005–. ABC.

The Handmaid's Tale. 2017–. Hulu.

Hill Street Blues. 1981–1987. NBC.

Homeland. 2011–2020. Showtime.

House of Cards. 2013–2018. Netflix.

How to Get Away with Murder. 2014–2020. ABC.

Inside Amy Schumer. 2013–2016. Comedy Central.

Jessica Jones. 2015–2019. Netflix.

Joey. 2004–2006. NBC.

The Larry Sanders Show. 1992–1998. HBO.

Lipstick Jungle. 2008–2009. NBC.

Lost. 2004–2010. ABC.

Lou Grant. 1977–1982. CBS.

The L Word. 2004–2009. Showtime.

Mad Men. 2007–2015. AMC.

The Mary Tyler Moore Show. 1970–1977. CBS.

M*A*S*H. 1972–1983. CBS.

Master of None. 2015–2017. Netflix.

Masters of Sex. 2013–2016. Showtime.

Maude. 1972–1978. CBS.

Melrose Place. 1992–1999. Fox.

Miami Vice. 1984–1990. NBC.

Mrs. America. 2020. FX on Hulu.

Night Court. 1984–1992. NBC.

Nurse Jackie. 2009–2015. Showtime.

The Office. 2001–2003. BBC.

The Office. 2005–2013. NBC.

One Mississippi. 2015–2017. Amazon.

Orange Is the New Black. 2013–2019. Netflix.

Oz. 1997–2003. HBO.

Parks and Recreation. 2009–2015. NBC.

Phyllis. 1975–1977. CBS.

Rhoda. 1974–1978. CBS.

Roseanne. 1988–1997. ABC.

Saturday Night Live. 1975–. NBC.

Scandal. 2012–2018. ABC.
Scrubs. 2001–2010. NBC, ABC.
Sex and the City. 1998–2004. HBO.
The Shield. 2002–2008. Fox.
Show Me a Hero. 2015. HBO.
Sons of Anarchy. 2008–2014. FX.
The Sopranos. 1999–2007. HBO.
Strong Medicine. 2000–2006. Lifetime.
Top of the Lake. 2013–2017. Sundance.
Transparent. 2014–2019. Amazon.
Treme. 2010–2013. HBO.
True Detective. 2014–2019. HBO.
Unbreakable Kimmy Schmidt. 2015–2020. Netflix.
United States of Tara. 2009–2011. Showtime.
UnREAL. 2015–2018. Lifetime.
Veep. 2012–2019. HBO.
Weeds. 2005–2012. Showtime.
The Wire. 2002–2008. HBO.

FILMS

101 Dalmatians. 1996. Dir. Stephen Herek. Buena Vista Pictures.
All the President's Men. 1976. Dir. Alan J. Pakula. Warner Bros.
Amadeus. 1985. Dir. Milos Forman. Orion Pictures.
Bridesmaids. 2011. Dir. Paul Feig. Universal Pictures.
Bringing Up Baby. 1938. Dir. Howard Hawks. RKO Radio Pictures.
Dangerous Liaisons. 1988. Dir. Stephen Frears. Warner Bros.
The Dark Knight. 2008. Dir. Christopher Nolan. Warner Bros.
The Devil's Advocate. 1997. Dir. Taylor Hackford. Warner Bros.
The Devil Wears Prada. 2006. Dir. David Frankel. Twentieth Century Fox Film
    Corporation.
Fatal Attraction. 1987. Dir. Adrian Lyne. Paramount Pictures.
Harry and the Hendersons. Dir. William Dear. 1987. Universal Pictures.
Inside Out. 2015. Dir. Pete Docter and Ronaldo Del Carmen. Walt Disney Pictures.
Mamma Mia! 2008. Dir. Phyllida Lloyd. Universal Pictures.
Mean Girls. 2004. Dir. Mark Waters. Paramount Pictures.
Michael Clayton. 2007. Dir. Tony Gilroy. Warner Bros.
Primal Fear. 1996. Dir. Gregory Hoblit. Paramount Pictures.
Willy Wonka & the Chocolate Factory. 1971. Dir. Mel Stuart. Paramount Pictures.

INDEX

comic female body, 16, 44–45, 57, 93, 106–8, 110, 114, 122–27, 133, 136, 218, 231

complex female character, 29, 140, 143, 185, 188, 192–93, 222, 225, 228. *See also* strong female character

complexity, 23, 25, 49, 84, 117, 141, 157, 179, 189, 194, 226; aesthetic, 143, 147, 149, 178; character, 23, 141, 143, 193, 198, 200, 222; narrative, 17–21, 49, 147, 186–87, 192; political, 49, 147

complex television, 2, 18, 21, 147, 178–79, 186–92

consumer citizenship, 6, 90

consumer culture, 7, 24

consumerism, 13, 35, 90, 172, 216

Cooper, Brenda, 211

Coriolanus, 177

Cox, Laverne, 8

Cox, Nicole B., 172

Cranston, Bryan, 222

Crazy Ex-Girlfriend, 14

Creeber, Glen, 83, 100

Crenshaw, Kimberlé, 7

Crider, Michael, 59

crisis: economic, 6, 48, 212; of patriarchy, 168, 208–9, 222, 224. *See also* masculinity: troubled / in crisis; recession

Cross, Marcia, 141

cross-dressing, 127

Crowder, Karen, 141

Crozier, Nancy, 160, 203

cruel optimism, 72, 76

Cuen, Leigh, 41

cultural hierarchies, 18–19, 21, 39, 46, 49, 53, 78, 104, 106, 145, 151, 173, 176, 184, 211; gendered, 2, 22, 26, 103, 141, 144–45, 154, 160, 185, 190, 214; of taste, 10–11, 19, 23, 34, 36, 45, 47, 53, 55, 58, 145, 156, 173, 176; of television, 18, 40, 47, 57, 78, 144, 159, 171, 186, 191, 214, 221

cultural value, 2–3, 9, 11, 13–16, 21–22, 24–27, 29, 33–34, 41–42, 45, 71–72, 75–76, 112, 140, 142, 144–46, 148–49, 151, 154–55, 157, 159, 161, 166, 173–74, 177–78, 181, 185, 190, 192, 213, 225, 227–31, 234; gendered, 9, 12; high, 20, 32, 34, 147, 181, 194

Cumming, Alan, 164–65

Curb Your Enthusiasm, 17, 55, 60, 107

Cybill, 94, 139

Czuchry, Matt, 193

D'Acci, Julie, 26–28, 32, 140

Dailey, Kate, 82

Dale, Alan, 104–6, 126

Daly, Jon, 76

Damages, 201

Dangerous Liaisons, 141, 201

Daniels, Greg, 71

D'Arcy, Caitlin, 202–6

Dark Knight, The, 68, 117–18, 122

Dasgupta, Sudeep, 11, 146, 186

David, Larry, 95, 229

Davis, Viola, 141

Davis, Wendy, 86

Deadwood, 20, 23, 32

DeCarvalho, Lauren, 172

DeGeneres, Ellen, 95, 139

Designing Women, 42

Desperate Housewives, 24

DeVil, Cruella, 201

Devil's Advocate, The, 207

Devil Wears Prada, The, 201

Deziel, Melanie, 171

diversity, 6–7, 81, 150, 160, 185; racial, 141; representational, 140, 150, 218

Division, The, 144

Dockterman, Eliana, 174–75

documentarism, 31, 132, 149–50, 178, 181, 216

documentary, 20, 36, 71–72, 97–98, 192–93

Donaghy, Jack, 58–59, 61, 64, 79, 85–88, 91–94, 114–18, 122

Donatelli, Cindy, 189

Douglas, Susan J., 36

Dow, Bonnie J., 9, 26–27, 32, 139, 205, 210, 226, 228

Doyle, Sady, 112–13

drag, 70, 120–21

drama: crime, 33, 147, 187; female-centered, 27, 142–43, 145, 147, 160, 166, 183, 185; highbrow, 146–47, 157, 216; high-concept, 146; male-centered, 168, 184, 189–90, 223–24; network, 167, 199; political, 156, 175; serialized, 187, 189; workplace, 143, 148, 202, 204 dramatic forms, 18, 140, 143–45, 176–77

dramedy, 3, 23–25, 30, 46–47, 55, 57, 153, 168, 175–76, 181, 184, 205, 211, 214, 216, 227–29, 231; female-centered, 47, 151, 176, 184, 199; postfeminist TV, 30, 45–46, 55–56, 58, 62, 64–66, 68–69, 111, 175, 184, 230. *See also* postfeminist: quality television

Draper, Betty, 223

Duberman, Amanda, 83

Dunham, Lena, 139, 175

Edgerton, Gary R., 34, 36, 41

edginess, 2, 15, 33, 36–37, 39–40, 62, 121, 229

Edwards, Stassa, 225

Elba, Idris, 179

Ellen, 94, 134, 139

Emmy Awards, 151, 154–55, 174, 177

Enlightened, 25, 175

ensemble cast, 28, 31–32, 57, 61, 129, 200, 208–10, 214, 230

Entertainment Weekly, 71, 77

Entourage, 38

episodic narrative structure, 20, 26, 31, 61, 144, 148–49, 166, 210, 212

Equal Rights Amendment, 228

Escobedo Shepherd, Julianne, 75

Ess, Ramsey, 117

Estefan, Gloria, 128

Evans, Florida, 44

Everett, Anna, 158–59, 163

everyman character, 72, 104, 126

everywoman character, 65

explicit content, 17, 19–20, 33–36, 40, 42–43, 45–46, 84, 107, 150, 180–81, 212, 214, 217–18, 220

Facebook, 171

Falco, Edie, 223

Fallon, Kevin, 47

Faludi, Susan, 5, 44

Family Hour programming, 30

fandom, 2, 41, 156, 159, 177, 188, 222–24; cult, 160; forensic, 2; practices, 158, 173

Fat Actress, 94, 107–8

Fatal Attraction, 201

Fat Albert, 92

female: body, 35, 44–46, 93, 103–4, 106–11, 114–15, 127, 136, 159, 216, 218, 220–21, 230–31; clown figure, 118, 120; collective, 209; comedian, 2, 65–66, 82, 95, 99, 101–3, 105–6, 110–13, 121, 131, 230; consumerism, 28, 217; experience, 133, 145, 147, 152; grotesque, 109–11, 113, 115, 120–21, 124, 126–27, 136, 218, 221, 230 (*see also under* femininity); subjectivity, 2, 6, 62, 84, 113, 140, 143, 145, 148, 151, 154, 166, 169, 171, 175, 184

female lawyer character, 141, 149, 166, 203–5, 208–11

female lawyer film cycle, 208–10, 212

female sexuality, 45–46, 107, 115, 211, 230

female success, 142, 168

Feminine Mystique, 234

femininity, 15, 28, 32, 44–45, 62, 102–3, 109, 111, 113, 118, 121, 126, 141–42, 161, 163, 166, 171, 179, 189–90, 201, 203, 215, 219, 221, 230–31; "failed," 62, 111, 116; grotesque, 82, 111, 114–16, 118, 121, 127, 181, 211, 218–19, 230 (*see also under* female); marginalized, 149, 181; mediatized, 211, 213, 219, 228; monstrous, 109, 113, 118, 120, 141; postfeminist, 8–9, 25, 44, 69, 88, 90, 111, 116–17, 194–95, 213, 219, 221–22, 226, 230. *See also* womanhood

feminism, 2–3, 5–9, 11–13, 16, 24, 32, 43–46, 58, 62, 69, 80–84, 87, 90, 93–96, 99, 101–2, 105–6, 110, 112–13, 133, 140, 143, 145, 147, 169, 183–89, 191–93, 195–97, 199–201, 203–5, 207–13, 215, 217, 219, 221, 223–26, 228–30; academic, 6–7, 143, 227 (*see also* feminist: scholarship); aspirational, 77, 85, 99, 123; "failed," 88, 94, 226–28; liberal, 29, 42–43, 61, 91–92, 99, 161, 194, 196–97, 207; lifestyle, 205, 226; popular, 7, 12, 34, 44, 49, 57, 62, 80, 88, 96, 99, 116, 161, 168, 191–92, 196; and postfeminism, 3, 8–9, 57, 89–90, 94–96, 184, 186, 190–91, 194, 215; second-wave, 5, 26, 36, 39, 44, 88, 101, 105, 126, 197, 200, 206, 208, 212, 226–27, 234; taken into

Peabody Award, 159
Peacock, Steven, 232–34
Peak TV, 16, 81, 234
performance, 16, 72, 96–99, 102–4, 108, 116–17, 120–21, 126–27, 130–31, 139, 141, 149, 156–57, 160, 163, 165–66, 169, 183, 198, 203–4, 230. *See also* comedy: performance
Perkins, Ann, 123, 127, 131
Perlman, Ron, 40
Petro, Patrice, 22, 172
Phyllis, 27
Pine, Geneva, 207
Pinkman, Jesse, 229
Piper, Helen, 186
Plimpton, Martha, 161
Poehler, Amy, 2, 12, 70–71, 79–80, 83, 89, 96–102, 110, 124–28, 133, 136, 183, 230
poetics, 186, 188, 191
Poniewozik, James, 81, 223
pornography, 34–36, 45, 103, 158
postcolonial, 8, 196
postfeminism, 2–10, 13, 15–17, 23–24, 30, 36, 45–46, 48, 57, 64, 69, 73, 80, 83, 88–91, 93–96, 100, 109–10, 113, 115–16, 150, 184, 186, 188, 191–92, 194–95, 200–201, 205–6, 210–11, 215–17, 222, 224–25, 228, 233–34; "choice," 5, 83, 91, 100, 193, 204–5, 228
postfeminist: chick flick, 74, 127; media culture, 6, 9, 11, 88, 201; quality television, 25–26, 47 (*see also* dramedy: postfeminist TV)
postmodern culture, 11, 32–33, 36, 59, 159, 189, 191
postnetwork television, 23, 34, 42, 48, 55, 70–71, 85, 142
postrecessionary media culture, 8, 96, 99, 142, 168, 192, 224
prestige television, 6, 13, 31, 34–35, 38, 46, 59–60, 73–74, 81, 139–40, 145–48, 154, 160–61, 167–68, 171, 174, 176–78, 181, 184–85, 187, 191–92, 194, 197–98, 201, 204, 211, 215, 222–25, 227–28
pretty/funny concept, 66, 103
Primal Fear, 207
profanity, 20, 35–40, 43, 107
Prudom, Laura, 229
Purvis, Tony, 145–46

queer theory, 64, 120

Rabinovitz, Lauren, 27, 139
race, 7, 27, 29, 43–44, 48, 61, 69, 85–86, 89, 133–34, 140, 158, 160, 171, 174, 178–79, 181, 196, 207, 212, 217–18
racial politics, 13, 20, 28, 133, 150, 160, 197, 207, 227
racism, 42, 74, 86, 197, 207
Ramsay, Debra, 172–73
ratings, 31, 58–59, 75, 171
Raymond, Adam K., 97–98
Reagan-Bush era, 30
realism, 7, 20, 26, 28–29, 64, 72, 96, 100–102, 121, 131, 140, 144–46, 149–50, 159, 171, 178, 181, 185, 187, 193, 214–16, 218, 220, 230–31, 233
recession, 13–14, 48, 142, 205. *See also* crisis: economic
Rex, Grace, 202
Rhimes, Shonda, 158–59
Rhoda, 27, 42
Richards, Mary, 28, 42, 60–61, 79
Rodrigues, Sara, 99–100
Rodriguez, Maddie, 99
Rolle, Esther, 44
romance narrative, 5, 55–58, 62, 65–66, 82–83, 105, 116, 118, 132, 158, 205, 210, 213
Romney, Jonathan, 168
Rorke, Robert, 149–50
Roseanne, 44–45, 84, 94, 193, 213
Rossitano, Frank, 93
Rowe Karlyn, Kathleen, 18, 27, 40, 43–46, 56–57, 95, 103, 105, 114, 128, 144, 201, 218
Russo, Mary, 109, 218
Ryan, Maureen, 32, 75, 81, 229

Sandberg, Sheryl, 99–100
Santo, Avi, 35, 42, 47
Santz, Horatio, 126
Sarandos, Ted, 154, 214
satire, 1–2, 13, 30, 54–57, 60–62, 64, 68–72, 75, 79, 82, 84–86, 89–91, 95–96, 98, 101, 106–7, 110–12, 118, 120, 127, 175, 192, 199, 230
Saturday Night Live, 62–63, 70, 89, 96, 126, 136
Savigny, Heather, 7
Scandal, 158–60
Scharff, Christina, 90

170, 184, 196, 198, 210–13, 215, 217–18, 231; streaming, 11–13, 15–16, 48–49, 154, 169, 195–96, 229–30; studies/scholarship, 2–4, 10–12, 17–19, 22, 146, 169, 186, 190–91, 232, 235
Television Academy, 154, 176, 178
Teller, Jax, 39–40
Teller, John, 40
30 Rock, 2–3, 12–13, 48, 54–71, 74–75, 77–91, 95–96, 99–101, 106, 110–12, 114–16, 119, 124, 127–28, 131–36, 144, 175, 183–84, 192, 196–97, 200, 203, 211, 226–27, 229–30
Thompson, Ethan, 96
Thompson, Robert J., 18, 43, 59–60, 62, 68
Thornham, Sue, 145–46
Tierney, Maura, 197
title sequence, 54, 149, 151, 180, 216–17, 219. *See also* opening credits
Top of the Lake, 14, 49, 142
Traeger, Chris, 123
tragedy, 18, 72, 177, 179–81
Traister, Rebecca, 88, 94
transgender feminism. *See* feminism: transgender
transgender mainstreaming, 8
transgender panic, 120
transgression, 10, 15, 24, 33–35, 37–38, 40, 42–46, 48–49, 57, 107, 109–10, 115, 120, 132, 139, 141, 175–76, 221
transnationality, 13, 225
Transparent, 14, 49, 229, 231
Trantham, Holly, 75
Travers, Ben, 151
Treme, 178–79
True Detective, 23
Trump, Donald, 6, 228
Twitter, 159, 171, 177, 197–98

Unbreakable Kimmy Schmidt, 14, 56, 95
United States of Tara, 25
UnREAL, 227, 229
unruliness, 44–46, 109, 113, 119–20, 132
unruly woman, 44–46, 114, 121
utopia, 70, 75–77, 79–80, 87, 96, 100–101

VanDerWerff, Todd, 81, 170
Variety, 70, 79, 229
Veep, 14, 73, 107, 194

Veronica Mars, 188
Viruet, Pilot, 154, 176
Vulture, 98, 166

Wallenstein, Andrew, 171
Waller-Bridge, Phoebe, 225–26, 231
warmedy, 29, 60, 78, 123, 132
Warner, Helen, 7
Warren, Suzanne "Crazy Eyes," 177
Wasicsko, Nick, 179–80
Weeds, 25, 153, 175, 181
Weekend Update, 89
Weidhase, Nathalie, 8
Wheatley, Helen, 10
White, Lara, 161–64
White, Mimi, 233–34
White, Rosie, 64, 70
White, Skyler, 222–24
White, Walter, 141, 185, 222–23, 229
Wicking, Christopher, 31
Wilkes, Karen, 90
Williams, Linda, 34–35, 77, 103, 145, 158–60, 162, 179–80, 187, 189
Willy Wonka and the Chocolate Factory, 68
Winch, Alison, 107, 175, 201
Winfrey, Oprah, 63, 85–86
Wire, The, 23, 32, 77, 150, 155, 178–80, 187, 233
womanhood, 2, 6, 9, 13, 24, 64, 84, 87–88, 98, 116, 127, 143, 148–49, 151, 177, 180, 195, 211, 215–16, 227, 233; Black, 8, 43, 85, 101, 133, 141, 146, 177, 179–80, 185, 197, 207, 215, 218–19; Latina, 85, 179–80, 215; white, 2, 5, 9, 25, 62, 85, 194–95. *See also* femininity
women's liberation movement, 27–28, 192–93, 230, 234
workplace, 28–29, 31, 72, 75, 91, 128, 133, 142, 193, 195–96, 200, 205, 213; comedy (*see* comedy: workplace); narrative, 110, 143, 195

Yabroff, Jennie, 99–100
Yes Please, 99
Yonkers, 178
York, Charlotte, 64
Yuan, Jada, 208

Zborowski, James, 10–12, 23, 186, 232–34

ABOUT THE AUTHOR

Julia Havas is lecturer in media at De Montfort University, Leicester. She has published in the journals *Television and New Media, MAI: Feminism and Popular Culture*, the *VIEW Journal of European Television History and Culture*, and *Animation Studies* and has contributed chapters to the anthologies *Hysterical! Women in American Comedy, Binge-watching and Contemporary Television Research*, and the *Routledge Companion to European Cinema*. Her research focuses on Anglo-American television, the gender and race politics of popular media, streaming culture, Hungarian film and television, and the transcultural travel of media.

CPSIA information can be obtained
at www.ICGtesting.com
Printed in the USA
LVHW051735100322
713135LV00013B/1629